D1405389

ROYAL WIVES

THE EMPRESS MATILDA
Daughter of Henry I. Copied from the only known portrait of her—her
great seal in the archives of Durham Cathedral.

HEATHER JENNER

✦✦✦

Royal Wives

St. Martin's Press

New York

AFFILIATED PUBLISHERS: Macmillan & Company, Limited,
London - also at Bombay, Calcutta, Madras and Melbourne -
The Macmillan Company of Canada, Limited, Toronto.

CONTENTS

LIST OF ILLUSTRATIONS

ACKNOWLEDGMENTS

1   *Radio Times Hulton Picture Library*
2   *National Portrait Gallery*
3   *Mansell Collection*
4   *Paul Popper Ltd.*

Introduction

PEOPLE AND their affairs have always interested me more
than things, so much so that my husband is convinced that if
only atomic power could be explained to me in terms of one
electron falling in love with another I would become an
expert physicist. My first matchmaking effort was when I was
five and insisted that my best girl friend, also aged five, should
become engaged to my second-best boy friend aged six. The
engagement did not last, but I still think that it would have
been an excellent match.

At school history, because it should have been about people,
was my favourite subject, but I found it tantalizing. We seemed
to concentrate on treaties, battles, and coalition governments,
all of which left me cold unless there were personalities
involved. The only treaties I wanted to hear about were the
marriage ones, and then I wanted to know what happened
when some unfortunate little princess was sent away from her
country to marry a man whom she had never met before and
whose language she probably did not speak. The dates that
intrigued me were the family ones, when the kings and queens
were born, when they married, and when their children were
born and died. These were hardly mentioned unless the
marriage brought about the end of a war or the king produced
no heir.

Sometimes a human touch was introduced. It had to be
allowed that Henry VIII had six wives and we were even taught
a little rhyme to help us remember their correct order. It
went: 'Divorced, beheaded, died; divorced, beheaded, survived.' The chief emphasis was laid on Henry's breaking away
from the Roman Catholic church rather than the life he lived
with his queens. Anne Boleyn, I gathered, deserved what she
got; but Catherine Howard didn't because she was just silly

and flirtatious. It came as a surprise to me later when I found out that Catherine Parr, whom I had been led to believe was dull and virtuous, married Thomas Seymour three months after Henry's death, and that he had not only courted her before her marriage to Henry, but had been courting her step-daughter Elizabeth since. It was also mentioned that Charles II had mistresses—they were called favourites—but Nell Gwynn was made to seem the most prominent and was represented as a jolly orange-throwing girl made more or less respectable because she had a kind heart and persuaded Charles to found the Chelsea Pensioners. Hints of other scandals and indis-cretions I came across in Shakespeare; but as we studied his works in expurgated editions I found them baffling. Not sur-prisingly my history reports said, 'Shows no interest, could do better'. Personally I thought that my teachers could have done better too.

I start this book with William the Conqueror because he made England into a kingdom and our Queen is his descendant. Four times the descent was continued through women. Matilda, the only surviving child of Henry I, was the mother of Henry II the first of our Plantagenet kings. Henry VII, the first Tudor king, the grandson of a Welsh squire and a Valois princess who were probably never married, claimed the throne through his mother Margaret Beaufort, the great grand-daughter of John of Gaunt, and strengthened his claim by marrying Elizabeth Plantagenet the daughter of Edward IV.

Their eldest daughter Margaret married the King of Scot-land and was great grandmother to James I, our first Stuart king. James's daughter Elizabeth married the Elector Palatine King of Bohemia and she was the grandmother of George I, our first Hanoverian king. Portraits of the five women concerned are given in my frontispiece and Plates I to IV.

I end the book at William IV, partly because he died exactly 750 years after William I, which makes a nice round date, partly because there has been so much written about Victoria and Edward VII, but chiefly because by the nineteenth century it had become much less politically important whom our kings or queens married than it had been in other centuries. I have omitted all account of the three of our rulers who never married at all—William II, Edward VI and Elizabeth I.

It mattered very much indeed to William the Conqueror whom he married; he had to establish himself and it was important to him to have a wife with some prestige. Henry I married a Princess with English blood to get the English on his side. Henry II made a love match with Eleanore of Aquitaine; she was also one of the richest women in Europe and between them they became more powerful than the King of France. The rest of the Plantagenets, except for the last two, Edward IV and Richard III, found their wives chiefly abroad; some of them brought money and peace, others were a liability. The mother of Henry IV was English, but died before she came to the throne. Of the Tudors two out of six of Henry VIII's wives came from the continent and Mary married the heir to the Spanish throne. The Stuarts' Consorts were all foreign princesses, but after them the English allowed no more so-called Protestant kings with Catholic consorts and the Hanoverians limited themselves to marrying women from insignificant German states who brought neither money nor influence to this country. Queen Victoria married her children and grandchildren into most of the royal families of Europe, but this did not stop the First World War when her relations found themselves on opposing sides. At the end of that war the two greatest Emperors, the German and the Russian, were both turned off their thrones, to be followed in 1931 by the King of Spain and in 1946 by the King of Italy. Now, on the whole, reigning families try to marry people who will be acceptable to their subjects rather than those who will add to their political power. This factor was strong enough to cause King Edward VIII to abdicate for love—the first time in our history that this had been done by any of our kings.

When I handed this book to my publisher his comment after reading it was, 'The kings hardly seem to count.' I did not mean to give this impression; my aim has not been to detract from them as leaders, fighters, or statesmen, but to write about them as husbands and family men in as factual a way as possible. The kings of course did count in this way too. During the first centuries about which I have written they had absolute power; and although some of them treated their wives badly, on the whole (considering how and why many of the marriages were arranged), they got on remarkably well. I hope that I have given a fair picture.

London   H.J.
November 1966

1 - *William the Conqueror*

Born 1027, died 1087. Became king of England 1066. Married Matilda of Flanders (born 1031, died 1083) in 1053.

WILLIAM THE CONQUEROR established law and order in England by a ruthless and calculated singlemindedness. We remember him as the King who made England so law-abiding that a man could safely walk across it carrying a bag of gold. He showed the same determination in the courtship of his wife as he did in the subduing of this country.

In contrast to the rest of his life the circumstances of his early days were more romantic than those of any other king we ever had, and they read like a fairy story. He was born as the result of a love affair between Robert—'the Magnificent' or 'the Devil' according to how people felt about him—the second son of Richard 'the Good' of Normandy, and Arlette, the spirited daughter of a tanner. William was staying at his Castle in Falaise when she caught his eye as she was washing clothes in the river and he was riding past on his horse. He sent for her father to arrange for her to be smuggled into the castle in the discreet way that befitted her humble station in life. She would have none of this and insisted on having the drawbridge lowered and being ushered in in state. When William was born she must still have been considered of importance because she was very ill and her serving women were so concerned that they crowded round her and left the baby struggling on the floor. Somehow he managed to get his breath,

13

let out a yell and survived, to struggle for the rest of his life.

After this initial effort the next few years were the easiest he ever had. Robert succeeded to the dukedom—many people said that he had poisoned his elder brother to do this—and tiring of Arlette married her off to a local nobleman. William he kept with him and at the age of eight, as he had no legitimate children of his own, Robert presented him to his noblemen as his heir, saying as he did so: 'He is little but he will grow.' Robert then went off on a crusade but luckily took the precaution of putting William into the care of King Henry I of France before he went, because he died a few months later while still away.

As William was a bastard, there were other more legitimate claimants to the dukedom. King Henry kept his word and helped him sometimes, but he had troubles of his own and as William grew more powerful he became jealous. William's way of living was hazardous, two of his guardians were murdered, and he frequently had to fight for his life.

This upbringing agreed with him and by the time he was eighteen he had not only established that the dukedom was his, but had grown to be physically one of the strongest men of his age. Nobody but he was strong enough to draw his bow, and it was said that he could hit a target when riding at full speed. He became a champion of chivalry and when he was riding at speed 'to see him reining in his horse, shining with sword, helmet and shield and brandishing his lance was a pleasant yet terrible sight'. He could be gentle and charming when he chose to be, but would fly into a rage if crossed and would take revenge with the utmost savagery.

He now decided that he needed a consort. His choice fell on Matilda, daughter of Baldwin V of Flanders. She was about fourteen and a good match, as her father was rich and her mother the sister of Henry, William's erstwhile protector. What was more, she was not engaged to anybody else, which was unusual for a rich heiress in her teens; for in those days they were bargained for from the cradle. She had been in love with a young, good-looking, fair-haired Saxon nobleman, Brihtric Meaw, whose father was the rich Lord of the Manor of Gloucester and who had been sent to her father's court by Edward the Confessor; but Brihtric turned her down.

Matilda had had a very different upbringing from that of William. She had lived in the comparative security of her father's court and was reputed to have all the usual accomplishments of a great lady of the time. Whether she was beautiful or not it is difficult to judge. A chronicler of the day said that she was 'even more distinguished for the purity of her manners than for her illustrious lineage and she united beauty and gentle breeding with all the graces of Christian Holiness'. Most great ladies were accounted beautiful; her manners were not always pure and gentle, nor were her graces of Christian Holiness always to the fore; like most women of that time, she had a tough streak.

The first time that William proposed she refused him on the grounds that he was a bastard. Baldwin again seemed to have allowed her to make her own choice, which was unusual for a father of those days. But he may not have been so much a liberal-minded father as a cautious one—her suitor had not completely established himself and was not then so powerful in France as he was to become later.

William was furious at the refusal. He was used to getting his own way and was also touchy on the subject of his birth. Not long before, some townsmen in Normandy had mocked him because he had tanner's blood, so to teach them a lesson he had them flayed alive and had their skins hung on a wall as animal skins were when they were being cured. He was, on the other hand, used to having to fight for what he wanted and he persisted in his courtship for seven years. Some time during that period he either stormed into her apartments and seized her by the hair and knocked her about; or, another version says, he knocked her off her horse and rolled her in the mud. Whichever he did, it was effective, because when her father asked her during the wedding festivities why she had changed her mind about William, she replied, 'Because I did not know the Duke as I do now, for he must be a man of great courage and daring to have beaten me in my own father's palace.'

By the time they were married he was more eligible than

she was. At twenty-one she was getting a bit old for the marriage market, but he was by then recognized as the greatest fighter of his time and had become one of the most powerful men in France.

The wedding took place at Notre Dame d'Eu in 1053. Baldwin gave his daughter a handsome dowry and there were great festivities which he and his wife attended. After these were over and his in-laws had gone back to Flanders, William took his bride on a tour round Normandy to show her to his subjects. They had not had a Duchess for a long time and were pleased with the idea and charmed by her grace and demeanour. The only flaw was that William's illegitimate uncle, the Archbishop of Rouen, had persuaded the Pope to forbid the marriage on the grounds of consanguinity—Matilda was the granddaughter of Eleanor of Normandy, who was William's aunt. William retaliated by accusing the Archbishop of selling church plate to supplement his income, and was so successful in this that the Archbishop was deposed. The Pope's displeasure could not have upset them much, because they had already had several children before his dispensation arrived in 1057.

From whatever motives William married Matilda, he became a most devoted husband, if an absent one, and seems to have been faithful. Most of his contemporaries had acknowledged mistresses and bastards but he had none. They lived mostly at Caen and the hall of their royal palace was one of the most magnificent in Europe. They lived in state but were not extravagant. William never cared for elaborate dress, believing that men should wear clothes that 'fitted to the form of their bodies, leaving them ready to run, ride or do anything that was to be done', and he and his Norman knights dressed accordingly. They took the education of their children seriously. They put the sons into the care of Bishop Lanfranc and under him Richard, the second son, became a real scholar.

Matilda was fond of such feminine occupations as embroidery and, during the thirteen years before the Conquest, had three sons, Robert, Richard and William, and one or two daughters. In all their married life she had ten children who survived babyhood.

Anybody at that time who had property had to defend it by the sword; but William went further than that—he was ambitious and determined to acquire as much power as possible, so in consequence was away a great deal fighting battles. While he was away Matilda had to be Regent. In those days nobody talked about women and careers, but a wife was often the only person whom her husband could trust, so she had to take over in his absence.

William had had thoughts about England before he married Matilda. He had been there in 1051 and said afterwards that Edward the Confessor, who had no male heir, had promised him that he should succeed to the throne. His claim to it was in some ways rather better than Harold's, who, although he was legitimate, was only the second son of Earl Godwin, while William's Aunt Emma, on his father's side, was Edward the Confessor's mother.

He also said that Harold had sworn, during a banquet held in his honour in Normandy, that William should have the throne. To make this promise more binding, William had hidden a sacred relic under the table and also promised Harold one of his daughters as a wife. As none of his children could have been more than twelve and Harold must have been in his forties, it does not sound as if the match would have had a happy future, and does not show William in a good light as a father. Harold cannot have thought much of the pact, because as soon as he got back to England he married somebody else and when Edward the Confessor died, proclaimed himself king.

William, determined to get his own way as usual, gathered together an expeditionary force. This was held up at St. Valérie by unfavourable winds, so Matilda planned a surprise and arrived in a splendid ship called *Mora* which had as a figurehead a bronze figure of their third son William.

She then stayed in Normandy while he conquered England, where he was crowned without her on Christmas Day 1066. In March 1067 he rejoined her in Normandy, where they proclaimed that Lent should be a festival that year to celebrate his conquest and return. They then toured Normandy together until September, when he returned to England. She remained behind as Regent again, this time with the help of her eldest son Robert—who was then thirteen years old. At the end of the year she came over to England and was crowned Queen—the first consort of an English king to be called Regina. The Saxon queens had simply been styled 'Wife of the King'. William was crowned again, to make the occasion more important and maybe to help to stress Matilda's slight claim to the throne as a descendant, through her father, of Alfred the Great. Despite the joyous occasion and the fact that she had been happily married to William for fourteen years, the tough side of Matilda's nature came to the fore and she took a belated revenge on Brihtric. She not only had him stripped of his lands and honours and imprisoned, but she deprived Gloucester, his town, of its civic liberties and charters.

Their fourth son Henry, their only son to be born in England, was born in Yorkshire in 1068, and Matilda settled on him the lands that William had given her in England and Normandy. In 1069 William sent her back to Normandy again to act as Regent with Robert, because there was so much trouble in England that he did not think that she was safe. As it happened she wasn't safe in Normandy either, because the new King of France attacked her, and William had to stop fighting the Scots to go to her aid.

After this, things were never quite the same between them. He spent more and more time in England and she in Normandy. There was even a hint of scandal in the family. The Norman ladies complained that their husbands had been spending too much time in England and that they were not always faithful while they were away. William himself was accused of having tried to seduce the wife of the Governor of Winchester and also of having had an affair with the daughter of one of the Canons of Canterbury—priests in the Roman Catholic church were allowed to marry until twenty-five years later than this date. Some authorities say that he did then in fact have an illegitimate son known as Peveral, Lord of Nottingham and Derby, and some say that the mother was a daughter of the founder of the Collegiate of St. Martin-le-Grand.

Again Matilda was said to have lapsed from her gentle Christian spirit and had the canon's daughter put to death and hamstrung—the Governor of Winchester's wife she seems to have ignored. After this William is said to have lost his temper with Matilda and beaten her so hard with his bridle that she died. If he did beat her he did not kill her, because she lived for another nine years. If he really had beaten her with such success before he married her, he might have tried the same thing again.

Whatever happened they lived together affectionately enough in Normandy in 1074, but not for long. Like many powerful men he would never be definite about which of his sons should inherit what after his death, and this caused dissension amongst them. Robert, who had been Regent in Normandy for some time and had been led to believe that he was to be its future ruler, did not appreciate it when his father came back on a brief visit and took over from him. Understandably enough he didn't like it either when, after his fiancée died, William took her dowry for himself.

They began to have a lot of quarrels and the whole family suffered. Once, young William and Henry threw dirty water over Robert from a castle window when he was walking in the courtyard with some friends. He was always jealous of William, who was his father's favourite, and, mad with rage, although the two younger brothers were only sixteen and eight respectively and he was twenty, he chased them sword in hand, and the King had to rush in, also sword in hand, to stop him. Immediately before this Robert had demanded the Duchies of Normandy and Maine from his father, who had refused them, and the water incident seems to have brought things to a climax; he rushed away from the court to his uncle, Matilda's brother Baldwin, who had quarrelled with William years before over money, loved to make things as difficult for William as he could, and willingly promised his help.

Matilda took sides with Robert against her husband and sold her jewels to send him money. He had always been her favourite son, and during the last few years she had seen more of him when they were acting as joint Regents than she had of William. William was hurt but restrained when he found out about this, and wrote her a reproachful letter in which he said, 'The woman who deceives her husband is the destruction of her house.' To which she replied, 'I pray you not to be surprised if I feel a mother's tenderness for her first-born.' He was reputed to have taken revenge not on her but on her private agent, Sampson, whom he had imprisoned and blinded.

His troubles with Robert continued. They fought against each other in battle and Robert threw him from his horse, a thing that had never happened to him before. William bellowed with rage, and Robert, who had not realized who he was until then, instead of pressing his advantage helped him to his feet. Robert won the battle, but they patched up a peace and in 1079 William took him to England to keep an eye on him, leaving Matilda behind again as Regent.

By this time her health was waning and family events did not help it. Her second son Richard died hunting in the New Forest and was buried at Winchester, and her favourite daughter Constance, the wife of Alan of Bretagne, died almost immediately afterwards. On 2nd November, 1083 she too died at the age of fifty-two.

She was outlived by three sons, Robert, William, and Henry; and four daughters, Cecilia, Adelaide, Adela, and Gundred. Cecilia was an abbess, Adelaide a nun, Adela married Stephen of Blois and was the mother of Stephen, King of England, and Gundred married Earl Warren. William was heartbroken after her death, his temper got worse than ever, and he had terrible fits of depression. His second son William, his favourite, who had fought with him against Robert, was the only person who could deal with him during these moods. He also was said to have given up hunting as part of his mourning, but as he had got tremendously fat and his health was not too good it probably was no very great sacrifice.

His own death was a mixture of farce and tragedy. He had been ill in bed and Philip, the King of France, taunted him by saying that 'King William, his cousin, was laid low in child bed' (a reference to his enormous stomach), adding, 'Oh what a number of candles must I provide at his going to church, certainly I think 100,000 will not suffice.' William, who had not lost his old fire, replied, 'Well, I trust when I shall be churched that our confine shall be at no such cost, but I will help to find him 100,000 candles myself and light them too, to some of their paines if God grant me life.'

God did, and the next July, when the French corn and grapes were most promising, he went into France and set fire to the cities and countryside and even to a church. His revenge killed him. The heat of the fire gave him fever, his horse trod on a bit of burning timber and he fell off. He died at Hermentrude, near Rouen. None of his sons were with him, and the nobles who had been round him went to pay homage to Robert, who was in Germany. He was left alone except for his servants, who plundered his house and left his body naked on the floor, as he had been at his birth sixty years before.

2 - Henry I

Born 1068, died 1135. Became king 1100. Married Matilda of Scotland (born 1079, died 1118) in 1100; secondly Adelicia of Louvaine (born 1103, died 1151) in 1121.

WILLIAM RUFUS was a homosexual who never married. The second surviving son of William the Conqueror, he managed to get to England before his elder brother Robert, who was in Germany, and became king. When, thirteen years later, he was killed hunting in the New Forest, Henry happened to be in another part of the forest, so he had not far to go to seize the royal treasure at Winchester and claim the throne, which he did with great promptitude. Robert, in the wrong place as usual, was in Sicily on his way back from the Holy Land.

Like his second brother Richard, although without so much justification, as Henry was a man of action rather than a scholar, he was nicknamed Beauclerk. Born in 1068, the only one of the Conqueror's sons to be born in England, he could speak Saxon as well as Norman French. The Conqueror left him £5,000 in silver, and Matilda left him her lands in England. Robert promptly borrowed £3,000 of the money and William Rufus seized the lands as soon as he conveniently could. Robert at one time imprisoned him and at another joined Rufus in besieging him; and to escape from them Henry had to wander round Germany for some years with only four retainers. With no money or influence it was entirely due to his prowess as a fighter and his hard cunning that he survived. This struggle for

22

existence left him a shrewd and ruthless negotiator who had no hesitation in being unscrupulous if the occasion arose.

He was described by Holinshed as 'strong of body, fleshie, of indifferent stature, black of hair and in manner bald before, large eyes, face comely, well countenanced and pleasant to beholders especially when he was disposed to mirth'. Presumably 'in manner bald before' meant that his hair was receding. In character he was said to excel in the virtues, wisdom, eloquence and valiance, which notwithstanding were somewhat blemished with the number of vices that reigned in him: as covetousness, cruelty, and fleshy lusts of the body. Like his father, he was inclined to go to fat, but he liked hard exercise and as a boy had run so fast that Rufus had nicknamed him 'Deerfoot'. In manner he was much quieter than either Robert or William Rufus and, far from being a homosexual, he had more acknowledged illegitimate children than any other English king, even surpassing Charles II. They were thought to number twenty, many of them born before he became king.

After he had been crowned he wasted no time in finding a bride, choosing Edyth, known as Matilda or Maud after she became Queen, daughter of Malcolm, King of Scotland, and Margaret, the granddaughter of Edmund Ironside, elder half-brother to Edward the Confessor. William Rufus had fought her father who had been killed in battle, after which she and her sister had been sent to live in the care of their aunt, the Saxon Princess Christine, Abbess of Romsey. The aunt put up a strenuous resistance to the marriage and declared that both girls had taken the veil. At first Matilda had resisted too, possibly because of Henry's reputation with women; but her brother, Alexander the Fierce of Scotland, persuaded her that it was her duty in the interests of her family and country to marry Henry and secure peace. A rhyme of that date does not make her sound loth to do this:

> Special love there has been as I understand,
> Between him and the fair King's daughter, Maud of Scotland,
> So that he willed her to wife and the Bishops also,
> And high men of the land advised him thereto.

She may have fallen in love with him because he was vital and attractive. Henry too had a large heart and a catholic taste in women, so may easily have been in love with her, at any rate for a brief period.

She certainly denied that she had taken the veil and said about her aunt: 'As often as I stood in her presence I wore the veil, trembling as I wore it with indignation and grief, but as soon as I could get out of her sight I used to snatch it from my head and fling it on the ground and trample it underfoot, that was the way and none other that I was veiled.'

Archbishop Anselm, one of the bishops who 'willed her to wife', married them on Sunday, 11th November, 1100, after which she was crowned. At the wedding the Archbishop said from the pulpit that she was free from religious vows, and explained that in those rough times many girls had to put on veils, made of coarse black cloth or serge, to protect themselves from the attentions of the Norman nobles.

By nature and temperament she and Henry were opposites, except that they both had a love of music. Despite her spirited defiance of her aunt, she was deeply religious and devoted to good works, and during Lent she would walk barefoot to Westminster Abbey every day and there wash and kiss the feet of the poor. Henry was less religious and got so impatient and bored with long church services that, when he found a priest who could get through Matins and Mass quicker than the others, he called him 'a priest fit for a soldier' and made him Bishop of Salisbury.

The marriage was popular with the Saxons, but not with the Normans, who nicknamed them 'Godric' and 'Godgifer', Saxon words meaning God's Prince and God's gifts. This was presumably sarcastic, possibly because Henry cut down on the extravagances of the Court in which William had indulged. He cut his hair short and wore simple clothes as had the Conqueror. In William's Court and in his brother Robert's in Normandy they had worn long garments 'like women's, which hindered walking or acting of any kind', and 'let their hair grow long like women'. They also 'copied the mien of women', though handicapped by the 'long pointed shoes with curved points like the horns of rams or the tails of scorpions' that they wore. These shoe fashions had an unromantic origin, as they had been invented by Count Fulke of Anjou to hide the swellings of his gouty feet.

Matilda produced a son, William, in 1101, more or less as Robert landed in England and tried—helped by the discontented barons—to conquer it from Henry. The two armies met and Robert although stronger in numbers, was persuaded to treat, partly, it was said, because when he heard that Matilda had just had a child, he said that he would not fight against a woman in childbed.

In the treaty Henry agreed to give up most of his lands in Normandy and pay Robert a pension of three thousand marks. Robert then stayed at the English Court for six months and, though he was often drunk, he and Matilda got on well together and spent a lot of time in each other's company. Like many virtuous women she could be quite unscrupulous if she believed that her cause was right; she was said to have taken advantage of Robert when he was in his cups, and, preying on his kindness and courtesy further, persuaded him to make over to her the pension that Henry had promised him, by pleading that she was badly in need of money.

In 1104 she produced a daughter, whom they christened Matilda. In 1105 she was left as Regent of England while Henry went over to Normandy to fight Robert. He defeated him at the battle of Tenchbrai and brought him to England, keeping him under open confinement until he died twenty-eight years later.

Henry had put England into good order and was now trying to do the same in Normandy, so he spent a great deal of his time there while she stayed in England. He took over with him Robert of Gloucester, his favourite illegitimate son, whose mother was a French woman, Sybil, daughter of Burgess Robert Corbet of Caen.

The Queen was supposed to have had two more children, Richard and Euphemia. As they were named it is probable that she did so, but they must have died in infancy. Queens in those days usually had more than four children and Matilda was still young, but she and Henry saw less and less of each other and she never produced another heir.

He plainly liked having his illegitimate children at his court, and perhaps because of this he did not seem to worry too much about having only one legitimate son. Not all his bastards were as biddable as Gloucester. Henry was nearly killed fighting against the husband of one of his illegitimate daughters, Joanna, in Normandy. He was so furious that she should be on the opposing side that he blockaded her in a tower and, instead of giving her safe conduct to leave, as was often the chivalrous custom of the day, she had to take off her clothes and swim a moat full of muddy water to escape.

Matilda must have known about his illegitimate children now, if she had not done so before, and presumably accepted the situation as part of married life, as they seem to have drifted apart rather than to have quarrelled. She led her own life and, although concerned for the poor, liked it to be luxurious and lived in great state at Winchester, devoting herself to charity and religious observances and acting as Regent when necessary.

In 1109 the little Matilda, then aged five, was betrothed to Henry V of Germany and sent to that country to be educated. In the same year Robert of Gloucester was married to the daughter of a powerful Norman called Fitz-Hayman, and their descendants played a part in English history for many generations, one of them, Adelicia, becoming the first wife of King John, and another the husband of Joan of Acre, daughter of Edward I.

In 1112 Henry and Matilda were together at Winchester. In 1117 Henry had to go to Normandy again to quell another revolt and this time took his legitimate son William, then aged sixteen, with him. Matilda died in 1118 while he was still there, so that none of her family were with her. Except for her bold stand against her aunt, her charity and religion and her tricking of the unfortunate Robert, she remains a shadowy figure, described as devoted rather than beautiful. In a quiet way her charities did good. She founded a hospital at St. Giles-in-the-Fields in Christchurch, and also had roads and bridges built when she was acting as Regent.

In 1120 Henry married William to Alice, the daughter of Fulke of Anjou, of the gouty feet. In the same year he himself became betrothed to Adelicia of Louvaine, daughter of Godfrey of Louvaine, Duke of Lower Lorraine and Brabant. Her nickname was 'The Fair Maid of Brabant'. She was descended from Charlemagne and was beautiful and accomplished.

In between the engagement and the marriage Henry suffered a terrible tragedy. On 25th November William was drowned on the *White Ship* coming back from Normandy. The voyage had started merrily enough. William and his friends had been drinking and he ordered wine to be given to the crew, who got drunk, so that the ship hit a rock and sank. William got into a small boat, but heard Matilda, the Countess of Porche, one of his illegitimate sisters, shouting for help and he went back to rescue her. The boat became overloaded and it sank too, taking with William and Matilda, Lucy, daughter of Henry's sister Adela and sister of Stephen later King of England, and an illegitimate brother of William's Richard. Stephen himself was meant to have been on the *White Ship* but had changed his mind at the last moment and not embarked.

When Henry heard the news he fainted and stayed unconscious for several hours. He was said never to have smiled again. All the same, he did not let sorrow dim his eye to the main chance; he tried to seize William's widow's dowry, which made her father so angry that he married off another of his daughters to William Clito, Robert's son and Henry's nephew, and later helped him in Normandy against Henry. Alice went back to her father and became a nun.

Henry and Adelicia were married at Windsor on 21st June, 1121. Impatient as usual, he called in the speedy Bishop of Salisbury to perform the ceremony. The Archbishop of Canterbury, an old and much slower man, heard about this and insisted on doing it himself. Then Henry tried to save time over Adelicia's coronation and got the Bishop of Salisbury to do this very early in the morning; but the Archbishop of

Canterbury arrived just before he had finished and did it all over again.

Adelicia was eighteen and he was fifty-three, morose and bad-tempered; by then he had become a great snorer rather than a great lover. She was a perfect wife; he appears to have been very fond of her, and saw that she was with him as much as possible. Almost immediately he had to go to Wales because there was trouble there, but he rejoined her at Winchester when he had dealt with this, and in 1123, when he had to go to Normandy to quell the Fulke and Clito rebellion, he sent for her after he had defeated them, to be with him at Rouen, where she had the doubtful pleasure of seeing him make savage reprisals against his enemies.

She took a great interest in his menagerie at Woodstock, which had in it lions, leopards, camels, lynxes, and a porcupine, and she collected material to write about his life and great deeds. He had given her a 'goodly dowry' and later gave her the County of Shropshire, Arundel Castle, and the Isle of Wight. By 1126 he had given up hope that they would produce an heir and sent for his daughter Matilda, now a widow, to come to him in England. She and Adelicia, who were about the same age, may have known each other before, as the Emperor Henry, Matilda's husband, had helped Adelicia's father defend his State of Louvaine.

They now travelled from Normandy to England together and became lifelong friends, and on many occasions Adelicia tried to keep the peace between father and daughter, which must have required great tact, as Matilda's temper was as hot as Henry's. As soon as they got home Henry proclaimed to the people that they could only be governed by English blood if they acknowledged Matilda as their future queen. Without much enthusiasm they did this, and Stephen, her cousin, was one of the first to pay her homage. Henry then double-crossed the English people and, instead of keeping her in England, where they could get to know her, he arranged a marriage between her and Geoffrey, the son of his enemy the Count of Anjou and brother of the unfortunate Alice. This was unpopular with everybody for good reasons.

To play for time Matilda pleaded with Henry that she was still in mourning for the Emperor, but he knew well that she had never been fond of him and brushed the excuse aside. The three of them spent Christmas at Windsor, with Matilda shut up in her apartments and Adelicia acting as go-between. Henry won in the end and sent her over to Geoffrey in charge of Robert Earl of Gloucester. They were betrothed on Whit Sunday, 1127, but she refused to marry Geoffrey immediately as her father had ordered, and Henry himself had to go over in August and personally lead her to the altar.

By 1130 Henry had become subject to nightmares, which were so strong that they were more like hallucinations. He used to wake up, rush out of bed and, seizing a weapon, brandish it to drive off imaginary assassins; this must have made married life even more trying. In 1133 he went to Normandy and in the summer celebrated the birth of his grandson. In 1135 he was staying at the Castle of Lyons near Rouen and went out hunting. He got overtired and overheated and then ate a heavy meal of lampreys, his favourite food; this brought on violent indigestion and a fever, from which he died seven days later at the age of sixty-seven. Robert of Gloucester was the only member of the family with him, and he carried out his last instructions, which were to take sixty thousand marks out of Henry's treasure chest at Falaise for the funeral, and to be the protector of Matilda, whom he had named as his heiress.

Adelicia remarried in 1138. Her new husband was William d'Albini, who had been wooed by the dowager Queen of France, but he preferred Adelicia. Stephen made him Earl of Sussex and they lived at Arundel and had seven children during the eleven years of their married life. Four of them were sons and the youngest was called Henry after the late king. Adelicia always looked on Matilda as the rightful queen and never went to Stephen's court, but her husband did and helped to bring about the Treaty of Wallingford in 1153 which settled that Henry II (Matilda's son) was to come to the throne. She died in 1151, a woman who had been much loved and respected.

3 - Stephen

Born 1097, died 1154. Became king 1135. Married Matilda (Maud) (born about 1103, died 1151) about 1114.

THE EMPRESS MATILDA, as she was called, naturally considered that she was the heiress to the throne after her father's death. She had been proclaimed so three times, and the nobles, her cousin Stephen among them, had sworn fealty to her.

She had had a curious life. Betrothed at the age of five to Henry V the Emperor of Germany, a man twenty-one years her senior, an unattractive character, treacherous, with an enormous love of power and an ungenerous nature, she had been sent to his country immediately after the betrothal to be educated there and had been married to him when she was only ten and he was thirty-one. By the time she was twenty-one she was a widow. Her husband had spent most of their married life quarrelling with the Pope and fighting other countries in Europe. They had had no children.

In 1126 her father sent for her after the death of her only brother, when it had become apparent to him that he would have no children by his second wife. Soon after she reached England he had her proclaimed his heir for the first time, and almost immediately after that packed her off to marry Geoffrey of Anjou. Nobody was happy about this, including the prospective bride, who had real cause for complaint. She was now expected to marry a man ten years her junior. It is true

I. MARGARET BEAUFORT
Mother of Henry VII.
Artist unknown.

II. ELIZABETH OF YORK
Wife of Henry VII.
Artist unknown.

III. MARGARET TUDOR
Queen of Scotland.
From an original
by Holbein.

IV. ELIZABETH OF BOHEMIA
From an original painting by
G. Honthorst, 1642.

that later he became known as 'the Handsome' but at the time of the marriage he was only twelve years old to her twenty-two. He was also only a Count, while she had been an Empress. The English were unhappy because they felt that they had been tricked by Henry. He had told them that the only way for them to be governed by an English sovereign was to accept her, and now she was being sent away to marry a foreigner. Worse still, what little they had seen of her they had not liked. Although she was beautiful her training at the German court had taught her to be imperious and distant and she was by nature fiery-tempered. The Normans were furious because the Angevins were their traditional and much-hated enemies.

After her father got his own way and forced her into marriage again, she and Geoffrey led a miserable existence, but for political reasons Henry was determined that they should stay married. Three times he had to intervene to patch up the differences between them, and once she left Geoffrey and he was made to write a humble letter to her, begging her to come back. He complained of her rudeness and her proud and haughty manner, and she complained about more or less everything. All the same, in 1133 she produced her first son, Henry, when Geoffrey was nineteen. While she had been in England, it had been noticed that she had been strongly attracted to her cousin Stephen, and there always existed a strong rumour that this child was in fact his. Later, when it happened to suit them, both Matilda and Henry claimed that he was Stephen's son. In 1135 she produced a second son, Geoffrey, and in 1136 a third, William. After the birth of her first son her father had her proclaimed heir for the third time; the second time had been just after her wedding.

When Henry died Matilda was looking after Geoffrey, who was lying at death's door in Anjou, and she could not get over to England at once. Her reluctance to leave her husband on his sick-bed was not so much due to wifely devotion as to her unreadiness to fight for her throne in England; she was unsure of her allies and the real feelings of the English people and did not want to leave Anjou and jeopardize her sons' inheritance there.

Stephen had no such complications or doubts: he rushed across the Channel from France and claimed the throne, explaining away his vow of homage to Matilda by saying that it had been taken under coercion and hinting that, as she was the daughter of a professed nun, she was illegitimate anyhow. He conveniently disregarded the fact that his own wife's mother had been in the same convent and taken the same vows.

He was not churlish by nature. He was gentle, courteous unless in a temper, liberal-minded, and had a love of easy and pleasant living. He was attractive to women and had been a favourite of his uncle, Henry II. He was said to be the handsomest man in Europe, his chief rival to that title being Matilda's husband, who was seventeen years his junior.

He was fairly well accepted by the English when he claimed the throne. They preferred a king to a queen, especially a queen without an adult heir, and they had seen much more of Stephen and Maud than they had of Matilda. His claims to the throne were good enough for those days when might was right, as he was the third son of Adela, daughter of William the Conqueror and favourite sister of Henry I. His father had been Stephen de Blois and, as the eldest son of his marriage was an idiot, Thibaut the next, inherited his estates. Maud's mother had been Matilda's mother's sister and her father Eustace of Boulogne. She was the only child, so, after Eustace's death, Stephen became Count of Boulogne in her right.

Maud was very unlike her beautiful but aggressive cousin Matilda and a much better wife. She was a plain woman some six years younger than her husband, with a gentle firmness of character. Like the other women of her mother's family she was fond of good works. She had great determination and put up with Stephen's occasional infidelities—he was known to have two illegitimate children, but does not seem to have had a notorious mistress or to have been a great womanizer so much as just a charmer; and she helped him when he was in difficulties, which he was for most of his reign. The English, especially the Londoners, liked her much better than Matilda, partly because of her gentler manner and partly because they did not feel that she was such a foreigner. She and Stephen had spent a lot of their married life in England. Henry had built a palace, Tower Royal, which he had given them on their marriage; it was situated somewhere between Cheapside and Westminster, and they had lived in it for a great part of their married life. Before they came to the throne they had had two children who had died.

Stephen was crowned on 26th December, 1135, and Maud three months later on 22nd March, 1136. Immediately their troubles began and went on practically until his death. The English soon found out that he was a weakling, not nearly ruthless enough for those times, and also vacillating. To make himself more popular with the English he abolished the Danegeld—the law which was a tax on land. Very soon he found that this was not practical, so he enforced the law again, which made him doubly unpopular. He also ill-advisedly allowed the nobles to fortify their castles, which made them independent of the Crown. They started rebellions, and the Welsh and Scotch saw their chance to start their own as well.

Ignoring the state of the country, which had become chaotic because of all this, Stephen managed for a brief period to indulge his love of luxury. He celebrated Easter of 1157 with Maud at Westminster in greater magnificence than any of the other Norman kings had ever attempted. Later in the year Maud produced a son, Eustace, and later still Stephen fell into a mysterious stupor, lying so lifelessly that at times they thought that he was dead. When he recovered he had to go to the defence of Boulogne because Geoffrey, who had also recovered, was attacking it. While he was away rebellion broke out in England. The cathedrals of Rochester, York and Bath were burned and Dover Castle seized. Maud, left on her own, took an active part, got her Boulonnais sailors to besiege Dover and won it back. Later, Maud had another son, William, who also lived to manhood.

By 1139 Robert of Gloucester had persuaded Matilda that she should come over to England and with his help claim her throne. Her landing arrangements went wrong and she only escaped being captured by Stephen by rushing to Arundel, where her stepmother, Adelicia, harboured her. Stephen could have captured her there but did not do so, some said because they had been lovers. Matilda did not have such delicate feelings and took advantage of his chivalry to escape and join Gloucester in Bristol, from where she set up a rival government and started to rule.

She must have bitterly hated both her cousins. Stephen had usurped her throne and Maud, her quiet, mousy little cousin, had married the only man to whom she had been attracted. In consequence of these feelings, when early in 1141 she took Stephen prisoner she treated him badly and ordered him to be kept in rigorous confinement at Bristol Castle; it was said he was sometimes in chains. Maud made desperate efforts to get him back. She tried pleading personally with Matilda, offered never to see him again and promised that he would retire to a monastery. Matilda coldly refused these terms, and Maud then offered herself and Eustace in exchange but again without success.

Matilda then moved to London but, disregarding Gloucester's counsels of moderation, made the fatal mistake of upsetting the Londoners. Instead of trying to get on good terms with them, she upbraided them for being traitors and demanded money because they had taken Stephen's side. They disliked her so much that when Maud appeared on the outskirts with an army they rallied to her and Matilda had to leave hurriedly from the banqueting hall of Westminster Palace where she was having her lunch. She managed to escape, but got so exhausted that she had to be placed in a litter at the end of her journey and tied to it so that she would not fall out. Another version was that she was put in a coffin and pretended to be a corpse.

Gloucester was captured and Maud used him to bargain for Stephen, who was sent back to his wife in November 1141, and in 1142 had the same sort of mysterious illness that he had had in 1137. As soon as Gloucester was set free, he went over to France to get help from Geoffrey—who had been having a splendid time without his wife and had no wish to go anywhere near her. He had had the satisfaction of fighting his family's old enemy, Normandy, in her name, and by 1144 had won it back. In 1142 he was winning more battles and had acquired a reputation for charm and dashing good looks as well as for his fighting prowess. Nothing would induce him to go to England, but he sent over instead Henry, who had been living in Anjou all this time and was then about nine years old. While Gloucester was away Stephen felt better again and besieged Matilda that Christmas in Oxford Castle. She had to escape in the snow. In 1147 Gloucester died just before Geoffrey recalled Henry to Normandy. She sent Henry back but this may not have been entirely because she was being obedient so much as a wish to make certain that Henry ruled there rather than his father, as in 1149 she handed over to him her lands in Normandy. Maud now retired from fighting altogether. Stephen was in good health again and her eldest son Eustace was old enough to fight for him. She took more and more to good works, but her health was bad and she died in 1151, the same year as Geoffrey died of a pleuritic fever.

By 1153 everybody was tired of fighting, and after the Battle of Wallingford Henry and Stephen met to treat together. Stephen had already fallen off his horse three times that day, which was described as a bad omen and may possibly have not made him feel his best. On this occasion Henry told Stephen that once, when Matilda had been ill and thought she was dying, she had admitted to him that Stephen was his father. Whatever happened, they made peace. Matilda gave up her claim to the throne on condition that Henry and his heir reigned after Stephen's death. This so infuriated Eustace that he rushed off pillaging the countryside and died of a fever, or some said because he choked on a piece of meat out of sheer bad temper. His younger brother, William, inherited Boulogne and his parents' personal lands in England and was given the earldom of Surrey.

Henry's nickname to most people was Fitz-Empress. This did not necessarily imply that he was illegitimate. 'Fitz' meant 'son of' and, as his inheritance through his mother was better than through that of his father's, he probably encouraged the nickname. Henry, his grandfather, as if to emphasize his claim to the throne, had called himself Fitz-Conqueror. Earlier, at the battle of Egilaw Heath, in which Henry had opposed Stephen, Matilda had intervened and said to Stephen: 'What is it you are about to do? Is it meet the father should destroy the son, or the son kill the sire? For the love of the most high God, fling down your weapons from your hands, sith that (as thou well knowest) he is indeed thine own son; for you well know we twain were acquainted before I wedded Geoffrey.'

As Henry was born six years after she had married Geoffrey, this speech was not strictly to the point. Whether Stephen left the throne to Henry because he believed he was his son, or because the country was in such a terrible state and he was tired of fighting, or because he felt guilty of seizing the throne from Matilda, or a combination of all three, is uncertain, but he carried his liberal-mindedness and courtesy so far that once, when Henry was fighting against him and had not enough money to pay his troops, Stephen paid them for him.

Geoffrey also appeared to be on good terms with Henry. He not only handed over Normandy to him when Matilda told him to, but went with him to the Court of France when he went to swear his allegiance to the French king. After his death the second son, Geoffrey, tried to claim Anjou on the grounds that he was the eldest legitimate son, but Henry then became very much Geoffrey's son and inherited the province.

From the point of view of a family likeness it would be difficult to say which of the two was his father. Both of them were tall, fair and good-looking, while Henry was sturdier and more like the Conqueror in build.

Matilda, once she had given up her claim to the English throne, became a changed character. She acted as Regent for Henry in Normandy, governed it with great discretion and was known as the 'Lady of the English'. She died, loved and respected by the Normans, in 1167.

Stephen died of a stoppage of the bowels in October 1154. His chief tragedy was that he fought for the best part of twenty years to establish himself as king, though quite the wrong sort of person to hold position at that that time. In a more peaceful age he might have been quite a good ruler.

Matilda was never happily married and, if she did have a love affair with Stephen, cannot have had much satisfaction from it, as they fought so long and bitterly.

4 - Henry II

Born 1133, died 1189. Married Eleanore of Aquitaine (born 1122, died 1204) in 1152.

ELEANORE WAS one of the most beautiful women of her time, dark and vivacious, highly sexed, and blessed with vitality and robust health. She was also a great heiress. She came from the land of troubadours and Courts of Love and liked to have a voluptuous and luxurious court around her. Her grandfather had been a great seducer of women and had abandoned his wife in favour of a noblewoman whose picture he had painted on his shield. When a bishop expressed disapproval of this, he replied that he wanted to carry his mistress at least figuratively into battle, since she had carried him so satisfactorily at less public times. Her parents died young, and her grandfather suddenly reformed his ways, made over to her all his estates and went on a pilgrimage to St. James of Compostella in Spain, where he died. This left her one of the richest women in Europe and in 1137, when she was fifteen, a marriage was arranged between her and Prince Louis of France, the heir to the French throne. From a political point of view it was an excellent match, but in other ways it was doomed to unhappiness and failure. Louis the second son of the King of France had been destined for the church until his elder brother Philip died. He was neither a man of action nor a clear-headed thinker, and the only thing that really interested him, apart from Eleanore, who fascinated him for a short time, and producing an heir to the throne, was church ceremonies.

To begin with he and Eleanore found in each other an attraction of opposites. He loved her beauty, warmth and vitality and she his restraint, exquisite manners and good taste. His father died almost immediately after their marriage and Louis became king. Eleanore had a daughter, Marie, who took after her mother in becoming 'renowned in the annals of courtly love'. Eleanore and Louis had already begun to grow apart and the differences in their characters were beginning to tell. No heir followed Marie, and by the time the child was three Eleanore was restless and Louis wanted to go on a crusade. Their ideas about how this should be done differed. Louis wanted the crusade to be austere and reverent but Eleanore turned it into a glittering court outing. She collected a mass of ladies whom she made dress as Amazons, and took along troubadours and enormous piles of luggage.

In Constantinople she had a splendid time being entertained by the Empress of Greece, who held state dinners, garden parties and water fêtes in her honour. At Antioch she and her followers ate exotic foods and there were complaints from the bishops that her court was lascivious; and she had a flirtation—rumour said that it went further than that—with her uncle, Raymond of Antioch, yet another man reputed to be the most handsome of his age. Louis took her away quickly because of the scandal that this was causing, only for her to become too interested in a magnificent Saracen, Emir Sal-Addin. Frustrated again, Eleanore, now patently bored with Louis, began talking about divorce on the grounds of consanguinity and went to Rome to try and get it arranged. The Pope did his best to keep them together and, as if trying to make them take the hint, gave them a present of a magnificent bed.

After all this Louis now had no love left for Eleanore but did not want to let her go because of her money, rather than for any religious feeling about the sanctity of marriage. He was so suspicious of her that he would not let her go to Aquitaine, and she languished at his court and complained of the cold north and its boredoms. Almost as if to aggravate her further he became more and more religious, wore plain clothing and shaved off his moustaches and long curls, so that she taunted him with looking 'more like a monk than a King'.

In 1150 she had a flirtation with the good looking Geoffrey who brought Henry to court to swear his allegiance. In 1151 after Geoffrey's death, Henry came back to the French court. In between his visits she had had another daughter. After his arrival things moved quickly, and one wonders exactly how the conversation went between Eleanore and Louis when she broke the news that she was pregnant again and he must have known without any possible doubt that the child she was carrying was not his. Whatever she said, the matter was urgent. He divorced her on 18th March, 1152, on the grounds that she was his fourth cousin. She and Henry were then married at Poitiers on Whit Sunday, 18th May, 1152, and their son William was born on 20th August, 1152. It is interesting to speculate what would have happened if the divorce had not been hurried through in time and the boy had been born while Eleanore was still married to Louis; he would ostensibly have been heir to the French throne.

By falling in love with Henry, who was as unlike Louis as it was possible to imagine, Eleanore went to an opposite extreme. He was a man of action, as highly sexed as she was and eleven years younger. And yet, apart from physical attraction, one cannot imagine what they had in common. Her court was luxurious and pleasure-loving, while his was reputed to be the most slovenly and uncomfortable in Europe. He delighted in being for ever on the move and spent days at a time entirely occupied with public business. Peter of Blois, who had been his tutor, wrote: 'When King Henry sets out of a morning you see multitudes of people running up and down as if they were distracted, horses rushing against horses, carriages overturning carriages, players, gamesters, cooks, confectioners, morris dancers, barbers, courtesans and parasites.' He also inherited his grandfather Henry I's love of animals and liked to take round with him a bear. Energetic and restless by nature, a tendency to fat made him eat very little, to be uninterested in food, and to take a great deal of exercise. Peter de Blois describes his colouring as ruddy, sub-rufous or pale red, in stature middle and his head round. He goes on to say: 'His head is of such quantity that to the neck, and to all the body, it accordeth even proportion. He has a fine, clear colour whilst he is pleased, but through a disturbance of heart like sparkling fire or lightning with hastiness. His head of curlie hair, when clipped square and in the forehead sheweth a lyonous visage, the nostrils even comely, according to all the other features. High vaulted feet, legs able to riding, broad bust and long champion arms, which telleth him to be strong and hardy. In a toe of his foot a nail groweth into his flesh, and in harm to the foot ever waxeth. His hands through his large size, sheweth negligence, for he utterly leaveth the keeping of them; never but when he beareth hawks, weareth he gloves. He likes standing, even doing so when he eat sometimes.'

Whatever his parentage he inherited the Angevin temper. The Conqueror and his descendants had had rages and melancholy expressions, but Henry exceeded all this and used to roll on the floor and bite mats and the legs of chairs and tables and anything else he could find, when he was really displeased. At other times he could be pleasant and good-tempered. He was a sound administrator, had a quick wit and a good memory, and could be learned, wise and liberal.

Eleanore must have been passionately in love with him. However dull it must have been, she was the Queen of France and in 1151 Henry's prospects were not particularly good. Normandy had been subdued by his father and handed over to him by his mother, but it was a turbulent country and preferred to be ruled by its own Duke rather than by a King of England. As soon as his father had died, his brother Geoffrey had disputed his claim to Anjou, and Stephen and Matilda did not agree on the succession to the English throne until 1153.

For him the marriage was advantageous, for, although Eleanore had lost her reputation, she still had her lands and money, and once Henry was established, she and Henry together were more powerful than Louis. He was probably tremendously attracted to her—one imagines that it would be difficult for a man not to be—but, like his grandfather Henry I, Henry was promiscuous; as early in their married life as 1153, according to Richard of Devizes, a son of his, Geoffrey, was born of a 'common English whore named Ykenai or Hikenai, who scorned no filthiness'. Henry was fond of the child who went into the Church and was well-educated, and in 1181 Henry made him Chancellor of England.

Their coronation took place six weeks after Stephen died, on Sunday, 19th December, 1154. Eleanore was by far the richest queen that England had ever had. She brought in luxuries that they had never known before, and encouraged trading in wine between Aquitaine and England. She brought over as her trousseau forty-two gowns of silk, linen and wool, many of which were richly embroidered; fourteen pairs of shoes, six of them richly embroidered with gold thread; five mantles of various colours bordered with various ermines, a profusion of veils and, very sensibly, ten warm undershirts.

Her courts she held at Bermondsey, Winchester, Woodstock and Westminster. She was fond of having mystery and miracle plays performed and, apart from a slight breath of scandal in 1155 when she was back in Aquitaine and thought to have looked on a troubadour called Ventadour with too much favour, she seems to have settled down quietly to an exemplary married life. During the next fifteen years she had eight children. William, who was just born in wedlock, was followed by Henry in 1154; Matilda, who later married Henry the Lion, Duke of Saxony, ancestor of the Hanoverian kings, was born in 1156, the same year that William died aged four. Richard was born in 1157, Geoffrey in 1159, Eleanore in 1162, Joanna in 1165, and John in 1167.

In 1160 Henry left Eleanore as Regent in England while he went to Normandy, where there was trouble. Later in the year he sent for Eleanore and his eldest surviving son Henry and married him at the age of six to Marguerite, daughter of Louis by his second marriage to Constance of Castile. An astounding arrangement when one thinks of what had previously happened. Having taken away the French king's wife, he seemed determined to marry his own sons to Louis's daughters. In 1162 Alice, another daughter of Louis, this time by his third wife Alice of Champagne, whom he married six weeks after Constance died, was betrothed to Richard.

By 1164 Henry and Eleanore had begun to quarrel because of his unfaithfulness. By then she was forty-two and had already had eight children, six by him and two by the King of France, and he was only thirty-one, hot-blooded and approaching his prime. The courtesans in his court were probably significant, as he does not seem to have had numbers of acknowledged mistresses or illegitimate children, as had Henry I. His best known mistress was Rosamund Clifford, who bore him two sons. He also had a recognized son called Morgan, whose mother 'The lady of Sir Ralph Blewer' was presumably Welsh. There grew up a legend about Rosamund— Rose of the World—and her death. Henry was supposed to have loved her dearly and to have had a labyrinth built for her at Woodstock; as Eleanore frequently held her court there it was a dangerous thing to do and she found them out. One story goes that Eleanore became suspicious and traced Henry there by a silken thread from a ball of floss that had got stuck in his spur when he was going to see his paramour. The story had different endings: some say Eleanore had her stabbed to death, others that she had her poisoned; and another version goes that she retired to a convent and died there twenty years later.

To begin with Henry and Eleanore just quarrelled; there was no serious rift between them, but after her last child was born the rift widened. Her subjects in Aquitaine became restive because they had not seen her for so long, and she went on there from Normandy and stayed for six years until 1173. She was thus away when Becket was slain, but when she did come back to England she was with Henry when he did penance for this crime at Canterbury.

Henry's troubles increased, many of them aggravated by Eleanore, who had grown to hate him. His sons were high-spirited and wanted their inheritances, and she sided with

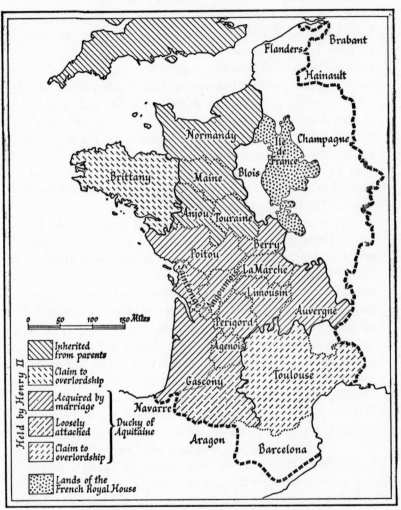

Reproduced from *King John* by W. L. Warren; by courtesy of Eyre & Spottiswoode Ltd.

European possessions of Henry II about 1170.

them. Like William the Conqueror, he was loth to give them any responsibility. He did have Henry crowned at Westminster as future King of England in imitation of the Capet kings, who had had their heirs crowned in their lifetime; but Henry, or Fitz-Henry as he was called, does not seem to have been overcome by filial affection at the gesture. During the banquet held afterwards his father waited on him as part of the traditional ceremony and, handing him a dish, said: 'There is no prince in Europe who has such a server at his table;' to which the prince replied in an aside to the Earl of Leicester: 'No great condescension for the son of an earl to wait on the son of a king.'

In 1170 Henry II fell into such a violent rage and made himself so ill that he thought he was going to die, and made a will. He left England, Normandy, Maine and Anjou to Henry; Aquitaine to Richard; Bretange to Geoffrey, who had married Constance, the heiress of that country; and John was left dependent on his brother, as had been Henry I. Richard was crowned King of Poitou and became more and more his mother's favourite and under her influence. Henry adored John, the youngest, and had him at his court surrounded by mistresses, courtesans and bastards.

Henry had at first been only too pleased to have Eleanore out of the way ruling her own country; but now that he had discovered that she was plotting against him with her sons he decided that he must keep an eye on her and in 1173 ordered her back to England. She tried to get to Paris disguised as a page boy, which, as she was then fifty-two, was rather ambitious. Her idea was to get her ex-husband Louis's help against Henry; as he was jealous of Henry's power, this was not such a wild idea as it seems. She was captured and held at Bordeaux until Henry arrived and took her back to England with her daughter-in-law, the French princess, Marguerite Fitz-Henry. Eleanore was then kept a prisoner, mostly at Winchester, for the next thirteen years.

From this time onwards the family squabbled among itself much in the same way as the Conqueror's had done. Henry tried to keep his sons with him; Fitz-Henry, although he was married by this time and eighteen years old, used to sleep in the same room, and actually escaped from it in the middle of the night to go and join in a fight against his father. He died in 1183 and left no heir.

After his death Richard became the oldest surviving son. His father showed no signs of proclaiming him heir, told him that he was to hand Aquitaine to John and still kept his fiancée, to whom he had been engaged for eighteen years, away from him. She was now twenty-three and Richard twenty-six. It was rumoured that she was Henry's mistress, and that he was going to obtain a divorce from Eleanore and marry her himself. That he did not do this was attributed to the fact that Eleanore was now sixty-three, old for those days, and he may have thought that she had not much longer to live.

In 1186 he let her go back to Aquitaine, as the people there were clamouring for her and had become difficult and discontented. Probably to keep mother and son apart he took Richard with him on a tour of Southern England.

In the same year Geoffrey was killed tilting in a tournament in France. Eleanore came back to England in 1187 and the pair became united in their dislike of their daughter-in-law Constance, Geoffrey's widow, who had produced a son, a few months after her husband's death. Eleanore did not like the idea of her acting as Regent for her baby son, although it was through her that they claimed Brittany, and Henry was becoming more and more determined that John should inherit land. One of their quarrels with Constance was a petty one over the child's name; Eleanore and Henry wanted him to be called Henry, but Constance did not. To make matters worse, before his death Geoffrey had been plotting with Philip, the French king, against his father, and both Philip and Henry claimed the child as their ward.

Only too pleased to make more trouble for his father, Richard sided with Philip and between them they defeated him in battle, drove him out of Le Mans and burnt it to the ground. Henry had been born there and felt the loss deeply, but seemed to blame God more than his son or himself for his defeat, and said, 'O God, thou hast shamefully taken from me this day the city which I loved most on earth, in which I was born and bred, where lies the body of my father and that of his patron saint; I will requite thee as I may.'

He got so worked up that he flew into one of his terrible rages which made him ill, and his suffering was greatly increased when he learned that John had deserted to the enemy. 'Can it be? John, my darling child, my very heart, for love of whom I have incurred all this misery. Has he indeed forsaken me?' he said. He then turned his face to the wall, whispering, 'Let things go now as they will, I care no more for myself nor for the world,' and gradually slipped into a delirium, watched over by the only son who had any affection for him and been consistently loyal—Geoffrey the Bastard. He frequently called down curses on Richard and John, and at the last had a haemorrhage and died in agony.

Eleanore survived him for fifteen strenuous years. Unabated in vigour she travelled round Europe controlling her two surviving sons. She stopped being a trouble-maker and seemed to grow in wisdom; many a time she had to smooth over difficulties made by their greed, cruelty, and thoughtlessness. There was a warmth and vitality about her even in her old age which her children, except perhaps for Joanna, did not seem to inherit. She was besieged when fighting a battle at the age of eighty, and at eighty-two took the veil and died two years later in 1204.

5 - Richard I

*Born 1157, died 1199. Became king 1189. Married Berengaria of Navarre
(born 1165, died 1230) in 1191.*

RICHARD I CARED less for England than any king we ever
had. Although he had been born at Oxford he had spent
most of his life with his mother in Aquitaine fighting for or
against his father and brothers on the Continent. He looked
upon England as a source of income, and during his reign of
ten years spent only six months in this country.

His passion was for fighting, and in his lifetime he became
a legend for his courage and leadership, also for his cruelty.
Tall, over six foot, with long legs and arms and a good figure,
he had reddish fair hair, a restless energy and a violent
temper. He often drank too much and, although physically
very strong, never enjoyed great good health: he suffered
from agues, fevers and skin diseases all his life. He loved
music and was a keen troubadour; he had a great love of
clothes and liked his surroundings to be neat and orderly
even when he was campaigning, and when he was not he
liked them to be beautiful and luxurious, often taking part
in the decorating of them himself.

In those ways he was like his mother, but unlike her he
had a coldness of character which made even his cruelty
dispassionate and deliberate rather than hotblooded. The
Aquitaines hated him as a ruler, especially after he had
quelled their rebellion and killed the prisoners he had taken

by cutting them down with the sword, and drowning or blinding them to make an example; many of his allies had no love for him either. The only person who had any influence over him was Eleanore, his mother. He had always been her favourite and had been brought up to believe that he would be the heir to her possessions. He certainly had one illegitimate child, Fulk, from an affair in his youth with Joanna St. Pol, and was thought also to have had as his mistress Maenz de Montagnac, whose favours he shared with Alphonso of Aragon, Raymond of Toulouse and various others. As well as this he was a homosexual; he was not so much highly-sexed like his parents, just amoral.

In the by now traditional manner of his ancestors the first thing that he did when his father died was to seize his treasure, this time from Chinon; then he crossed to England to seize what money could be found there and to liberate his mother Eleanore. After he was crowned he sold a few bishoprics to raise money and fined those noblemen who did not want to go with him on the crusade on which he had set his heart. If they did not pay enough he put them in prison.

Before he died Henry had arranged for John, Richard's younger brother, to marry Adelicia, the granddaughter of Robert of Gloucester, Henry I's illegitimate son. The marriage had been delayed because Baldwin, the Archbishop of Canterbury, forbade it on the grounds of consanguinity; but they married at Michaelmas and John was given estates in England and left behind as one of the Regents.

Eleanore decided that Richard must be married too. His fiancée Alice was still in England, twenty-six and unmarried, but Eleanore hated her, and Richard, far from being a pressing suitor, had only demanded his bride when he particularly wanted to aggravate his father. In 1188, when they were on very bad terms, he did so and, when Henry refused to hand her over, said, 'Now I believe what had seemed to me to be impossible.' After which remarks Henry became speechless and his face went first deadly pale and then purple.

After Henry died, Alice's brother Philip demanded that he should marry her. Richard refused, saying that he would not marry his father's whore, and accused her of having had a daughter as the result of their liaison. A French rhyme of the time said:

> Then spoke King Philip, and in grief said,
> 'My sister Alice is now forsaken,
> Since one, of more riches, of Navarre hast thou taken.'
> When King Richard understood what King Philip had sworn,
> Before clergy he stood and proved on that morn,
> That Alice to his father a child had borne,
> Which his sire King Henry held for his own,
> A maiden-child it was and now dead is.

Richard kept Alice prisoner at Rouen and the poor woman was not married off until the age of thirty-five, when her bridegroom was a French nobleman; for her dowry she was given the country of Ponthieu. Curiously enough, it was her descendants not Richard's, who ruled England in the end, as she was the great-grandmother of Edward II.

Eleanore decided that Richard should marry Berengaria, the daughter of Sancho 'the Wise', King of Navarre. She had been born in 1165, eight years after Richard and has been described as 'virtuous and fair', 'a renowned, beautiful and prudent virgin', but also as 'more learned than beautiful'. Her brother Sancho, 'the Bold or Strong', who had succeeded his father, was a great hunting and fighting companion of Richard's. Richard visited their court in 1177 when Berengaria was twelve and she was supposed to have fallen in love with him while he was there. Now Eleanore swept her off to Brindisi while Richard got himself out of his engagement to Alice. She took her on to Messina and handed her over to Joanna, her youngest daughter and Richard's favourite sister, now the widow of William 'the Good', King of Sicily, whose chief pleasure had been oriental slave girls. To Joanna, Eleanore is recorded as having said, 'Fair daughter, take this damsel for me to the king your brother and tell him I command him to espouse her speedily'. It was said that 'Queen Joanna held her dear. They lived as doves in a cage'. Eleanore then went back to England to see how John was behaving. She was sixty-nine and seemed to thrive on travelling round Europe, exhausting and dangerous as it must have been.

The wedding took place on 12th May, 1191, at Limassol. Berengaria was crowned Queen of England and Cyprus at the ceremony. Richard seems to have stolen the scene at the wedding by looking 'happy and splendid' and wearing a rose-coloured satin tunic with a cloak of striped silver tissue, a scarlet bonnet brocaded with gold, while the hilt of his sword and baldric were covered with jewels. She is described briefly as 'wearing a mantilla'. He celebrated the occasion by starting a Knightly Order of the Blue Thong, who wore bands of blue leather round their left legs, and whose first object was to protect the Queen.

Before the wedding a most curious thing happened. In Messina Richard came before the bishops half-naked and in sackcloth, with a scourge in his hand, and did public penance for his unnatural sins. How public the penance was and whether Berengaria knew about it it is difficult to say, nor if she knew about the appalling cruelties he had committed when subduing the island. Almost as soon as the wedding was over Richard set sail for Palestine, and Berengaria and Joanna followed him in another ship; with them went the King of Cyprus's daughter, some said because Richard wanted her as his mistress, others that she was simply a hostage.

They remained on Crusade for fifteen months. Almost as soon as they landed Richard became ill with fever and boils, and his hair fell out and his skin peeled as if he had a vitamin deficiency. He was so weak that he had to be carried to the battle of Acre on a litter.

In July they were all in the royal palace at Acre and Richard was quarrelling with all the other leaders. In August Richard perpetrated another of his terrible acts of cruelty by way of revenge on Saladin. He ordered all the Moslem survivors of Acre and their women and children to be brought before him and then gave the order that they should all be butchered. After they were dead the corpses were mutilated.

After this Richard ordered the Crusade to move on without any women and children except the ones who worked as washerwomen and such like. Joanna, Berengaria and the little Cypriot princess were left behind, and they did not meet again until October, when they were all in Jaffa.

It was in Jaffa that he suggested to Joanna that she should marry El Saladin's brother El Adil. She flew into a temper and said that she was not going to marry an infidel, and they had a fine family row, which she won. The rainy season then came upon them, so the fighting stopped and he saw something of his wife, but as soon as he was able he started to fight again until August, when again he fell ill. He also heard that John was intriguing against him in England. He was not making any progress in Palestine, many of the Crusaders were ill, a lot had gone home and the remainder were quarrelling. He decided he must leave.

He sent Berengaria and Joanna away in advance and followed in another ship. There were rumours that he and Berengaria were not getting on well. Some said that she had had a miscarriage brought on by witnessing his atrocities, others that she found out about his vicious life. They had only seen each other for about four months during the seventeen months they had been married and some of this time Richard had been ill; they were not to meet again for four years.

Berengaria and Joanna got safely to Rome, where Joanna fell in love with Raymond, Count St. Gilles, whom she married. Richard was not so fortunate; after a month at sea he was shipwrecked on the Adriatic coast. He took to the road and tried to disguise himself by letting his hair and beard grow long, but was captured and held prisoner by the Duke of Austria, one of the chief people with whom he had quarrelled in Palestine. For weeks nobody knew where he was or even that he was in trouble. Then Berengaria saw a jewelled collar or belt of his on sale in Rome which she recognized as his. Two monks found out that he was the Emperor's prisoner. Blondel de Nesle, a troubadour, discovered exactly where he was held when he heard Richard's voice singing from a tower.

Eleanore made frantic efforts to get him released and wrote curious letters to the Pope, confessing her past sins and begging for his help. The Pope was on her side without the letters, and so was the German Diet and a great deal of Europe, who thought it was wrong for the Duke of Austria, who was the lay head of Christendom, to keep captive the leader and brave fighter of the last Crusade. When they were in Palestine Richard was said to have lost his temper with the Archduke and publicly kicked him, which probably accounted for his un-Crusaderlike actions. If he did, the kick cost England a lot of money, as the Duke demanded a tremendous ransom. Eleanore managed to collect it, though John spent a great deal of what he collected in England on himself.

After one year, six weeks and three days of captivity, Richard was set free and landed in England in the spring of 1194; he had been away for four years, three months and nine days. He rushed round England putting things in order and then went back to Normandy and on to his Angevin territories; he made no attempt to go to Berengaria but rejoined his old hunting, jousting and drinking companions. One day when he was hunting in Normandy a hermit stopped him, preached him a long sermon about his way of life, and ended up by saying that unless he repented his end and punishment were close at hand. Almost immediately after this, during Easter 1195, Richard became very ill indeed and got such a fright that he sent for all the monks round him, made another public confession, and said that if Berengaria would forgive him he would never forsake her again. She did, and until his death she was with him on his campaigns. It is likely that it was by this time only a marriage in name, if it had ever been anything else. Although she was only thirty-one and he thirty-nine, Richard seemed so positive that they would not have children that he proclaimed Arthur, Geoffrey's son, his heir, and tried to persuade Constance, the child's mother, to send him to be brought up in England.

Three years later he died besieging the Castle of Chaluz. An arrow from a crossbow got him in the shoulder, and his physicians cut it out so clumsily that he died of the wound.

Berengaria lived for another thirty-one years and died at Le Mans in 1230. Really the most remarkable thing about her was her name, and the fact that she was the only Queen of England never to set foot in England. The chief thing that one knows about her after Richard's death was that she had great difficulty in getting her money, first out of John and then out of Henry.

6 - King John

Born 1167, died 1216. Became king 1199. Married Adelicia of Gloucester (date of birth uncertain, died 1217) in 1189. Divorced 1199. Married Isabella of Angouleme (born 1186, died 1245) in 1200.

JOHN INHERITED the nastiest characteristics of both sides of his family. The cunning that he inherited from his father was more like outright dishonesty; he had little of his father's energy but plenty of his violent temper. He inherited from his mother his love of pleasure and luxury but, unlike her, he was over-extravagant, and by the time he came to the throne there was not much money left. Although educated in England—he had been born there on Christmas Eve 1167 and had been brought up in his father's court more than in his mother's—he was 'French' in outlook and temperament. He loved rich foods, good wines, of which he drank too much, music, women, amusing companions and gambling—his favourite game was backgammon. He collected jewels and rivalled Richard in his fondness for clothes. One Christmas he was described as wearing 'a red satin mantle embroidered with sapphire and pearls, a tunic of damask, and a girdle set with garnets and sapphires, while the baldric across his shoulder to sustain his sword was set with diamonds and emeralds and his white gloves adorned, one with a ruby and one with a sapphire.'

His chief merit was that he had good taste and was fond of literature. In looks he was shorter than his father, about five feet six inches, was inclined to fat but, unlike his father, did not do anything about it; and he had a drooping left eye. Although he had been his father's favourite he had been nicknamed by him 'Lackland' because Henry never succeeded in finding him any country to rule.

Henry had tried various ruses to get him land. When John was four years old he negotiated to get him engaged to a daughter of the Count of Maurienne. When the Count asked about money Henry, who never liked paying, promised that John should have lands which he had already given to Fitz-Henry. Fitz-Henry objected and started a rebellion. Later, Henry tried taking Aquitaine away from Richard and giving it to John but that started another rebellion.

Shortly before his death he had given him £4,000-worth of land in England and arranged for him to marry Adelicia, a rich heiress and one of the three daughters of the Earl of Gloucester and a granddaughter of Robert of Gloucester, Henry I's illegitimate son. As her father had had no heirs and her two sisters had married, she was styled Countess of Gloucester, and when John married her in 1189 he took the earldom to himself. On his marriage Richard gave him £1,000 a year and, after his coronation, the Duchies of Cornwall, Devon and Somerset. The Church was against the marriage from the first on the grounds of consanguinity, and the original date of the ceremony was postponed for a few months. John must have gone through with it simply because he thought that it was the most advantageous way at that moment to secure land and money; he quite obviously had no other use for Adelicia and she never appeared in public as his wife. So little indeed did he think of the marriage that, without going through any form of divorce, in 1192 he contemplated rescuing and marrying Alice, the French princess who had been Richard's fiancée and was imprisoned by him at Rouen. In 1199 he did get an official divorce from Adelicia but kept her a state prisoner until 1213, when he sold her to Geoffrey de Mandeville for 20,000 marks. After Geoffrey died in 1215 she married Hubert de Burgh as his second wife a few days before her own death on 14th October, 1217, a year after John's.

After Richard's death Arthur of Brittany, the son of Geoffrey, the third son of Henry and Eleanore, should have inherited the throne. Richard had named him as his heir and had tried to persuade Constance, his mother, to send him to England to be educated. Constance hated Eleanore and had refused to do so. When Richard died she was having matrimonial adventures herself and had just eloped from her second husband, the Earl of Chester and, without a divorce, 'married' Sir Guy of Thouars, which possibly took her mind off claiming Arthur's rightful inheritance, and in 1201 she died having a baby.

John wasted no time in claiming the throne and Eleanore supported his claim. He rushed to Chinon and seized the treasure and then went back to England, leaving Eleanore as Regent over his French estates. He was crowned at Westminster on 27th May, 1199.

Early in 1200 he stopped at the castle of Lusignan on his way to Aquitaine. There he met and fell in love with Isabella of Angoulême, the rich and beautiful heiress of her father, Count Aymer of Angoulême. She was in her early teens and engaged to Hugh de Lusingan; she had been sent to the home of his uncle, Arthur de Lusignan, to be educated. Hugh was away and John determined that, betrothal or not, they should marry. In this he had the approval of her parents, who thought that he was a better match than Hugh, so they made an excuse for her to go back to them, and she and John were married at Bordeaux on 24th August, 1200. John was then thirty-two years old and she was fourteen.

Hugh, when he came back, challenged John to a duel, but John refused to fight himself and said that he would appoint a champion to meet him, to which Hugh replied that all champions were cut-throats and let the matter drop. The Pope, too, expressed his displeasure at the marriage because of her former betrothal, but John must have been used to papal disapproval of his marriages by that time and was not too worried.

Isabella was brought to England to be crowned. Although extravagant in his own dress, John did not seem to encourage

her to make a great show. For her coronation she was given
three cloaks of fine linen, one of scarlet cloth and one of grey
pelisse. After this they went back to France and stayed at
Rouen, where they ate splendid dinners and stayed in bed
until noon. Kings at that time were expected to get up at
about five o'clock in the morning, and the story went round
that she had enthralled him by witchcraft.

This easy life was interrupted by Hugh de Lusignan, who,
seeking his revenge, combined with Arthur, who had legitimate grievance against both John and Eleanor, to besiege
Eleanor in her castle of Mirabeau in Poitou. For once John
took prompt action. He had a strong filial feeling and he now
marched night and day for forty-eight hours to her rescue.
He took Arthur and his sister, Eleanor, prisoner. Eleanor
was well treated and died a natural death in 1241. Arthur died
soon afterwards in mysterious circumstances. Some said that
John ordered that he should be blinded and then killed;
others that he ordered him to be castrated and that the shock
killed him; and another story was that, when he was drunk,
he killed him himself and, putting a stone round the body,
sank it in a river. Whatever happened the custodian of Falaise
Castle where Arthur was held prisoner, a man called Hugh de
Burgh, was very much rewarded. After Arthur's death de
Burgh was given lands and manors and later married the
unfortunate Adelicia, John's first wife, as his third, and after
her the King of Scotland's sister.

In November John had to go and put down more rebellions
in the south of France and left Isabella, then about sixteen, in
charge at Chinon, where she was attacked by rebels, and in
January 1203 he had to rush to her rescue. He had lost
Normandy and by 1206 most of the rest of his lands in France.

He spent the Christmas of 1204 with Isabella at Canterbury.
She had not yet produced a child and her hold over him had
already weakened, and his eye began to roam. He already had
three acknowledged bastard sons, Oliver, Richard and Osbert,
and one or two daughters, one of whom married Llewellyn of
Wales, who fought against him in 1211. These had been
born before his marriage to Isabella but now he took other

mistresses. This naturally upset Isabella, who was quick-tempered, sensual and spoilt, and they began to have quarrels. She was not the only person who was upset, the barons did not appreciate it either when he tried to seduce their wives or daughters.

During the next twelve years he caused several scandals, one when he tried to seduce the wife of a nobleman called de Vesci by a trick. He borrowed de Vesci's ring and sent it to the country to his wife with a message saying that her husband was dying and that she must go to London to King John. De Vesci met his wife on the way to London and substituted a prostitute for her. John next day said to de Vesci, 'Your wife is very pleasant in the silence of the night.' De Vesci told him about the substitution and then 'quickly ran from the King's wrath'. Another scandal occurred over Matilda the Fair, the daughter of one of his barons who caught his eye in 1214. She did not reciprocate his feelings, so he abducted her and incarcerated her in the White Tower, where some said, he had her poisoned because she had resisted his advances.

In 1207 Isabella produced her first child, a son; between then and 1216 she had four more children, Richard born in 1209, Joanna 1210, Isabella 1214 and Eleanor in 1215. This did not stop their quarrels getting worse and he accused her of being unfaithful; he was reputed to have assassinated two of her lovers and to have had their bodies hung over her bed. Whether he really went as far as this or not is uncertain, but in 1212 he followed the Plantagenet habit of imprisoning wives, and kept Isabella at Gloucester Abbey with her most recently born daughter Isabella until 1213. Her other children he took away from her because he said she was immoral. After her father had died and she had inherited Angoulême he let her out of prison. Her mother came over to England to pay them a visit, and the three of them went back to Angoulême. They came back to England again for Christmas, which they spent at Windsor in great style; John had sent in as provisions 2,000 capons, 15,000 herrings, 1,000 eels, 1,000 pounds of almonds and 6,000 gallons of wine.

In June 1215 he left Windsor Castle to sign the Magna
Carta. As he showed no signs of abiding by it, the barons
asked Philip to come over and rule England. Philip did not
do so but sent his son Louis over with an army, which landed
on 16th October. Neither side seemed to know what to do
after this; Louis seemed half-hearted and John moved about
from place to place and 'lost his luggage in the Wash'. He
had had gout in 1215 and had been ill with dysentery since
then; he had also fallen into frequent rages as he became
more and more thwarted and frustrated. He went to the
Abbey of Swinshead, where some said that he ate too much
fruit and drank too much wine, fell into his last rage and
died; others that the monks poisoned him. Whichever it was,
he became seriously ill and was carried on a litter to Newark,
where he died on 19th October, 1216.

Isabella was not asked to be Regent to her young son
because her reputation was so bad, and in 1217 she took
her daughter Joanna over to France to marry her to her
erstwhile fiancée Hugh de Lusignan. Hugh was away on a
Crusade, but in 1220 he came back and, preferring the mother
to the daughter, married her instead.

Isabella tried to put this all on a very high plane and wrote
to Henry III.

'To our dearest son Henry, by the grace of God King of
England, Lord of Ireland, Duke of Normandy and Aquitaine,
Isabella, Countess of Anjou and Angoulême sends health and
her maternal benediction.

'We hereby signify to you that when the Counts of March
and Eu departed this life, the Lord Hugh de Lusignan remained
alone and without heirs at Poitu; and his friends would not
permit that our daughter should be united to him in marriage
because her age is so tender, but counselled him to take a
wife from whom he could speedily hope for an heir; and it
was proposed that he should take a wife in France, which if
he had done, all your land in Poitu and Gascony would be
lost. We, therefore, seeing the great peril that might accrue
if that marriage should take place (when other counsellors
could give us no better advice) ourself married the said

Count de March; and God knows that we did this rather for your benefit than our own; and we earnestly pray that you will restore to him (Hugh de Lusignan, Count de March) his lawful right: that is Niort, and the castles of Exeter and Rockingham which your father, our former husband, bequeathed to us.'

Neither Henry nor his Regents were much impressed by this letter and did not give Hugh the castles; but she did produce the heirs. She had five sons and three daughters by this marriage and greatly preferred these children to those of her marriage to John.

In 1245 she was accused of hiring assassins to murder the King of France, Louis, who had succeeded his father Philip. Louis called a Congress to go into the charge to which she was now bidden. The story goes that she waited outside on her horse and then galloped away when she saw a witness whom she knew was her enemy, go into the court.

Her excuse for her sudden flight was that she had been insulted because, when her husband had gone to do homage to the King and Queen, they did not receive her for three days, and when they did they did not ask her to sit down. After her flight she went back to La Marche, stripped the castle of everything and had it sent to Angoulême. She then shut herself into her room, would not see the Count for three days, and only came out when he promised to start a rebellion against the king.

The whole episode upset her so much that she was said to have attempted to kill herself with a dagger, but somebody seized it and stopped her. Hugh again wanted a duel, this time with Louis's brother, for his wife's honour, but he declined, saying that Hugh was too treason-spotted. This so upset Isabella that she took the veil and died in 1246. Since 1216, when Henry came to the throne, she was an almost permanent nuisance to him, but he always treated her with the greatest respect.

7 - Henry III

Born 1207, died 1272. Became king 1216. Married Eleanor of Provence (born 1222, died 1291) in 1230.

HENRY III WAS handicapped all his life by his family. When he was only nine years old he succeeded to the throne of England and had to rule a country that had been first ruined by his uncle, King Richard, and then by his father, King John. He also inherited from them three women who were no help at all. Richard's widow Berengaria was perpetually demanding her pension because payments had always been behind; Isabella, his mother, made trouble all over Europe and expected him to welcome and support her second family, although he had scarcely known her and hardly knew them; and Eleanor, his sister, demanded bigger and better dowries, and her quarrels with him about these aggravated his misunderstandings with Simon de Montfort, her second husband.

Physically he was not well-endowed. He had a drooping left eye like his father; like him too he was plump and inclined to indolence, and most years had tertian fever. He had a much nicer nature than any of his immediate ancestors; his instinct, unlike some of his forebears, was to treat women well rather than badly, and he was a devoted father and family man. He had the family temper but was kindly by nature rather than cruel. Like his father he had a great love of luxury and had 'French' tastes, but by this time had few French possessions to help to pay for them.

He was crowned on 28th October, 1216, and because he was so young England was ruled by a Regency. By 1223 he was allowed some say in the government of his country, and in January, 1227, he announced that being now of age he would rule himself. In 1225 and 1226 there had been three attempts to find him a bride. First he had tried to marry a daughter of Leopold of Austria, then a daughter of the King of Bohemia, and lastly a daughter of the Count of Brittany, Peter of Dreux. These attempts fell through chiefly through the hostility of the King of France, who had no wish to see the King of England become powerful again in Europe.

In 1231 he tried to marry the sister of the King of Scotland, but her elder sister was married to Hugh de Burgh. This old henchman of King John's was now a man of great importance and power, and the barons were determined that he should get no nearer to the throne, so they were against the marriage.

Between 1231 and 1235, while making his biggest efforts to get married, he was in such money difficulties that he had to pawn the crown jewels in France, and it was only with the greatest effort that he managed to raise the money to get them back. In 1235 he actually got married by proxy to Joan, daughter of Simon Count of Ponthieu. The French king forbade this too, but curiously enough did not mind Henry marrying his own wife's younger sister a year later in January 1236. Possibly because the family had little power and no money he thought that a weak King of England bound to him by close family ties, would be a decided asset.

Eleanor of Provence was the daughter of Raymond de Bérenger, Count of Provence, and his wife, the daughter of Thomas of Savoy. Her nickname was 'La Belle'. On both sides of her family they had good looks, charm and talent— they all wrote poetry and songs and loved beauty and literature —but none of them had any money, a commodity of which Henry was also desperately short. Eleanor was devoted to all her relatives and liked to have as many as possible of them in England, and so did Henry, who was fascinated by them and put them into positions of power.

There was some difficulty about her dowry, as nobody in

her family had any money, and at one time the marriage was
nearly off when her father said that he could not pay the
20,000 marks that Henry demanded. Henry took fright at
this and told his negotiators to get her, whatever it cost.
He was going to give her the reversion of Isabella the Queen
Mother's dowry, but there was no immediate settlement and
she did not get any money for a long time. Undaunted by
lack of funds, Henry arranged for her to have the most
magnificent wedding that the English had yet seen, when they
were married at Canterbury on 6th January, 1236. For the
ceremony he wore cloth of gold which had just been invented.

She was then fourteen years old and he was twenty-nine.
She came to Westminster for her coronation sixteen days
after the wedding; the Londoners swept the streets and her
chamber was redecorated in her honour. Among the things
which Henry gave her were nine chaplets for her hair, a
great crown and jewelled girdles. Her sister Margaret, Queen
of France, gave her an ostentatious but virtually useless
present—a peacock made of silver which had a tail set with
sapphires, pearls and other precious stones. It was meant to
carry sweet waters, which were forced out of its beak into a
silver basin.

Henry paid for some of this with the money which he
should have given as dowry to his sister Isabella, who had
just married the Emperor of Germany. The English people
had enjoyed the festivities of the wedding and the coronation, but they did not like footing the bills nor the crowd of
foreign retainers that came over with her. Richard, the king's
brother, suggested that Henry should follow the example of
the King of France, who, after marrying her sister Margaret,
had sent away her entourage. Henry wasn't strong enough
in character to do so even if he had felt so inclined, which
he didn't because he liked them. They were witty, charming
and French and ameliorated his life and his rather dull court.
Also he adored Eleanor, and she was only really happy with
her family about her. As he said later in life, 'he never could
do enough to testify his love for the Queen and her family'.

In 1238 his sister Eleanor married Simon de Montfort.

She had continually blamed Henry for not insisting that the Marshal family, into which she had married when younger and been widowed, should pay her more of her dowry which she claimed they owed. William Marshal had been Henry's Regent and was rich, and she had married his son. Added to her bitterness about this and other money matters, she and Eleanor la Belle disliked each other. Eleanor may have been jealous of the Queen because until her arrival she had reigned at court without competition.

There was no open disagreement with Henry until a year after she and de Montfort married. Edward, the first child of Henry and Eleanor, was born on 16th June, 1239, and christened on 16th July. It was a family affair; de Montfort and Eleanor were in high favour at the time of the christening ceremony, and he was godfather. At the churching of the Queen which took place a month later, a public affair with a solemn procession from Westminster Abbey, the king suddenly flew into one of the family rages and, in front of the court, accused de Montfort of having seduced his sister Eleanor before they were married, and ordered his attendants to turn him out of the palace. She was pregnant, and they were hustled away in a boat.

Three months later the king and queen were at Woodstock and an attempt was made on Henry's life. A mad poet called Ribault rushed into the presence chamber and demanded that Henry should hand over the crown to him, as he insisted that he was the rightful king. Courtiers led him away and Henry told them to treat him gently because he was mad. They seem to have treated him too gently, because in the middle of the night he stole into the king's chamber with a knife and hid himself under the bed. The king, fortunately for him, was in the queen's chamber and nobody would have known anything about Ribault, except that later in the night he went berserk and, yelling insults about the king, stabbed the bolster. This time he was made captive and later executed at Coventry.

Two years after Edward was born they had a daughter, Margaret. Henry was then persuaded by his stepfather, Hugh, to fight with him against Louis; they were soundly beaten, and Henry's half-brothers, the Lusignans, swarmed to England to take shelter in his court, so he had to support them too, also his half-sister Alice de Lusignan, whom he married to John de Warrenne, Earl of Surrey. This must have been an unwanted extra burden, as he already owed so much money in Bordeaux that he had had to stay there longer than he had wanted while he raised enough to pay his bills. He did not help his money problems by living with Eleanor and their large court in Bordeaux, as if he was celebrating a victory rather than recovering from a defeat. To get the Jews to lend him money to help him out of his difficulties he threatened them with expulsion from London if they did not produce the sum. He had succeeded in doing this by October 1243, when he and Eleanor came back to England with a daughter Beatrice who had been born to them whilst they were away. In this year Richard of Cornwall, who had become a widower, married the queen's youngest sister Sancha.

The Queen's relations were now well established. Thomas of Savoy, one of her uncles, was made Archbishop of Canterbury, and another, Peter of Savoy, Earl of Richmond. Peter built the Palace of Savoy, and there is a plaque about him on the wall outside the Savoy Hotel, which is on the site of the old building. It says: 'Here Peter lodged the many beautiful ladies whom he brought in 1247 from the Courts of Europe to marry them to his wards, a large number of rich young English nobles,' which was a most lucrative trade.

In 1244 Eleanor's uncle Thomas behaved disgracefully. He forced himself into the diocese of the Bishop of London and tried to make the monks there receive him. They did not want to do so, so he hit one of their friars in the face, tore off his cape and trampled it underfoot. When the monks tried to put up some resistance he beat them too, and during the scuffle they discovered that he was wearing armour under his bishop's robes. The monks complained to Henry, but he was so besotted by the family that he would not even listen to them, let alone punish the culprit. The Londoners were furious about this and, whether to try and placate them or

not, Henry weighed the royal children in silver and distributed
the sum amongst the poor children of London. He seemed
to have repented of this the next year and, after the birth of
his second son, Edmund Crouchback, imposed a fine on
Londoners of 1,500 marks, because he said that they had
sheltered a man whom he had banished.

In 1245 Isabella, his mother, died. This must have been a
blessed relief, because as she got older she became more and
more of a trouble-maker, and now she was dead Eleanor got
her dower lands, which might have helped them a bit with
their own money difficulties if she had not handed most of
the money over to her relatives. They had now been married
for ten years and his devotion to her had increased rather than
waned. The same could be said of his debts, which were
enormous, and the state of the country which was chaotic.

More and more pressed for money, he thought of schemes
to raise it and in 1249 he had the brilliant idea of sending
the Queen and Prince Edward out to dine with the rich men
of the City of London, who were meant to pay for this great
honour with gifts. Eleanor improved on this and used to
take her relations too, who used to complain if they did not
get rich gifts as well.

In 1250 he publicly took the Cross as a pilgrim at Westminster and asked the population to contribute money to
this enterprise. Although he was known as a religious man,
many of his subjects looked upon it as another of his schemes
to help him get out of his debts. At another time he wanted
to go on a crusade with Louis, but Eleanor refused to leave
her life of comfort, and he could not bear to go without her
so the plan fell through.

In 1251 on St. Dunstan's Day the queen was in her apartments at Windsor with some of the royal children, when the
chimney above the room that they were in was struck by
lightning and reduced to dust.

In 1252 he had to pay the Pope money to make his marriage
to Eleanor valid because of his proxy marriage to Joan of
Ponthieu, who had herself been married for years to the King
of Castile and whose daughter Eleanor became the bride of

Edward, Henry's son, two years later in 1254—to which marriage the Pope raised no objection. In 1253 Henry went to France and was regally entertained by his brother-in-law Louis, and Eleanor had a daughter, Katherine, who died in infancy and was buried with her four little brothers who had been born and died since the birth of Edmund in 1245. In all she had nine children.

In 1254 the family incurred even further expenses. Eleanor went with Edward to Burgos for his marriage to Eleanor of Castile. Henry settled £1,000 per annum on the bride in case Edward should die before he did, and gave a great feast for them in Paris. The Princess came back to England before Edward and had a suite of rooms with glazed windows, a raised hearth, a chimney, a wardrobe and an adjoining oratory; the apartments were hung with valuable tapestries. She arrived in England on 17th October, 1255. Again the citizens liked the show but not the bill that followed, nor did they like the Spaniards who came with her. They did not have them for long, because almost immediately after Edward arrived in November 1255, he took her back to Bordeaux to complete her education. Eleanor was seriously ill in 1255, and her illness was said to be aggravated by worry about her daughter Margaret, who with her husband the Scots king was being kept a prisoner. They were not kept prisoner for very long and came to stay with her mother at Windsor while Henry was still in France.

When he came back to England again Henry, as usual, was looking for money. Eleanor was said to have become less extravagant by then, but her needs were still great and an account for her necessities included, 'In silks, mantles, upper garments, linen hose for her ladies, and other miscellaneous expenses for her wardrobe, one hundred and four score pounds, eleven shillings and twelve pence halfpenny. In jewels for the Queen's use to wit, eleven rich garlands, with emeralds, pearls, sapphires and garnets, of the value of 145 pounds, 4 shillings and 4 pence.' She seemed at one time to have pawned her jewels in England and Edward, under the pretext of making sure that they were secure, broke into the treasury and stole £10,000 of the people's money which they had left there for safe keeping.

Henry's temper by this time was irascible; like all his family he got worse as he got older, and he must have been difficult to live with. Although there was no sign that he quarrelled with Eleanor he did so with everybody else, and in particular with de Montfort who led the barons against him. In 1259 he was very ill in Paris with some sort of fever, and again in 1261.

The Londoners hated Eleanor more and more. While Henry was away and she acted as Regent, she taxed them even more heavily and seemed to feel no scruples about how she got money for her immediate needs or those of her family. She showed no mercy to them even when there was a famine and many of them were starving. In 1263 they were so enraged that the Queen became frightened and tried to leave the Tower where she was and get to Windsor by barge. The people saw her trying to escape and shouting, 'Drown the witch!' threw mud and rotten eggs, and large stones to try and sink her, so that the queen was forced back to the Tower. Edward I, who was very fond of his mother, never forgave the Londoners for this. In 1264, during the Civil War between Henry and de Montfort, Henry took her over to France for safety, and she did not come back to England again until after the Battle of Evesham.

Now for the only time in his life, Henry's name was to be associated with a liason. He captured in battle the Countess of Gloucester wife of his brother Richard's stepson, and at once released her, remarking that he did not make war on ladies. This seems innocuous enough but the incident caused Queen Marguerite of France to write to him that: Though desiring the society of her sister his queen, she would hasten her departure to him according to his request; because she feared that on account of his long delay he would marry some other lady and that as long as the Countess of Gloucester remained in his vicinity, she should be impatient till she knew that her sister had joined him.

It is difficult to put this letter down to lighthearted banter in view of the fact that the lady almost certainly had an affair with Edward later, so it is possible that she may not have been the most chaste of countesses.

Eleanor certainly came back to England as soon as she could and Henry gave her the custody of London Bridge. This charge she also abused, as she took money from the Londoners but did not keep the bridge open.

After this, for the last years of his life, Henry became more and more ineffectual and Edward virtually ruled England. In 1264 Henry was so ill that he nearly died, and his illness left him so weak that his convalescence lasted several months. At the beginning of 1272 his brother Richard died and ten months later, in November, he followed, and was buried in the old coffin of Edward the Confessor, of whom he had been a great admirer.

In 1276 Eleanor became a nun and spent the rest of her days at Amesbury. In 1275 she had been very ill; a physician from Provence was sent to her and she recovered, to outlive all her children except Edward and Edmund. She died in 1291.

8 - Edward I

Born 1239, died 1307. Became king 1272. Married Eleanor of Castile (born 1244, died 1290) in 1254. Married Marguerite of France (born 1279, died 1317) in 1298.

EDWARD I INHERITED the drooping eye and fierce temper of his father and grandfather but otherwise was as unlike them as is possible to imagine. He was six feet two inches and handsome; when he was young he had light silvery hair, which grew darker as he grew older, and he talked with a slight lisp. 'His head spherical; his eyes round, gentle and dove-like when pleased, but fierce as a lion and sparkling with fire when he was disturbed; his hair crisp or curling, his nose prominent and raised in the middle; his chest broad, his arms agile, his limbs long, his feet arched, his body firm and fleshy, but not fat,' wrote one chronicler of the times.

As a child he was inclined to be delicate, but unlike his father and grandfather he was austere rather than 'French' in his habits. As he grew up he was seldom ill, and ate and drank very little. He was interested in architecture, but had no great love of literature or luxury, and his only intellectual entertainment was chess. He was a good swordsman and horseman and reputed to be the best lance in the world. His passion when he was not fighting was hunting and hawking. He was incapable of disloyalty, but could be ruthless.

During the first part of his life he had a streak of wildness and lawlessness. His mother had encouraged him in her schemes to get as much out of the English as possible, and at her instigation he was even reputed to have robbed merchants of their goods. He never fully forgave the Londoners for their attack on her.

He married Eleanor of Castile at Burgos in October 1254. She was the half-sister of the reigning King of Castile, daughter of Joanna of Ponthieu who had been contracted to Henry years before, and granddaughter of Alice, Richard I's spurned fiancée.

To begin with their marriage was only in name, because she was only ten and he fifteen. She arrived in England without her husband on 17th October, 1255, with such a scanty wardrobe that Henry had to send her money and jewellery, which did not please the English, who must have thought that their next queen was going to follow the pattern of their present one. Edward followed her over on 29th November, 1255, and in 1256 they both went back to Bordeaux and she did not come back to England until after the Civil War against de Montfort was over.

When they were reunited both of them were grown up. He had proved himself as a warrior and she was a lovely woman of twenty, gentle and considerate in her ways. She became known as the queen in whom 'strife ever found a peacemaker', and her nickname was 'the faithful'. He was not yet faithful. He had an affair with the Countess of Gloucester, creating a court scandal which lasted for several years and must have been going on between 1265 and 1270, during which time Eleanor had their first three children, John, Henry and Eleanor. Henry III was so delighted with his beautiful little grandchildren that he increased their mother's allowance.

In 1270 Edward went on a crusade, the last English king to do so, and saying 'Nothing should part those whom God have joined,' Eleanor accompanied him. Before she went, she and Eleanor of Provence toured England together, visiting various shrines; at Dunstable they offered an altar cloth at the shrine of St. Peter as a thanksgiving for the health of her young children. Luckily for England Eleanor of

Provence did not infect her daughter-in-law with her avariciousness, and Eleanor the Faithful became one of the best-loved of all our queens when her husband ascended the throne. Their pilgrimage was especially pathetic, because before she came back to England the two little princes had died.

They spent the winter in Sicily and there heard of the death of one of their young sons, Henry. They then went on to Acre, where their daughter Joan was born and Edward was seriously wounded in the arm by a Saracen with a poisoned dagger. There are two varying stories about the faithful Eleanor and this incident: one was that she sucked the poison out of the wound, and the other that she was so upset that the surgeon dealing with the wound asked for the lady to be carried out because she was so hysterical. In 1272 they went back to Sicily and heard of the death of their other son, John, and of Henry III. Edward was much more upset about the death of his father than of his son, about whom he said philosophically, 'I may get more children but never another father,' which can scarcely have been comforting to the young mother.

Far from following the example of the rest of his family and hurrying home to seize the royal treasure, Edward took his time and they made a leisurely journey back. They went first to Rome, then on to Bordeaux, where Alphonso, their third son, was born. They then stopped in Lyon, where Edward jousted, and lightning killed two of his courtiers who were standing just behind him. After this they went to Paris, where he did homage for his French possessions, and then they spent a year in Gascony while he suppressed a revolt. They did not reach England until the following year, when they were crowned at Westminster on 19th August, 1274, one year and nine months after his father's death.

After the coronation Edward put his affairs in order, and in doing so spared nobody. He subdued the Welsh, hanged two hundred Jewish moneylenders and reorganized the legislation of England. Eleanor spent most of her time at Windsor, and by 1278 had had two more daughters, Margaret, and

Mary—the latter the only one of her children to live to the age of fifty.

Their domestic life sounds happy if hearty. Edward, now that he had settled down, was primarily a man's man, with his love of jousting, hunting and hawking. He had simple tastes and enjoyed a certain amount of horseplay. He bet a laundrymaid that she could not ride to hounds and be in at the death of the stag. She did and was, and won forty shillings. Another time he paid out £14 to the women of his household who, according to some custom of the day, on an Easter Monday lifted his chair off the ground and would not put him down until he promised them that sum. He liked chess and once for no apparent reason changed his seat just before a lump of ceiling fell down where he had been playing.

In 1282 the Welsh rose up again, and Eleanor went with Edward on his campaign to subdue them. In 1283 their daughter Isabella was born. They were still in Wales in 1284, where on 25th April another son, Edward, was born at Caernarvon Castle in a very small, dark room, only twelve feet long and eight feet wide, hung with tapestries to make it more luxurious. As soon as she was able Eleanor moved to the more luxurious Conway Castle. Shortly after Edward's birth their only other surviving son, Alphonso, died, so Edward became the heir.

They went back to London for Christmas and then on to Gascony for three years, where her daughters Beatrice and Berengaria were born. While they were there their daughter Mary, now eight, became a nun at the Abbey of Amesbury, where her grandmother Eleanor had taken the veil. Edward was against this, but Eleanor had made a promise that she would give this daughter to the church and he gave way to her. Their daughter Margaret was married to John of Brabant. At the wedding Edward became irritated by a squire and struck him, for which he had to pay £13 6s. 8d. compensation. When they came back to England in 1289 they had another daughter, Blanche.

The next year he went off to fight the Scots. Eleanor, ever

faithful, although ill with fever tried to follow him. At
Hardely near Grantham her condition worsened and she
became seriously ill. Edward rushed back from Scotland to
try to be with her but she died on 29th November before he
got there. They had been married for thirty-six years and
had had thirteen children, of whom six were sons, only one
of whom had survived. Edward was inconsolable after her
death and followed her corpse back to London; the journey
took thirteen days, and at each stop he erected a cross to her
memory.

His trials as a widower grew upon him and he must have
longed for Eleanor to help deal with their daughters. Just
before her death Joan was married to the Earl of Gloucester,
who had divorced his over-gay countess, with whom Edward
had had the affair. They had to have special permission to
marry from the Pope as they were nearly related, and one
wonders if the Pope knew all the circumstances. Gloucester
died not long after the marriage and Edward arranged for
her to marry the Count of Savoy. Joan had other views and
before this could happen, secretly married one of her departed
husband's household. Another of his daughters threw him
into such a rage when he was discussing with her her wedding arrangements, that he flung her coronet away from him
in a burst of anger, and the Keeper of the Privy Purse wrote
in his accounts: 'To make good a large ruby and an emerald
lost out of the coronet, when the King's grace was pleased to
throw it behind the fire.'

By 1294 Edward was looking for another wife and tried to
get Blanche 'the Fair', the sister of Philip 'the Fair' of France
to be his second queen. He asked his ambassador in France
to give him a detailed description of her appearance, her face,
manner and the turn of her waist, which he did, but Philip
refused to let her go on the grounds that she was too young,
and offered instead his half-sister Margaret, aged fifteen, a few
years older than Blanche but still forty years younger than
Edward. At the same time they agreed that his daughter,
Isabella, should become betrothed to young Edward at a future
date.

The wedding of Edward and Margaret was held up for four years while they got a dispensation from the Pope on the grounds of consanguinity. Not long before the wedding Edward fell off his horse when he was fighting against the Scots and broke two of his ribs, but fought on without any apparent ill effects.

Margaret was by no means fair like her half-brother and his family; she had a slightly hooked nose and was plain but good. She was also tactful and needed to be, because Edward was becoming more and more difficult. Many of his contemporaries were dead, his heir, instead of being in his thirties as John, his eldest son, would have been if he had survived, was only fourteen. His new wife was only five years older, so he was a very lonely old man. Added to this he was terribly short of money, a persistent worry. Physically he was still a magnificent specimen of manhood, he hunted and could leap into the saddle by putting his hand on it. He had lost neither his teeth nor his hair, though his eyesight was not as good as it had been.

Margaret spent the first few months of her married life in isolation in the Tower of London because a smallpox epidemic was raging; when that was over and she was allowed out, she was never crowned, possibly because of the expense. She became very friendly with her stepdaughter Mary, the nun, who was with her when her first child, Thomas of Woodstock, was born, and she was so ill that she nearly died. The child was delicate at first and she had great worries about feeding it; it had a wet nurse from France but could not keep her milk down; when an English one was provided he did better. In 1302 she had another son Edmund, and later a daughter, Eleanor, who died a few months after she was born.

In 1303 Margaret travelled to the borders of Scotland to be near Edward while he was fighting that country, and was moved to York for safety, where Edward paid her a visit. She went north again in the winter and spent Christmas with him at Dunfermline. She stayed in Scotland for some time, because in 1305 she watched the siege of Stirling from an oriel window built specially for her and her ladies in the king's house in the town; and a bill was sent in to Edward for a feather bed for her use. Edward was hit by an arrow, but it cannot have wounded him badly, because he pulled it out himself, spat on it and demanded that the archer who had fired it should be captured and hanged.

His health after this declined and he became really ill at the end of 1305, having to be carried on a litter to a tournament at Westminster—the biggest that England had ever seen. He partially recovered and went back to fight the Scots but got dysentery and was so weak that he had to be carried on a litter into battle. At Carlisle he bravely got off the litter and on to a horse, but the effort killed him. He died on 7th July, 1307, at Burgh on Sands and was buried at Westminster with his first wife Eleanor. He made two dying wishes to Edward: one to be kind to his half-brothers Thomas and Edmund, and above all to treat with respect and tenderness his mother, Queen Margaret. The other wish, which he made before the barons, was: 'That as soon as he was dead the young King should take his body and boil it in a cauldron till the flesh departed clean from the bones; and then to bury the flesh and keep still the bones, and as often as the Scots should rebel against him, he should assemble his people against them, and carry with him the bones of his father.' In that way the old king felt sure that the Scots would always be defeated. The young Edward was said to have sworn that he would do this, but in fact never carried out this barbaric wish.

Margaret lived another ten years and she and Edward II were always good friends. She went with him to France when he married her niece Isabella in 1308, and while she was alive tried her best to keep their marriage together. She died at Marlborough in 1317.

9 - Edward II

Born 1284. Became king 1307. Murdered 1327. Married Isabella of France (born 1292, died 1358) in 1308.

EDWARD II HAD a strange, lonely boyhood, and it is easy to understand how he became attracted to the first of his notorious favourites, Piers Gaveston. Born when his mother was forty years old and his father forty-five, he was their fourth son, but because his two eldest brothers had died before his birth and the third one a few weeks afterwards, he became his father's heir almost immediately and was watched over by both his parents with care and anxiety.

His mother died when he was six and his father did not marry again until eight years after this. His new stepmother was only seven years older than he was. She became his friend and a good influence in his life, and softened the effect of his by now irritable and terrifying father. The old king was anxious to do his best for him, but Edward showed little taste for either war or governing, and to try and make him less dreamy and more manly Edward I provided Piers as his companion.

Piers was the son of a Gascon squire, a robust, keen-witted and unscrupulous boy, who soon brought out the worst in the young prince. Edward was naturally dreamy and quiet but had the same taste for horseplay as his father and enjoyed occasional rowdiness. He once paid his sergeant, Jack of St. Albans, money for dancing on the table, and somebody

77

else for falling off his horse in a funny way; he liked to gamble and lost large sums playing chuck-farthing and pitch-and-toss. All this sounds innocuous, but his court was disorderly, 'full of ruffians, parasites and ribalds. They spent the night in jesting, playing and banqueting' and also in 'other filthy and dishonourable exercises'. For these Piers was the chief procurer. Edward's more wholesome tastes were for rowing, swimming and having baths, which was unusual in the Middle Ages. King John, who was fastidious, used to have one every three weeks.

Piers also used his irreverent wit against the nobles and did so in public. He nicknamed Warwick, who foamed at the mouth, 'the Wild Boar'; Lancaster, who liked his clothes to be picturesque, 'the Stage Player'; and Pembroke 'the Jew'. That the old king was worried about the relationship before he died is certain, because he sent Piers away. Edward got him back on succeeding to the throne, and one wonders what the sophisticated Gascon had to say about the dead king's savage instructions about his bones.

From a very early age there had been plans to get Edward married. He was first betrothed to the Maid of Norway but she died when he was six. In 1294 it was agreed that he should marry Isabella, the King of France's daughter, at the same time as Margaret, the King of France's half-sister, became betrothed to his father. His betrothal did not take place until 1303 when he was nineteen, and they were not actually married until 1308, when he was twenty-four and his bride sixteen. The wedding took place in Boulogne with great magnificence, and the Dowager Queen Margaret went with him to France. There were four kings at the wedding besides Edward: those of France, Navarre, Sicily, and the Romans.

They made a fine-looking pair. Edward had a proud, upstanding appearance and bright curly hair. He talked easily and could be amusing. She lived up to the family nickname 'the Fair' in the sense that she was beautiful, though in colour she was dark as she had inherited the southern skin from her mother and the Moorish look that went with it, rather than the fairer skin of her father. She was by far the best-bred queen that England had yet imported. Her father was the King of France and her mother the Queen of Navarre.

She was sent to England with an extravagant trousseau fitting to her station. She had 'two gold crowns ornamented with gems, gold and silver drinking vessels, golden spoons and fifty silver plates. Her dresses were made of gold and silver stuff, velvet and taffetas. She had six dresses of green cloth, six of rose-scarlet, and many costly furs. For linen she had 419 yards, and the tapestries for her chamber were elaborate with the arms of England and France woven in gold'. Both Isabella and her father gave Edward presents of jewels as well. This must have been a nice change for the English, who had had two penniless queens, Eleanor of Provence and Eleanor of Castile.

Edward left Piers as Regent when he went to his wedding. He had already made him Earl of Cornwall and married him to his niece, the daughter of Joan of Acre and the Earl of Gloucester, who was one of the richest heiresses in the country. When Isabella and Edward arrived at Dover, Edward was so delighted to see his favourite again that he rushed towards him and, in full view of everybody, embraced him and covered him with kisses. The queen's uncles, who had accompanied her, were not pleased at this, and later Isabella was very much displeased when she found out that Edward had given Piers the handsome presents that had been given to him by her father.

It cannot have helped much that the arrangements for her coronation were put into Piers' hands and he mismanaged them abominably. His chief consideration was to make sure that he was more splendidly dressed than anybody else, including the king. Otherwise he took little trouble. The organization was so bad that one knight was trodden to death in the scrum, and the banquet was not only badly cooked but very late. The French guests went back to France full of complaints about the fiasco and the way that their princess had been insulted by the behaviour of Edward towards Piers.

The English nobles had had enough of Piers anyhow and, with the King of France on their side, forced Edward to send him out of England, which he did, making him Regent of Ireland by way of compensation. He came back after a year with an enormous retinue, but the nobles insisted that he must leave again, and this time he went to Guienne and Edward was not able to recall him until three years later in 1312, when he made him Secretary of State.

In Piers' absence Edward and Isabella had four years together without him, except for the one interruption when he came back, and, although they did not have any children during that time, they seem to have lived together amicably enough. It was only when he came back for good that Isabella wrote to her father 'as the most wretched of wives' and accused Gaveston of being the cause of all the trouble by alienating the king's affection from her and leading him into improper company.

When Isabella and Piers met they often clashed. She had a violent temper, had been pampered and spoilt all her life, and so had he. Once she appealed to Edward because she said that Piers had been rude to her, but Edward took no notice. All the same she and Edward cannot have been completely alienated, for in the New Year she became pregnant. Civil war then broke out in England and, because of Piers, the Earl of Lancaster, the king's half-brother, sided against the king and took the side of the rebel barons. Isabella's sympathies were with the rebels, but she found herself in the ridiculous position of escaping from York to Newcastle with Edward and Piers. Once there, despite her tears, Edward abandoned her and took ship with Piers to Scarborough, leaving Isabella to look after herself. Edward then left Piers at York while he tried to collect more forces in the Midlands. The rebel forces besieged York and forced Piers to surrender, which he did on condition that they would take him to the king. They broke the conditions, gave him a sham trial and hanged him.

Edward was consoled for his death by the birth of their first son and was at Windsor with Isabella for that event. The child, Edward, was born at three o'clock in the morning of 13th November, 1312.

For the next nine years they led an apparently normal married life. Soon after the birth of their heir they visited Aquitaine together, then they stayed with her father in Paris for two months, enjoying the luxury of life in his rich court. After this they paid a visit to Pontoise, where a fire broke out in their rooms so that they had to escape in their night-clothes, and everything except what they had on was burnt.

They were back in England in 1314 and Edward fought against and was beaten by the Scots at Bannockburn. Isabella stayed in the palace at Eltham, where she had their second son John. When Edward was brought the news of the child's birth he gave a handsome present to the knight who was the messenger, and as soon as she was able Isabella joined him in the North. In 1316 Edward gave money and some lands in Ponthieu to Isabella's nurse. In 1318 she had a daughter, Eleanor, and afterwards accompanied Edward on another campaign against the Scots. All this time her conduct is described as 'all that was prudent, amiable and feminine'.

The Dowager Queen Margaret died in 1317. She had been a restraining influence on both of them and, as misfortune would have it, soon after her death Edward started to be attracted by his next favourite, Hugh Despencer. Even so the king and queen remained on good terms for a few more years. In 1321 the king ordered dress lengths for her and her damosels and in 1322 she had another daughter, known as Joanna of the Tower because she was born in the Tower of London. In the same year, though, she met Roger Mortimer and was im-mediately attracted to this dashing, heterosexual extrovert, descendant of the wife of Richard of Normandy, grandmother to the Conqueror and proud of his ancestry. His father had died in his teens and Edward I had granted his tutorage to Gaveston's father. To redeem himself from him and marry whom he wished he had paid him 2,000 crowns.

Edward loaded Hugh with honours as injudiciously as he had Piers, and very soon the barons were against him, Roger Mortimer amongst them. Roger was captured in the spring of 1322 and imprisoned in the Tower of London; and his wife, and seven daughters were shut up in different convents scattered over England. He was still in the Tower at Christmas time, 1323, and Edward ordered that he should be executed, but reprieved him, possibly persuaded to do so by Isabella.

In 1324, with the connivance of Isabella, Mortimer escaped. The valet of the Constable of the Tower drugged the guards, Mortimer got through a hole in the wall that he had made leading to the royal kitchen, climbed the chimney and went over the roof and let himself down by a rope ladder. The valet then rowed him over the Thames, where some of his men waited with horses. He rode to Hampshire and took ship to Normandy.

Another rebellion broke out and Isabella was left to the mercy of the king and his favourite. Edward dismissed all her French servants and lessened her allowance and, when she complained about this to her brother, Charles the Fair, who had now become King of France, Edward retaliated by taking her lands in Cornwall away from her too, saying with perfect truth that she had plotted against him with the barons.

Their relationship was now as bad as it could be. She wrote more letters to Charles saying that it was all the fault, this time, of the Despencers, and Charles threatened Edward by saying that he would take away his possessions in France. This was so serious that Edward allowed Isabella to go to France in May 1325, to negotiate with her brother. There she joined Mortimer and other barons who had escaped with him and she arranged that Charles would accept homage from her eldest son, Edward, if the king made over to France the Duchies of Monthieu and Guienne. Edward II's affairs were at such a low ebb that he agreed and sent his son Edward over in September to pay homage.

To the embarrassment of Charles, Isabella then refused to go back to England and her affair with Mortimer became an open scandal. Edward II wrote to him: 'But truly dearest brother, it must be apparent to you, as it is to us and to all men, that she does not love us as she ought to love her lord.' He also wrote to his son, who was only twelve, saying about her: 'We have knowledge of her evil doings to our sorrow; how she devises pretences for absenting herself from us on account of our dear and faithful nephew le Despencer who has always so well and loyally served us, while you and all the world have seen that she openly, notoriously, and knowing to the contrary to her duty, and against the welfare of our crown, has attracted to herself, and retains in her company, the Mortimer, our traitor and mortal foe, proved attainted and adjudged; and him she accompanies in the house and abroad in despite of us, our crown and the right ordering of the realm.'

Eventually Charles threatened with banishment anybody who helped her, and she was warned that he was planning to send her and Mortimer back to Edward in England. At this news they all hurried to Hainault, where young Edward met Philippa, his future queen. After this, helped by the Count of Hainault, Philippa's father, they collected an army of 2,757 soldiers and landed at Harwich on 25th September. The common people flocked to them, and Edward II, who had offered £1,000 for Mortimer's head, was defeated and captured. The queen returned to Westminster on 15th December, summoned Parliament in the king's name and young Edward was proclaimed king. Only fourteen years old, he showed remarkable wisdom and would not take the throne until his father officially abdicated. This he did at Kenilworth Castle, where he handed over the crown and sceptre and was so overcome that he fainted. The crown and sceptre were brought back to London with the regalia and on 20th January, 1327, the boy was proclaimed king.

Isabella had the army with her and although she had not been appointed Regent, adopted the role and made Mortimer her prime minister. She sent her husband presents and pleasant little letters, but neither went to see him herself nor allowed her children to do so; in fact she had him moved to Corfe Castle because she thought that he was being too well treated where he was. Later he was moved to Berkeley Castle.

His journeys were made horrible by his captors. Used to splendid horses, he was forced to ride on a hack and to wear a crown of straw; used to a life of luxury he was forced to shave and wash in muddy water in an open field. On 22nd

September he was foully murdered. He was impaled with a hot iron, a death considered in keeping with his vicious habits. His cries of agony were smothered by a pillow.

For the best part of the next three years Isabella and her lover reigned and it was rumoured that she had had a baby by him. He became more and more overbearing, even towards the young king, did not bother to stand up in his presence, and kept a larger retinue than he had.

In 1330, aged 18, Edward took action. In October Isabella and Mortimer were living in Nottingham Castle. For the sake of appearances they slept in different parts of the castle, but he used a secret passage to get to her room. The seneschal of the castle told Edward about this and he sent a party of men to seize Mortimer from his mother's room. Mortimer was executed and for a time the Queen Mother was kept a close prisoner.

As she grew older she was allowed more freedom. She spent most of her time at Castle Rising in Norfolk and had plenty of knights and ladies in attendance on her. Edward visited her several times a year, and used to send her barrels of sturgeon, which was one of her favourite foods. She died on 22nd August, 1358, aged sixty-three and was buried next to the remains of Mortimer at Grey Friars with, oddly enough, Edward's heart on her breast.

10 - Edward III

Born 1312, died 1377. Became king 1327. Married Philippa of Hainault (born 1314, died 1369) in 1338.

SEVERAL YEARS before Edward III and his mother had stayed at the Court of Hainault Edward II had sent over an emissary to see if Philippa of Hainault would be a good prospective bride. He had reported: 'The lady whom he saw was not un-comely, hair betwixt blue-black and brown. Her head is clean-shaped; her forehead high. Her eyes are blackish-brown and deep. Her nose is fairly smooth and even, save that it is somewhat broad, her mouth fairly wide. Her lips somewhat full, especially the lower lip. Her teeth which have fallen and grown again are white enough, but the rest are not so white. The lower teeth project a little beyond the upper; yet this is little seen. Her ears and chin are comely enough. Her back well shaped, all her limbs are well set and unmaimed; and naught amiss so far as any man can see. Moreover she is brown of skin all over.'

In other words, no raving beauty but probably healthy. The bust of her in the National Portrait Gallery, the first of our queens whom we can see there, makes her look thick-necked and heavy, but pleasant, as she does on her tomb in West-minster Abbey. They may have been done when she was older and had put on weight, but one imagines that she was always pretty sturdy.

Edward is described as being charming and good-looking,

with brilliant gold hair, a high-bridged nose, and eyes that sparkled like fire when he was cross. His air and movements were kingly, he had the same sort of restless energy as Henry II but a far greater love of show, and he adored tournaments, pageantry and chivalry. He was almost effeminate in his love of jewellery, but was in other ways completely masculine. He could be very cruel, but he had a good brain and was open to reason, insomuch as he could be dissuaded by argument from acts of revenge and savagery. It is recorded that he liked books and bought one about romance from a nun at Amesbury which he kept as his own.

Philippa was one of four daughters and Edward preferred her to another one who was also offered to him as his potential queen. Isabella was in favour of the match and related to Philippa's mother, so as usual they had to have a dispensation from the Pope on the grounds of consanguinity.

Philippa arrived in England on 23rd December, 1327. Edward was fighting in the north and Isabella, who was in power, welcomed her, and then—to try and take the minds of the English people off the murder of her husband, Edward II —arranged magnificent celebrations for their wedding at York, where the ceremony took place on 24th January, 1328.

In July Isabella staged another show for the English, this time for the betrothal of her daughter to Prince David of Scotland. In 1329 Edward went to France to do homage again for his French possessions, and while he was away Isabella and Mortimer tricked, trapped and finally executed his father's half-brother, the Earl of Kent. This was the beginning of their downfall, for within a year Edward had had Mortimer hanged and Isabella put out of harm's way. From then on he reigned himself.

In June of that year their first child, Edward 'the Black Prince', was born to them at Woodstock. He was large and healthy-looking, and Philippa breast-fed him herself. The young couple were popular with the English and took their duties seriously. She inherited plenty of business acumen from her father, and started a weaving colony in Norwich to use the wool in which England was rich. Edward II had brought in a law saying that no cloth was to be imported, so weaving was very necessary.

In other ways too Philippa's personality asserted itself. Edward arranged a tournament at Cheapside. It was an elaborate affair and the courtiers rode through the streets in pairs, the men dressed as tartars and the ladies wearing red velvet tunics and white camelot caps. Unfortunately the stand on which the queen, her ladies and knights sat collapsed, which made Edward so angry that he ordered that the carpenters who had made the stands should be killed. However, Philippa pleaded with him and they were spared.

This was the first of her public acts of clemency. In 1333 she most unfortunately was not with him when he committed an appalling act of savagery. She had gone north with him when he was fighting the Scots and he had sent her away because she was considered to be in danger. The Scots found out where she was and besieged her. In retaliation Edward had murdered two young boys whom he held as hostage.

The next year she had a daughter, Joanna, and the year after, another one, Isabella, who was followed by a son, William, who died young.

Edward's father-in-law, the Count of Hainault, now pointed out to him that it was silly to fight against the Scots. These activities weakened his claim to the throne of France and more important still there was little plunder. To encourage Edward to start a really big war he sent him a jewelled helmet, but almost immediately afterwards died. This was a blow to Edward because the Count lent him money of which he was desperately in need.

Edward's claim to the French throne was through his mother, the only child of Philip IV to have children. After three of her brothers had been successively Kings of France her cousin Philip of Valois ascended the throne. Ignoring the Salic Law in 1337 Edward launched an attack on France and started the Hundred Years War. The faithful Philippa followed him round as best she could, having a baby pretty well every year.

In 1338 she had a third son, Lionel, who grew to be nearly

seven feet tall and whose daughter Philippa married the Earl of March and was the great-grandmother of Edward IV. Edward followed the pattern of the French Court and made his sons royal dukes, the first time that the title was used in England. Lionel was made Duke of Clarence.

In 1340 John of Gaunt was born at Ghent. He later became the Duke of Lancaster and the Lancastrians descended from him. Later, when John was older and many people were afraid of his ambition, a rumour was started that he was not really the royal child who had been born. The queen, they said, had overlaid the baby and, being too frightened to tell the king, had substituted another. This story does not sound at all in keeping with Philippa's character, and John of Gaunt when he grew up was said to look remarkably like Edward. Just after his birth another incident occurred. Edward arrived home to find all the royal children except John, who was with his mother, left with only three nurses. The commander of the soldiers who were meant to be guarding them had gone out to see his lady love, and the rest of the garrison had followed suit. Edward ordered the whole lot to be executed: fortunately for them Philippa was there and was able to persuade him to give them less severe sentences.

Edward came back to England again to fight the Scots and this time he was defeated. Philippa was not with him because he had left her together with the Earls of Derby and Salisbury in Flanders as security for the money that he had borrowed there. On his way down from Scotland he was stopped at the Castle of Wark, where, in the absence of her husband, he was entertained by the Countess of Salisbury. He is said to have been smitten by her charms and there are two versions of what happened. One is that she virtuously resisted him and that he went away rebuffed. The other that he went into her room at night and forced his attentions on her, and that when her husband was let out of pawn he 'reproached the king'.

Philippa came back to England in 1341 and gave birth to Edmund Langley, Duke of York. His son, the Earl of Cambridge, married Anne Mortimer, the great-granddaughter of

Lionel the Giant, and they were the grandparents of Edward IV. Thus in the space of a few years Edward not only started the Hundred Years War, but unwittingly produced the causes of the Wars of the Roses.

He was so poor that he had to stay in England for the next few years. He staged a tournament at Windsor in 1344 at which both Philippa and Isabella were present and during which the poor Earl of Salisbury was killed. After his death his widow took a vow of chastity. His son, the second earl, married in 1346 Joanna of Kent, later to become the wife of the Black Prince.

By 1346 he had managed to collect some money and went over to France again with his eldest son Prince Edward and won the battle of Crecy. The Prince fought wearing black armour and thus gained his nickname 'The Black Prince'. He had left Lionel the Giant and Philippa as Regents in England. The Scots attacked again and Philippa herself hurried north to fight them and, riding a white charger, defeated them at the battle of Neville's Cross. Having done this she hurried over to Calais and had to plead with her husband on her knees for the lives of the six principal citizens of Calais.

Edward's victories made him rich. As his father-in-law had said, there was plunder in France, and for once he had money to spend. Everybody in the court dressed in fur or velvet and he was able to hold tournaments and balls. It was during one of these, the story goes, that he was dancing with the Countess of Salisbury—Joanna of Kent later to be his daughter-in-law—when her garter fell off and he picked it up for her and started the chivalrous Order of the Garter. There was probably more to the story than that. Richard Coeur de Lion had started a similar order of knighthood, the order of the blue thong, and Edward—who encouraged jousting and tilting— had most likely already formed the Order and merely used the incident to cover up her embarrassment.

These celebrations were stopped in 1348 by the Black Death which swept England and killed one in three of the population, among them Edward's daughter Joanna, who was in Bayonne for her wedding to the son of the King of Castile and died the night before it should have taken place. This may not have been such a tragedy as it sounds as he later became Pedro the Cruel, so she might not have been happy if she had lived. Later in the year the truce that the French and English had made because of the Black Death ceased and the French attacked Calais. Edward went over to fight them as a knight under the command of the Governor of Calais, and beat the French champion in single combat. This was the sort of thing he loved doing, and in an excellent mood at dinner that evening he set the man free and gave him presents.

In 1350 he fought and defeated the Spanish fleet off Winchelsea and Philippa watched him from the cliffs—this must have been a harrowing experience for her because the ship he fought from sank during the action. After this he gradually left more and more of the fighting in France to the Black Prince who, after his victory at Poitiers, became a great national hero; he brought back lots of booty and, after capturing the King of France, demanded three hundred thousand crowns for his return.

Edward III did go over to fight again in France in 1359, taking his four surviving eldest sons, Edward, Lionel, John and Edmund with him and leaving little Thomas of Woodstock, aged five, behind as Regent. When they came back they celebrated the marriage of John of Gaunt, to Blanche, daughter of Henry Plantagenet the Duke of Lancaster, at Reading, where the celebrations went on for three days. On the fourth day they rode to London, where they held a tournament. Here Edward made another of his flamboyant gestures and arranged for the mayor and the sheriffs to order their herald to announce that their knights would fight against all comers. The challenge was accepted and when the five knights uncovered they turned out to be Edward and his four sons.

Two years later the Black Prince got married and this time Edward and Philippa were not pleased with the match. Joanna, his bride, one of the most beautiful women in England, had already been involved in a scandal. Two years older than the Black Prince and the second daughter of Edmund, the sixth son of Edward I, who had been put to death by Isabella and Mortimer in 1330, she had been secretly married when she was very young to Sir Thomas Holland. He had then gone off to fight the French and she married Salisbury; possibly she had been coerced into doing so because the other marriage would not have been considered a good match. When Holland came back from France he spent his plunder money on getting his wife back and a divorce was arranged between her and Salisbury in 1349. She had two sons by Holland before he was killed in France.

Joanna and the Black Prince were married on 10th October, 1361, in Windsor Chapel, and Edward invested him with the Duchy of Aquitaine, where they went to live.

The Black Death came back to England and again struck at the royal family. The Duke of Lancaster, John of Gaunt's father-in-law, died of it and so did his only sister-in-law, Matilda. These two deaths left him Duke of Lancaster in his wife's name and one of the richest men in England.

By 1364 Edward was fifty and had almost completely given himself up to a life of ease and luxury, enjoying hunting, building, and banquets. In 1367 the Black Death struck yet again and this time took John of Gaunt's first wife. In this year, too, the faithful Philippa developed dropsy. She had had twenty years of child-bearing, had become very fat, and long ago lost any looks that she might have had. Edward had taken up with various unimportant mistresses, but now met Alice Perrers, who was his paramour for the rest of his life.

Philippa took two years to die, and before she did so wrote a touching letter to her husband: 'We have, my husband, enjoyed our long union in happiness and peace and prosperity'—presumably she meant that they had not quarrelled, because his reign was scarcely peaceful and, come to that, it was not particularly prosperous—'but I entreat, before I depart and we are for ever separated in this world, that you will grant us three requests. I beg you will fulfil whatever engagements I have entered into with merchants for their

wares, as well as on this, as on the other side of the sea.
I beseech you to fulfil whatever gifts or legacies I have made
or left to churches wherein I have paid my devotions, and
to all my servants whether male or female; and when it shall
please God to call you hence you will choose no other
sepulchre than mine and that you will rest by my side in the
cloister of Westminster Abbey.'

She was not buried by his side but at his feet. She had
been one of our better queens, she had tried to do the best
that she could for this country by encouraging trade, and she
had been a wonderful wife.

After her death Edward, encouraged by Alice Perrers,
relapsed into indolence and self-indulgence, spending more
and more of his time at Windsor hunting rather than governing the country. He roused himself enough in 1372 to try
and re-invade France but was not successful, and by 1374
had lost all the lands he had gained. In 1376 came another
blow when the Black Prince died, leaving a young son as the
next heir. Edward, although only sixty-four, seemed to be in
his dotage. He stayed more and more at Skene with Alice.
Earlier she had been banished by Parliament because she had
been living so ostentatiously and extravagantly, wearing the
late queen's jewels and insisting on being attended by noble-
women. John of Gaunt had her brought back again because his
father was so unhappy without her. She was with him when he
died of a stroke in 1377. She was reputed to have stripped the
rings off his fingers before she left the death-chamber.

Edward was not a faithful husband, but he was not a
notoriously unfaithful one. On the whole one imagines that
Philippa created happiness for them and that, on her side at
least, there was devotion.

11 - Richard II

Born 1367, became king 1377, died 1400. Married Anne of Bohemia (born 1368, died 1394) in 1381, Isabella de Valois (born 1388, died 1410) in 1396.

IT WAS one of the tragedies of English history that John of Gaunt was the fourth son of Edward III rather than the eldest. One of the most colourful characters in history, of all Edward's sons he had the strongest health and character.

The Black Prince, who should have succeeded to the throne, died before his father. His early popularity had faded because of the terrible acts of cruelty he had perpetrated. The sack of Limoges in 1370 was a crime that was never forgotten, and he was hated in Aquitaine for his bad government and unreasonable acts, as his ancestor Richard Coeur de Lion had been before him.

Richard II was the second son of the Black Prince; the eldest one, Edward, died when he was six, Richard was born four years after. Richard was then brought to England and put into the charge of Sir Simon Burley and proclaimed heir to the throne as soon as his father died in 1376.

He was crowned on 16th July, 1377, and there were difficulties from the moment he came to the throne. The Black Death ravaged the country again, and although his grandfather had brought in plunder and money from ransoms, this had given the country a false and temporary prosperity that had left it worse off than ever. Richard's uncle, Thomas of Gloucester, continually plotted against him. John of Gaunt

93

was loyal, but he was unpopular with the Londoners, who hated his enormous wealth, and both they and Richard distrusted his intentions.

Richard had a taste for power and was extravagant. A pretty boy—good-looking in an effeminate way—he grew up to be tall and elegant, with golden hair covering his exceptionally small head. He had a quick temper and blushed easily when annoyed. Like Edward III he loved hunting, pageantry, building and jewels. In other ways he was a great deal more cultured than Edward had been. He was greatly attached to his tutor, Simon Burley, through whom he gained his love of reading, and by the time he was seventeen he owned a dozen books of French romances. He was particular about his personal habits and most probably invented handkerchiefs. The clerk who kept his accounts recorded: 'Clothe supplied in little pieces for giving the King for carrying in his hand to wipe and clean his nose.' He was a homosexual but, unlike his great-grandfather, Edward II, who had children by a wife who grew to hate him, he had no children by either of his wives, who both adored him. He was brought up by his mother with his two stepbrothers, the Hollands, and Robert de Vere, Earl of Oxford, who became the Gaveston of the reign, and whom Richard made first Marquess of Dublin, the first time the title had been bestowed by an English king, and later Duke of Ireland.

In 1380 when he was thirteen he became engaged to Anne of Bohemia, 'a blooming German girl', one year younger than him and the eldest daughter of the Emperor Charles IV by his fourth wife. She was born at Prague and Richard's tutor, Sir Simon Burley, was sent as ambassador to her father's court to arrange the match. The Emperor Charles knew little of England and sent Duke Primislaus over to see what it was like. He sent back a good report, but meantime the Emperor died, so his widow had to continue the negotiations, and gave her permission for the Duke to treat with Richard concerning the wedlock of 'that excellent virgin, the damsel Anne'.

Like the other Royals Anne was occasionally described as

beauteous, but she seems to have been on the stout side, with a pear-shaped face, a narrow forehead and bulbous cheeks. She was very keen on fashion and introduced new styles to the ladies of England. She and her entourage wore enormous horned caps studded with jewels. She also introduced side-saddles, which were made like a bench with a hanging step on which she could put her feet.

As they were both very young when they were first married it was reasonable to expect that the marriage would be in name only for a few years, but it is almost certain that it remained like this until she died thirteen years later, although they were devoted to each other. They had a good deal in common, they were both narcissistic in their love of clothes and luxury, although she was more sensible and less extravagant than Richard, who had one coat alone that was almost priceless because of the precious stones with which it was covered. They encouraged their courtiers to dress richly too; the men wore coats with long sleeves that trailed on the ground and were trimmed with fur and, as in the time of William II, shoes with long points, sometimes so long that they had to be held up by gold chains to prevent the courtiers tripping; they wore velvet bands round their hair which they grew long; their fingers were covered with rings and they wore scented gloves.

Anne must have met the favourite, de Vere, from the beginning, as he quickly divorced his wife and married one of her ladies-in-waiting; but, unlike Isabella of Angoulême, Edward II's wife, she became a friend of his and did not attempt to quarrel. She was on the whole surprisingly levelheaded, and a good influence on Richard. The English did not like her because of her foreign retinue and because she had no dowry.

In 1381 Richard proved himself a brave man during the Wat Tyler rebellion. In 1385 his mother, Joanna of Kent, died. As an English princess Joanna had been popular, especially with the Londoners, who regarded her as theirs, but she was a light-minded and frivolous woman in many ways and always scheming for the advancement of her Holland sons. She did show a serious side in so much that she was a convert of Wycliffe, and in this had something in common with the Protestant Anne of Bohemia.

Feeling was not so friendly between her Holland sons and Anne. Just before Joanna died Richard was fighting the Scots and sent another of his favourites—Lord Stafford—to Anne with a message. On the way Stafford was murdered by John Holland in revenge for one of the Bohemian archers killing his favourite squire. Richard was furious and ordered his half-brother to be executed. Joanna pleaded for his life and the worry of it all hastened her death. After she died, Richard pardoned Holland.

In 1386 Richard and Anne travelled round England together for several months, and they did not get back to London until 1387, when they ran into grave trouble. A council called 'the Lords Appellant', headed by Gloucester, was still ruling for Richard; this Council turned on de Vere, defeated him in battle and sent him into exile, from which he never returned. They also imprisoned Burley, one of the charges against him being that he had been given money to pay for Anne's journey to England but had not done so. Anne pleaded for him on her knees before the Council, but to no avail.

Richard bided his time and took his revenge a few months later. Entering the council chamber he suddenly asked Gloucester, who was presiding, how old he was. Gloucester replied, 'Your Highness is in your twenty-fourth year.' 'Then,' said Richard, 'I am old enough to manage my own affairs.'

To celebrate, he held a tournament at Smithfield that went on for twenty-four days. John of Gaunt was back in England and they made up their differences and he helped him rule. In 1390 Gaunt gave a big hunting party for them in Leicester Forest. This party lasted for five days: Gloucester was there as well and on the surface everybody seemed very amicable.

In 1392, in an attempt to raise funds, Richard tried to raise a loan from the citizens of London and, because they did not respond, appointed a warden to rule the city and moved his court to York. Anne helped patch up the quarrel and they moved back to London in great splendour, which was not tactful and did not please the Londoners. He was, they said, 'much given to excesses in apparel and the pleasures of the body.' His court was badly run: 'In his kitchen 300 servitors and everie other office. Of ladies, chamberers and launderers, 300 at the least. Gorgeously apparelled, not one of them kept within the bounds of their degree. Yeomen and grooms were clothed in silks, over sumptuous for their estate. Furthermore there reigned abundantly the filthy sin of leacherie and fornication, with abominable adultery speci-ally in the king, but most chiefly in the palace.'

Richard now became more and more extravagant and, worse still, the plague came back to England and one of its victims was Anne. She died at Shene Palace on Whit Sunday, 7th June, 1394. Richard was overcome by a savage grief. He never went to Shene Palace again and destroyed the wing of the palace in which she had lived. He gave her a splendid funeral, but his grief was so unmeasured that he struck the Earl of Arundel, one of the Appellants, in the face because he arrived late. This caused a terrible scandal because he did it in a church and drew blood.

After her death he drank a great deal, sometimes staying up all night, and used to sit on the throne in his chambers talking to nobody but watching them all. He became moody and more extravagant and to console himself further went hunting in Ireland, presumably with the Duke of that country, his old favourite de Vere.

Despite his great sorrow for Anne's death he almost imme-diately started arrangements to marry Isabella de Valois, daughter of the French King, and then only eight years old to his thirty. Her father, Charles VI of France, was an invalid, subject to attacks of inflammation of the brain. Her mother, Isabeau of Bavaria, was at that time merely renowned for her beauty, charm and luxurious taste in dress, but later became notorious for her licentious conduct.

The suggested marriage was hotly debated in the Hall of Eltham Palace. The English were against it because of their by now traditional enmity with France, and also on the grounds of age. In the marriage contract Richard was to give up his claims to the throne of France and to hand over Brest and Cherbourg. In return for this she was given an enormous dowry of 800,000 gold francs to be paid yearly in instalments. As he had no money he could not have fought the French for the throne anyhow, so for him it was a good bargain. As for her age he said 'that every day would remedy the deficiency of her age, and her youth was one of the reasons for his preferring her, because he could educate her and bring her up to his own mind, and to the manners and customs of England; and as for himself, he was young enough to wait for her'.

He got his way and the Earl Marshal of England went to France to arrange the terms of the marriage. At a carefully staged meeting he dropped on his knee before Isabella and said: 'Madame, if it please God, you shall be our Lady and Queen.' To which the child replied, 'Sir, if it please God, and my lord and father, that I shall be Queen of England, I shall be well pleased thereof, for I have been told I shall be a great lady.'

The marriage contract that they drew up said that she should be free to return to her native land with her retinue if her marriage was not consummated or if Richard predeceased her; and if either of these things happened she was to take back with her a portion of her dowry, jewels, and gifts as well.

At the wedding, which was on All Saints Day, 1st November, 1396, his narcissus complex came to the fore. It was the first time that he had been to France since his return from Aquitaine as a child, and he seemed determined to make a great show. In six weeks he spent £200,000, and during the voyage home there was a terrible storm in which he lost a lot of his property. Every day he wore more gorgeous clothes. Hers must have been gorgeous too and she brought to England with her an astounding trousseau. In it was a robe and mantle nnequalled in England, made of red velvet embossed with birds of goldsmiths' work perched upon branches of pearls and emeralds. She also had coronets, rings, necklaces and clasps worth 500,000 crowns.

She was crowned with great pomp and then sent down to Windsor in charge of a governess to be educated. Richard had spent so much on the wedding and the coronation that he was more in debt than ever, but this did not seem to worry him, and he indulged in a further orgy of spending, which was copied by his courtiers. Isabella's governess, Lady de Courcy, was as richly dressed as the little queen, and the bills for her upkeep were so enormous that even Richard disapproved and replaced her: but the tournaments he staged, his bodyguard, his household expenses and his patronage of art and letters increased.

In 1397 he had his revenge on his uncle, Gloucester. He asked the Lords Appellant to dinner; Warwick, the only one who accepted, was exiled. Two others, Gloucester and Arundel, he had arrested in their own homes. Gloucester was sent as a prisoner to Calais and died there, probably murdered on Richard's instructions, and Arundel was beheaded. John of Gaunt and Henry fled to France.

The next year Richard held a tournament at Windsor on St. George's Day. Forty knights and forty squires were to maintain the beauty of the 'virgin Queen of England'. Isabella dispensed the prizes and 'acquitted herself well'. In the same year his heir, the Earl of March, was killed in a skirmish in Ireland, leaving a son and a daughter, Anne, who married Richard, Earl of Cambridge, son of Edmund Dangley, Duke of York, son of Edward III; and they were the grandparents of Edward IV.

Early in 1399 John of Gaunt died. Richard promptly banished his heir, Henry, for life and took away his inheritance. He had by this time decided that he would go to Ireland, and at Whitsun held a feast at Windsor with the little queen before he went. Their actual parting took place outside the church at Windsor and he lifted her up in his arms, saying repeatedly, 'Adieu, Madame'. She was so upset at his departure that she pined for weeks afterwards. They never met again.

He had to come back in the summer to fight Henry, who had landed in Yorkshire and was marching across England towards the West Country. From Milford Haven he wrote to the little queen: 'My mistress and my consort, accursed be the man who separateth us. I am dying of grief because of it. My fair sister, my lady and my sole desire! Since I am robbed of the pleasure of beholding thee, such pain and affliction oppresseth my whole heart, that I am ofttimes near despair. Alas, Isabel, rightful daughter of France! You were wont to be my joy, my hope, my consolation. And now I plainly see, that through the violence of fortune, which hath slain many a man, I must be deprived of you; whereat I often endure so sincere a pang, that day and night I am in danger of bitter death. And it is no marvel, when I from such a height have fallen so low, and lost my joy, my solace, and my consort.'

He surrendered to Henry in August and was first escorted to Chester riding on a 'sorry' horse, then on to the Tower of London, from where he abdicated on 29th September. After that he was taken to Pontefract Castle and by Valentine's Day, 1400, he was dead. Some said that he was starved to death, others that he starved himself to death, others that he was killed in a fight with his attendants. Yet another story says that a band of Henry's men murdered him. Henry had said, 'Have I no faithful friend who will deliver me of one whose life will be my death, and whose death will be my life?' Like his ancestor Henry II, he had his wish interpreted literally, and Sir Piers of Exton rushed off with eight other people and did the deed.

Isabella was left a widow at the age of twelve. Tall for her age, slim, beautiful and graceful, as her father was having one of his mad bouts she was left in Henry's power. He did not want to fulfil the marriage contract and send a portion of her dowry, jewels and gifts back with her, so he tried to marry her to his eldest son, the future Henry V. This she steadfastly refused to do, and luckily for her her father became more or less sane again and insisted on having her back; and at about the same time Henry had the clever idea of claiming the ransom for the Black Prince's prisoner, King John of France, which had never been paid and cancelled out the dowry.

In June 1401, wearing the deepest mourning, Isabella left. She refused to speak to Henry when she met him, and was watched in silence when she rode through the streets of London on her way to Dover. Here she had to wait a month before she could cross the Channel because the weather was so bad, but she arrived in Calais on 28th July.

Henry persisted in trying to get her as a bride for his eldest son until 1406, when she became betrothed to her cousin, Charles of Angouleme later the Duke of Orleans, who was some years younger than herself. She wept bitterly at the wedding, but he was an exceptionally elegant and civilized man, and she grew to love him.

She died on 13th September, 1410, after the birth of a child. Orleans was heartbroken and wrote a poem on her death which said:

> Death! Who made thee so bold, alas,
> To take from me my lovely Princess?
> Who was my comfort, my life,
> My good, my pleasure, my riches!
> Alas! I am lonely, bereft of my mate.
> Adieu, my lady, my lily!
> Our lives are for ever severed.

12 - Henry IV

Born 1367, died 1413. Became king 1399. Married in 1381 Marie de Bohun (born 1369, died 1394); Joanna of Navarre (born 1369, died 1437) in 1402.

HENRY IV WAS born on 3rd April, 1367, at Bolingbroke, in Lincolnshire, to John of Gaunt, the fourth son of Edward III, and his first wife Blanche, the daughter of Henry Plantagenet, a descendant of Henry III. There had been three other children born before him: Philippa, who later married first John of Portugal and then Philip le Bon, Duke of Burgundy; John, who died in infancy; and Elizabeth, who was betrothed at an early age to the Earl of Pembroke, but preferred John Holland so much that she had to be quickly married to him to make their child legitimate.

Henry's father, John of Gaunt, had had three wives. Blanche, who died of the plague when Henry was only two years old; Constance, daughter of Pedro the Cruel, King of Castile, through whom John of Gaunt unsuccessfully tried to claim that kingdom and who died in 1394; and Katherine Swynford, sister-in-law of Chaucer, who became governess to Blanche's children after her death and whose own children by John of Gaunt were legitimized later by Richard II. It was from her that Margaret Beaufort, the mother of Henry VII, was descended. She had been married before and had children by her former marriage. John of Gaunt was one of Chaucer's patrons and paid him £10 a year.

John of Gaunt was a good family man and Henry got on

well with his brothers and sisters, whole, step, half, legitimate or otherwise. He was brought up to be religious, was carefully educated, and spent his time at Savoy Palace or at one of his father's country manors. He was keen on exercise and sport and used to play handball, a game similar to fives; an item in his accounts was 26s. 8d. paid to two members of the retinue of his uncle, Edward Langley, who beat him at that game. He also practised skill at arms, being unskilful enough to hurt one of his own retainers so badly that he had to give him a pension.

Nearly a year younger than Richard II, they were both made Knights of the Garter by Edward III in 1377, and from then on he was styled Earl of Derby as well as the Earl of Richmond, which he had been from the age of three. In appearance he was the opposite to his good-looking, effeminate cousin. He had none of Richard's flamboyance and charm, was stocky in figure and ruddy in complexion and grew a rough beard.

In 1381 he was married on 18th March, just before his fourteenth birthday, to Marie de Bohun, who was twelve. She was the great-granddaughter of Edward I and she and her sister shared one of the greatest fortunes in England. Her sister had married Thomas of Woodstock, Henry's mischief-making uncle who, because Marie had at one time intended to go into a convent, had imagined that his wife would get the greater part of the fortune, so was very much displeased when she changed her mind and married Henry.

John of Gaunt paid for the wedding—the duty of the bridegroom's father rather than the bride's in those days—and saw to it that it was an important affair. Richard II and Edmund Langley sent their minstrels, and Henry's eldest sister paid '£10–£18' to a Lombardy goldsmith for a present for the bride. Although they were both so young they had a son the next year, but it died almost as soon as it was born. Whereupon her mother took her home again, saying that she was too young for uncontrolled marital relations and that she was not to be returned to her bridegroom again until she was fourteen. John of Gaunt paid her mother one hundred marks annually for her keep while she remained in her charge, which was until she was about sixteen, as Henry went with his father to Calais and was there until 1385, when he was back in England and got a special mention for jousting at Smithfield, his chief rival in the tournament being his half-brother John Beaufort, one of the sons of his father and Katherine Swynford.

In 1386 he was appointed Warden of the County Palatine of Lancaster while his father was still away, and in 1387 was one of those who fought and defeated Richard's favourite, de Vere. He and Marie were living together again and in that year she had Henry, their first son to survive, at Monmouth, and nearly died in doing so. Hurrying to Monmouth to be at the birth, Henry was told the news that a son had been born by a ferryman, to whom he gave a bag of gold. He brought his family to London in 1387, and Thomas, Duke of Clarence, was born there. He was a healthy baby, but his elder brother was not, so they moved out to Kenilworth for the child to get the good air. Henry liked it there, the hunting was good and he loved his wife. They played chess together with a set of silver chessmen, and they were both fond of music; she sang to a guitar and he played a recorder, and they had a few years of quiet married life.

Marie was looked upon as a young lady of fashion. She had a 'popinjay', her dogs had decorated collars, and she chose the clothes of her little boys carefully. In 1390 she had another son, John, Duke of Bedford. Henry went over to Calais again and later in the year took part in the jousting. After this, as he had nothing to do in England, his father thought that he would be better in France because of the uncertainty of Richard's feelings towards them, so that he was almost permanently away from her. He came back for short visits, after which she always had another baby.

While Henry was in Calais he heard that there was a scheme to attack the lair of the Barbary pirates at Tunis, so he and John Beaufort and Thomas Swynford—Katherine's son by her first marriage—joined in the expedition. While he was away, his fourth son Humphrey, Duke of Gloucester, was born;

this time a sailor brought him the news and got only 13s. 4d., not a bag of gold. He was back in England in 1391 bringing three bears with him, and in 1392 he was sent to France on a peace mission and was there when his daughter Blanche was born. In 1393 he went off to Venice and Prague, where he was entertained by Wenceslaus of Bohemia, brother of his cousin Richard's wife, Anne. From there he went on to Vienna, Rhodes, Jaffa and Cyprus, where the king gave him a leopard. He got back to London on 5th July, 1393, and in 1394 Marie died giving birth to their sixth child and second daughter Philippa.

Marie was the only woman that he ever loved. There is no suspicion that he had any mistresses and his second marriage, which was more political than anything else, took place after his health had begun to deteriorate. For the next few years his young family were cared for in the country. The little boys at Tutbury, near Kenilworth, were in charge of a woman called Mary Harvey, who had been chosen by Marie before her death, and the little girls, at Bytham Castle in Lincolnshire, were looked after by a nurse called Joan.

At first he was on quite good terms with his cousin Richard who, when he married his second wife Isabella, daughter of the King of France, suggested that Henry should at the same time marry one of her relations. Later Richard turned against him, and when Henry accused the Duke of Norfolk of treason, at first said that the two should fight a duel but suddenly changed his mind and banished him. This killed John of Gaunt, who was a sick man anyhow, and died in 1398. Henry applied for his lands but Richard refused to allow him to have them. The lands were vital to Henry, and he landed in England to fight against Richard on 15th July, 1399. The country had been badly governed for so long that it was thoroughly discontented, and many rallied to him. He defeated Richard and was crowned King on 13th October. That Christmas young Henry was particularly ill when the whole family had a bad attack of food poisoning.

In 1401 he made a marriage treaty between his daughter Blanche and the Holy Roman Emperor, but notwithstanding his vast personal fortune his treasury was so poor that he could not collect enough to send her off with a dowry until 1404.

While he had been in exile Henry had met Joanna of Navarre. She was the second daughter of Charles the Bad and Jane of France, the daughter of King John, who had been taken prisoner by Edward III; so in many ways her claim to the French throne was as good if not better than anybody else's. Because he was without money or lands her father used treachery to try and gain his ends, hence his nickname, and on top of this he had the reputation of being a sorcerer. In 1386 Joanna had been married to John de Montfort, Duke of Bretagne, as his third wife; he had had no children by the other two, but made up for it with her, as she had eight in thirteen years: a daughter who died in infancy, followed by John, who succeeded his father; Marie, who was at one time engaged to Henry V but the French king broke it off and she married the Duke of Alençon; Blanche, Countess of Armagnac, and Margaret, Viscountess de Rohan, who both died young; Arthur, who was captured by Henry V and kept in England for years afterwards; Jules, who died when he was on a visit to England; and Richard, Count d'Estampes.

The Duke of Bretagne was years older than Joanna and bad tempered, but this did not stop his wives from being devoted to him, Joanna in particular. A story that may not have been true and could have been started by her malicious old father was in circulation about an affair between her and Oliver de Clisson, one of the duke's staunch allies, who had helped him establish himself in Bretagne and lost an eye in doing so. The duke, when he was told of their supposed love, was reputed to have ordered that Clisson should be murdered, but his instructions were not carried out, to his great relief, because he repented of his decision soon afterwards. Another version says that Joanna herself managed to persuade her husband that the scandal was not true and was able to patch up their friendship.

The duke died in 1399, and the wedding between Henry and Joanna took place by proxy at the Palace of Eltham on 3rd

April, 1402. The ceremony must have looked strange, because a man took the place of the bride and Henry put the wedding ring on his finger.

Joanna called herself Queen of England from the day of her proxy wedding, but she did not reach this country until January 1403, as Henry had not enough money to pay for ships to bring her over. When she did embark with her two youngest daughters, Blanche and Marguerite, they ran into a terrible storm and ended up in Cornwall. Henry must have raised some more money because, after the wedding had been publicly solemnized on 7th February, they had the usual feasting and jollities. Henry's half-brother, Henry of Beaufort, Bishop of Lincoln, performed the ceremony.

Whether they lived a proper married life together or not is doubtful. She was two years younger than he was, graceful, beautiful and extremely intelligent. She had been left as Regent in Bretagne, and Henry was said to have married her primarily because he wanted to gain control over the young duke, her eldest son; but she never allowed this to happen and one presumes that she realized that she would not be Regent for very long and would be better as Queen of England with a court of her own. Henry seems to have been fond of her and to have treated her generously. He gave her estates and special apartments from which to carry on her business affairs. When her second son Arthur came to England two years after they were married, he made him Earl of Richmond, the title he had formerly held himself. He stood up for her too when the lords objected to the disorderly state of the royal household, saying that 'all French persons, Bretons, Lombards, Italians and Navarese whatsoever be removed out of the Palace from the King and Queen, except the Queen's two daughters and Marias St. Parnesy, excepting like wise Nicholas Aldewyche and John Putian and their wives'. He pretended to acquiesce but allowed her to keep as well her Breton cook, two knights, a damsel, two chambermaids, one mistress, two esquires, one nurse and one chambermaid for the queen's daughters, and a messenger. She also kept eleven Breton launderers and a valet launderer. This annoyed Parliament, which at once demanded that she paid for her own journeys when she visited the king.

Almost as soon as they were married the French invaded the Isle of Wight, and shortly afterwards a rebellion broke out, headed by the Northumberland Percys. The Scots were also troublesome to him, and he had trouble with his wild young son, Henry. On top of all this his health started to deteriorate. He lived another ten years, but he was often seized with violent pains; terrible itchings and eruptions disfigured his face, and he went into comas and seemed to shrink in size. He also had a rupture of the intestines, and rumours went round that he had the pox, or leprosy. What he had was probably von Recklinghausen's disease; the wasting that would have accompanied this in those days without the help of modern drugs would have accounted for his shrunken appearance.

Joanna had her own personal troubles too. Besides having her retainers sent away she had to send her two little daughters back to their eldest brother because he had arranged marriages for them, and when her third son Jules came over to visit her he died. She spent a lot of her time at Leeds Castle but was with Henry when he died at Westminster.

He had been told by a fortune-teller that he would die in Jerusalem. His illness had been much worse for some time, but he had struggled up from Eltham to the shrine of St. Edward in Westminster. Here he collapsed and, becoming unconscious, was carried into a nearby room called Jerusalem. There he died.

Joanna had always tried to keep on good terms with her stepchildren, and after Henry's death she and Henry V got on fairly well together until his thoughts turned to the reconquest of France. Her family, including her sons, were against him in this, and Arthur was captured and brought back to London as a prisoner after the battle of Agincourt. A few years after that, when she was at Havering-atte-Bower in Essex, she was arrested on a charge of witchcraft and sent as a prisoner to Pevensey Castle, where she stayed for four years, and was deprived of her servants, money and dower lands, all this without any trial. One of the chief charges against her was that she was planning Henry V's death by sorcery, her chief accuser being her own confessor.

A document from the Parliamentary Rolls of the time said: 'Be it remembered, that upon information given to the King sovereign Lord as well as by the relation and confession of one Friar John Randolf of the order of Friars-Minors, that Johanne Queen of England compassed and imagined the death and destruction of our lord the King, in the most high and horrible manner that could be devised; the which compassing, imagining and destruction have been openly published throughout all England.' The document went on to advise that all her goods, rents and possessions should be confiscated, and the rents owing to her to be paid to the Crown.

Just before he died Henry V repented of his harsh treatment and sent her some dresses. Henry VI treated her with great respect; she got her dower back and lived at her favourite residence at Havering-atte-Bower again. She died in 1437 aged sixty-eight; 'in the same year died all the lions in the Tower, the which was nought seen in no man's time before out of mind.' She was not only the only queen of England to be tried for witchcraft, but she was the only one to have had eight children by a previous marriage.

13 - Henry V

Born 1387, died 1422. Became king 1413. Married Katherine de Valois (born 1402, died 1438) in 1420.

ALTHOUGH A delicate child Henry V was brought up to be a warrior. Like his father he was very keen on physical fitness and, like Henry I, said to be able to run as fast as a deer. He was probably, also like his parents, fond of music, because a harp was bought for him when he was ten. His father's half-brother, Henry Beaufort, was chiefly in charge of his education and, as Beaufort was Chancellor of Oxford, Henry studied there for a while. He liked gardening and as soon as he became king laid out a garden at Kenilworth. He liked astrology; he was also very religious. He was the first king of England to write all his letters in English.

By the time he was sixteen he was considered experienced enough to be left to rule the Welsh. He used his brain in subduing them and bribed many of them away from their allegiance with money and promises of pensions. At this age he was badly wounded in the face, so much so that he was scarred for life; but he refused to stop fighting, saying, 'How will others fight if they see me, a prince, the king's son, leaving the field for fear?'

His father was taken seriously ill in 1408 and Henry was called back to London, where he virtually acted as Regent for the last few years of his father's life and was accused by him of treachery and of trying to usurp the throne. During

the five years that he was living in and around London he
lived a wild life. At one time he and his friends deserted his
father's court altogether for Cheylesmore—near Coventry—
and there they were taken into custody for raising a riot.
Another time he was sent to prison for boxing a judge's
ears.

When he came to the throne at the age of twenty-six he
had become more responsible but his great desire was to re-
conquer France. He had very little justification for doing
this and was so poor that he had to pawn the crown jewels
and his father's beautiful crown to help pay for his army.
Before he could go to France he had to put down a rebellion
which had the object of putting his cousin, the son of the
Earl of March, whom Richard II had made his heir, on to the
throne. To prove that Richard was really dead he had his
corpse dug up and exhibited in robes of state and regal
ornaments and then re-buried in Westminster Abbey in the
same tomb as Anne of Bohemia.

Since his childhood there had been plans for his marriage.
Besides his father's efforts to marry him to Richard II's widow
Isabella, he was at one time pledged to the King of Norway's
sister, and at another to Marie, a daughter of his stepmother,
Joanna of Navarre. To strengthen his claim on the French
throne he was now determined to marry into the mad Valois
family.

The only daughter left was Katherine. She had had a
terrible childhood. Unlike her eldest sister Isabella, Richard
II's wife, who had been spoilt and cosseted by both her parents,
she and her brothers and sisters had spent a good deal of
time shut up in St. Pol, where they had had too few clothes
and insufficient food. Her mother, who had twelve children,
eight of whom she survived, no longer had any use for her
mad husband, and her behaviour had become a scandal. She
pilfered from the royal exchequer when she was Regent, was
fond of luxury when they had no money, was generally
frivolous and avaricious, and had lovers. Her father, Charles VI,
had been out of his mind with only occasional spells of sanity
since 1404.

Henry asked for an enormous dowry from the French king and a treaty providing that he should ascend to the French throne after the French king's death and be Regent in his lifetime. When the French king refused to hand over his daughter on those terms, Henry demanded the English provinces in France and said that if he was not given them he would take them by force. The French king must have been having one of his more lucid moments, because he replied, 'If that was in his mind he would do his best to receive him, but as to the marriage he thought it would be a strange way of wooing Katherine, covered with the blood of her country-men.' Louis the Dauphin chose that moment to send a cask of tennis balls to Henry, saying that 'they were the fitter playthings for him, according to his former course of life'. To which Henry replied, 'These balls shall be struck back with such a racquet as shall force open Paris gates.'

As good as his word, Henry left his brother Bedford as Regent, went over to France and in 1415 won the battle of Agincourt, bringing back with him as prisoner not only his stepbrother Arthur, but the widower of Richard's queen Isabella as well as Charles, Duke of Orleans, who was kept prisoner in England for twenty-three years because of his nearness to the French throne. He also gained the hand of Katherine on the terms he had asked, although the French never had enough money to pay the dowry.

Henry was slim, tall, good-looking, with a ruddy com-plexion, big nose and thin face, and fifteen years older than his bride. She was pretty although she had a long nose that was slightly hooked at the tip and rather too slanting features. She showed no traces of insanity, but was rather stupid. They were married at Troyes on 3rd June. During their first night together, following a French custom for royal marriages, a grand procession came to the bedside bringing them wine and soup.

Katherine's brother, the Dauphin, was still fighting against Henry, although her mother had made peace with him on behalf of the king, who had again become too mad to rule. A few days after the wedding Henry went off to the seige of

Montereau, where the French had been holding out desperately, and fourteen days later butchered the entire garrison.
Katherine remained with her parents a few miles away while
this was going on and he paid her frequent visits. The two
courts then went on to Corbeil, where Henry's brother's wife,
the Duchess of Clarence, joined them, and Henry's musicians
played to King Charles because it helped to soothe his madness.

They did not get back to England until 1st February, and
on 14th February Katherine had a splendid coronation and
feast. After this Henry had to go north and left Katherine
at Westminster, but sent for her to join him at Leicester to
celebrate Easter. He then went over to France again. She was
pregnant and before he left he warned her against letting their
son be born at Windsor because of a rhyme that went:

> I, Henry, born at Monmouth
> Shall small time reign and much get;
> But Henry of Windsor shall long reign and lose all,
> But as God will so be it.

Katherine disobeyed him and the child was born at Windsor. She placated him by writing a most loving letter and,
as he was still in France in the spring, he asked her to join
him there, which she did in May. The child was left in
England with his uncle the Duke of Gloucester.

In Paris Katherine held court and, disregarding the fact
that her mad father was still alive and her mother was with
him in Paris, she caused great offence by behaving as if she
were queen. Henry was already ill with the dysentery which
was to kill him. He neglected the disease and went on with
his campaign of subduing the French, but was so weak that
he often had to be carried on a litter. On 31st August, 1422,
he died. His corpse was brought back to Dover accompanied
by his sorrowing young widow.

Katherine was never to see France or any of her family
again. She was not made Regent. Henry VI's uncles and the
Beauforts managed the country, and the baby king was left
in her charge until he was five, after which time he was put

in charge of tutors. By then she had another interest in the form of Owen Tudor.

As an ex-queen of England and sister of the king of France—her father also died in 1422—Isabella at the age of twenty-two appeared to have no market value as a potential bride. She had taken her husband's side against her brother, so he had no wish to further her interests, and it must have suited Henry VI's Regents for her not to marry a powerful English nobleman who might have gained, through her, the ear of the young king.

When she fell in love with and had a child by an unimportant Welsh squire—Owen Tudor who 'did not possess more than £40 a year'—it is unbelievable that the Regents had no inkling of what was going on. In all probability they turned a blind eye to the affair as long as she was discreet, and were pleased that it precluded any chance of her being politically important.

Katherine first met Owen Tudor a few months after her husband's death, when making an elaborate pirouette while dancing before her, he fell into her lap. When or if they married is not certain. She found happiness with him, but the affair must have been fraught with anxiety, as it was a serious offence for a queen of England to have a lover. She had three sons by him: Edmund of Hadham, whom Henry VI made a knight in 1449 when he was nineteen; Jasper of Hatfield, born in the same week as Henry VI was crowned, so that Katherine could not be at the coronation and had to plead that she was ill with a fever; and Owen, who was also born at an embarrassing moment for her when Henry came back to England after his coronation in France. This time she could not avoid going to Westminster, where she had the child, who was taken away from her immediately, and put into a monastery where he stayed and became a monk. Her fourth child was a daughter, Margaret, who died shortly after she was born, when Katherine was already dying herself of cancer of the breast.

She died in 1437. Henry erected a tomb to her memory, the epitaph on it implying that she died a widow. He was extraordinarily good to her sons. He made Edmund Earl of Richmond in 1452 and married him in 1455 to Margaret, the daughter of John Beaufort, his Regent and the grandson of John of Gaunt and Katherine Swynford. Their son, who was born after Edmund's death in 1456, became Henry VII. Jasper fought valiantly for Henry all his life and was made Earl of Pembroke. He had his lands taken away when the Yorkists were in power, but they were restored to him after the battle of Bosworth and he was created Duke of Bedford.

Almost immediately after Katherine's death Gloucester, the king's uncle, tried to make Owen prisoner and sent for him to come to London. Owen went straight to Westminster where he took sanctuary, and was allowed to go back to Wales. Later he was captured there and sent to Newgate Prison, from which he escaped and Henry pardoned him and made provision for him. He later fought for Henry and was captured at the battle of Mortimer Cross in 1470 by the Yorkists and beheaded.

14 - Henry VI

Born 1421, died 1471. Became king 1422. Married Margaret of Anjou (born 1429, died 1482) in 1445.

KING OF ENGLAND at nine months old, born of the mad Valois blood on one side and a string of intrepid fighters on the other, Henry VI was a saintly character. His inclination was to pardon everybody and to help them if he could. He treated his grandfather's widow, Joanna, with far more respect than had his father, her stepson; covered up his mother's affair with Owen Tudor with tact and discretion; and after she died saw that her children from that affair were looked after and advanced. He was very modest, and when some girls were brought to dance before him with bared bosoms, he was so upset that he left the room to show his disapproval. His strongest swearword was 'forsooth' and he did not like his courtiers to use anything stronger. He did not like show and wore simple clothes and rounded boots like a farmer. In 1459 staying at the Abbey of St. Albans he gave his best gown to the prior, and his treasurer had to buy it back because it was the only good one that he had. Later in life when he was fetched from the Tower, where he had been prisoner, and restored to the throne for six months, he wore the same blue velvet gown the whole time. He loved to study and compose music, and wrote a Gloria and a Sanctus that were played. When he was at Windsor he liked to invite the Eton boys to talk to them and give them good advice; he also gave them a beautiful chapel. In appearance he was tall and slender like his father, but more delicate-looking.

The events in his reign would have been terrible enough for a robust king to bear, but for a gentle weakling suffering mentally and physically from nervous instability they were overwhelming. His regents, guardians and relations continually fought amongst themselves, and during his reign the Hundred Years War ended and the Wars of the Roses began.

He was first brought to court and presented to Parliament when he was a yelling three year old. When he was five he was knighted by his uncle Bedford; crowned King of England when he was eight; and of France when he was ten, after which the English steadily lost their possessions there. He had looked for a wife from an early age and had gone so far to send a painter over to the court of the Count of Armagnac to send reports back about his daughter's looks and accomplishments. Nothing came of this, so he settled on Margaret of Anjou, the daughter of René of Anjou, whose sister was married to Henry's uncle, Charles VII of France. It was a strange choice as, although René called himself the King of Naples, both the Sicilies, Hungary and Jerusalem, as well as of Anjou and Provence, in fact he had control of none of those lands and spent a great deal of his time as a prisoner of the Duke of Burgundy because he was so poor that he was unable to pay ransom enough to gain his freedom. René's mother, Yolande, had a tremendous influence over her weak-minded son-in-law Charles, and repeatedly urged him to fight against the English, and his wife Isabella was a brave, resourceful woman who repeatedly left her four children to raise money and fight for her husband. It is possible that Henry's Regents hoped that Margaret would take after her mother and grandmother and look after her husband's interests as courageously.

Margaret was their second daughter and fourth child, and was born on 23rd March, 1429, before either of her parents were twenty-one. Her betrothal to Henry took place in 1436, but the marriage was not until nine years later in 1445, when the Duke of Suffolk, descendant of Richard II's favourite, went over to France taking his wife with him, to stand proxy for the king and to bring his bride back to England. The proxy marriage took place at Nancy on 3rd March, 1445.

Margaret had been living with her aunt, the Queen of France, for several years and was very upset at leaving her. The King of France cannot have made her feel any happier. He rode part of the way with her and when they parted said, with his eyes full of tears, 'I seem to have done nothing for you, my niece, in placing you on one of the greatest thrones in Europe, for it is scarcely worthy of possessing you.' He then returned to Nancy, his eyes swollen with weeping, and she started on her way to England.

She arrived at Pontoise on 18th March and went on to Rouen, where they fêted her, but she then had to wait at Harfleur for several days because of rough weather. When she did sail on 9th April she was so ill that the wedding had to be delayed for several days after she had landed and did not take place until 22nd April.

There is a story that when they did meet, Henry tried to make the meeting romantic; disguising himself as a squire he handed her a letter from the king and remained kneeling while she read it, saying, 'A woman may be seen over well when she reads a letter.' When she realized who he was she was very upset that she had kept him kneeling.

The wedding took place at Titchfield and they travelled slowly back through southern England, feasting on the way. She was crowned on 30th May at Westminster Abbey and afterwards they had a three-day tournament. Parliament had to vote her a dowry, as she was penniless, and gave her land and money. Then Henry found that he could not pay for all the feasting they had had and had to ask his subjects for a loan.

The first two years of his marriage, his regents, particularly Beaufort, continued to do most of the governing. Margaret was pretty and quite accomplished and 'King Henry, new to the delights of female society, was intoxicated with the charms, the wit and graceful manners of his youthful bride'.

In her aunt's court she had not been the leading figure and their social life had been overshadowed by wars and quarrels. England was still peaceful and she could enjoy life to the full; the court, which had been subdued by Henry's austerity, blossomed again for a short time as she reigned over it. Unfortunately she was inexperienced, had been brought up in an atmosphere of intrigue, and had strong likes and dislikes which she did not trouble to disguise. Outside the pleasure-loving faction in the court she was not at all popular. She was yet another French queen with no dowry. A rumour was started that she and Suffolk had had an affair. This was unlikely, as he was fifty and she sixteen when he acted as proxy at her wedding, and his wife remained at court in a position of influence even after his death. What is more likely is that as he had always wanted peace with France, he was made the scapegoat for all England's troubles in that country, and executed. The Bishop of Salisbury, who had married them, was dragged out of his church by a mob and murdered. Then a rebellion started in Kent. Henry met the rebels at Blackheath and defeated them but Margaret would not let him follow up his victory and dragged him off to Kenilworth.

After several years of marriage she had produced no heir and there were two rival claimants for this position. York claimed through both his parents—his mother was the great-granddaughter of Clarence, the third son of Edward III, and his father the son of Edmund Langley, Edward III's fifth son. He himself had been Lieutenant of Ireland and after Suffolk's death in 1450 came back to England. The other claimant was the Duke of Somerset, John Beaufort, who was the grandson of John of Gaunt by his wife Katherine Swynford, whose father had been half-brother to Henry IV.

By this time Margaret, who was now twenty-one, must have known that her husband was nervously unstable and needed peace and quiet and protection. The fact that she would not let him fight at Blackheath seems to prove this point. In 1453 he became mad. By this time Margaret was pregnant, and Edward, their son, was born on 13th October.

Henry's madness took the same form as that of his grandfather and he became so ill that they did not attempt to show his son to him until April 1454. Even then he was incapable of understanding who the baby was and was not able to do so until January of the next year, when he had partially recovered.

Somerset was in Margaret's confidence and knew all about Henry's illness, but she did not trust York and all this time tried to keep him away from the king. In November 1454 he became Regent, but even so she managed to conceal the king's condition from him to a surprising extent.

By May 1455 things had come to a head and the first battle between the Yorkists and Lancastrians took place. The king ostensibly led the Lancastrians and was defeated at St. Albans in a battle that lasted less than an hour. Somerset was killed and York became all-powerful. The excitement was too much for Henry, for in November he went out of his mind again until 1456.

Margaret tried everything to get rid of York, she persuaded Henry to offer him the lieutenancy of Ireland again, but York refused the position. He now had an ally in his cousin Warwick, and Margaret hated both of them. If she had not been so against them they might very well have kept Henry on the throne and her life would have had a different ending.

From now on she became a desperate woman fighting a losing battle on behalf of her weak husband and her infant son. In this battle she did not mind about anything except the throne, and made the mistake of trying to get England's most deadly enemies on her side. She first appealed to Charles VII, who sent a fleet to Sandwich, which he sacked in 1457, hoping to catch Warwick's ships there. Next she appealed to the Scots. These methods lost her much-needed friends in England.

There was a temporary lull in 1458 and the king and queen took part in a procession from Westminster to St. Paul's, York leading the queen. By spring the next year the position had worsened again and the Yorkists and Lancastrians again fought against each other. This ended by Henry defeating York at Ludlow in October 1459, and York fled to Ireland and Warwick to Calais.

The Yorkists had collected their forces again by 1460 and this time, while Margaret and Henry were in Coventry, Warwick marched on London, which, except for the garrison in the Tower, put up little resistance, and then defeated Henry at Northampton. York then returned to London and set up a government in Henry's name.

Margaret stayed in the north with the little prince trying to recruit more men for their cause. She tried to bring the prince before the people and gave him as much nominal responsibility as she could, although he was only six. He was sent off with his father's half-brother to recruit and given the power to pardon rebels—other than those accused of high treason. In March 1463, his governess was dismissed because he was too old for the 'governance of women'. It became too dangerous for Margaret in the north of England and she had to flee to Scotland by sea. There she consented on behalf of England to give up land in the north if they would agree to help her.

When York arrived in London he ordered Henry out of his apartments and wanted to take the throne, but Warwick and the majority of his followers advised him against this, saying that they had sworn their oath of allegiance to Henry. Henry agreed that he should be king until his death, after which time York should be king instead of Edward.

While this was going on, the new Duke of Somerset had rallied the Lancastrian forces and soon after won the battle of Wakefield, at which York was slain, and his third son, the Earl of Rutland, with him. Warwick still had possession of Henry's person, but Margaret and Edward came down to St. Albans again with their army all wearing Edward's badge, and recaptured Henry, whom Warwick had taken with him to the battle. Henry knighted Edward on the field.

York's son, the former Earl of March, now the new Duke, later Edward IV, joined up with Warwick in London, which they still held. Margaret then appealed for foreign help again, this time to the French, who, because of their constant inter-ference on her behalf, became associated in the minds of the English with the Lancastrian cause and turned many of them against it. Having previously been against the claim of Edward's father to the throne, they now acclaimed Edward their king, and on Palm Sunday, 1st March, 1461, he sat on the throne and asked if the people wished him to rule. In reply they shouted 'Yea, yea!' On the 19th of that month he led an army against Margaret and in a battle which raged for ten hours defeated her at Towton. Henry, Margaret and Edward flew to the Scots for shelter, and it was there that Margaret and Edward were captured by robbers who, when they understood who their captives were, gave them shelter in a cave for two days.

Edward became engaged to the little Scots princess and Henry handed over to Scotland the county of Berwick. In return the Scots sent down a force which attacked the English and was not halted until it got to York. A bitter blow was then dealt to Margaret by the death of Charles VII, who was succeeded by his son Louis; he was a great deal more interested in uniting France than in helping her in her troubles. Margaret went over to France to plead her cause with him and at the same time saw her father, whom she had not seen for seventeen years. She and Louis met on friendly terms and the meeting was successful insomuch as he lent her money, forbade his subjects to trade with the partisans of Edward IV and sent 2,000 men to Scotland to fight for her. Her forces set off in boats in October but got scattered and landed at different places, so that nobody rallied to them and she was forced to retreat again to Berwick. In 1464 the Lancastrians, Henry among them this time, attacked Northumberland and were defeated at Hexham. They flew to Edinburgh, where Margaret and Henry parted, she and Edward for France and Henry to go into hiding in the Lancashire hills for a few months until he was captured by Edward IV.

The gentle Henry spent a few months living a hand-to-mouth existence until he was recognized by a monk and he and his two attendants, a doctor and a boy, were captured. He was taken to London, where Warwick met him at Islington and paraded him through the streets with his feet tied to his horse's stirrups. Here he stayed in the Tower for five years until Warwick quarrelled with Edward, defeated him in battle and put Henry on the throne again for six months. He was almost senile, unkempt and dirty when they fetched him from the Tower.

During these five years Margaret and Edward stayed in France. The Scots refused her any more help and she saw Louis gradually recognize Edward IV as king. Warwick was regally entertained by him when he was sent over by Edward and a marriage arranged between the Duke of Burgundy and Edward's sister, Margaret of York. In 1464 Edward announced his marriage to Elizabeth Woodville, which caused a rift between him and Warwick, so much so that he tried to prevent his brother Clarence marrying Warwick's eldest daughter. These differences were smoothed over until 1470, then Clarence combined with Warwick against Edward and Warwick went to France to see Margaret.

How he persuaded her to allow her son to marry his other daughter, Anne, it is difficult to imagine, but it must have been because she felt this was her last hope to get him on to the throne. Once the young prince and Anne were married she kept them with her as if they were hostages to guarantee Warwick's good faith.

Perhaps because of her innate distrust and dislike of Warwick she did not act promptly when he wanted her to do so. He had liberated Henry on 12th October, 1470, and in November the young Prince of Wales and Anne were married. In February 1471, Warwick expected Margaret and the young couple to arrive in England. For some reason or other Margaret delayed and she did not embark until March, when unfavourable winds held her back, so they did not actually arrive in England until April after Edward and his brother Clarence, who had gone over to his side again, had defeated Warwick. The first thing that she heard when she landed was that Warwick had been killed on 13th April at the battle of Barnet.

Worse was to follow on 4th May. The Lancastrian forces were defeated again and Edward the Prince of Wales killed on the battlefield. There are varying stories about how this happened: some say that he was simply found dead on the battlefield, others that Edward IV struck him and ordered him to be murdered. Margaret was near the field of battle but did not take part. She and her ladies were taken prisoner. On 21st May Henry VI was murdered, many said by the Duke of Gloucester, Edward's brother and later Richard III.

For Margaret life was finished. For eighteen years she had been fighting with great courage to keep the throne for her husband and her child. Naturally high-spirited and gay, only for the first few years of her married life had she been able to enjoy herself. She had tried to make the best of life even in the midst of her troubles. She always celebrated her victories with gusto, some said to the detriment of her cause and that instead of celebrating she should have followed up her advantage. Poor woman, she had few triumphs or moments of happiness to celebrate. The tragedy was that, if she had not felt so deeply against those whom she considered her husband's enemies, York and Warwick, they might well have kept him on his throne. Broken-hearted and with no motive to fight further, she was no longer a danger to the Yorkist cause. She was kept prisoner for a few months, first in the Tower and then at Windsor, after which time Edward IV allowed her to live with the faithful Duchess of Suffolk, widow of the Duke who had been so cruelly put to death. In 1475 Louis paid ransom for her and she went back to France and lived very quietly. She died of consumption on 2nd August, 1482, at the age of fifty-three, and was buried in the same tomb as her father, who had died just a few months before.

15 - Edward IV

Born 1442, died 1483. Became king 1461. Married Elizabeth Woodville (born 1437, died 1492) in 1464.

WHEN QUESTIONED about his claim to the throne Henry VI had said, 'My father was king; his father was king; I myself have worn the crown for forty years from my cradle; you have all sworn fealty to me as your sovereign, and your fathers have done like to mine. How then can my right be disputed?' Which was sound arguing except for the fact that his grandfather had no right to the throne in the first place. His descent was from the fourth son of Edward III while Edward IV's was from the third. Edward's family had never stopped fighting against the Lancastrians. His father and eldest brother had been killed doing so, and his grandfather had been executed by them for treason.

Born at Rouen, the son of the Duke of York and Cecily Neville—a lady who was nicknamed the Rose of Rouen and had eleven children and, according to gossip, many lovers—Edward IV spent his early life under the influence of his cousin, Warwick the Kingmaker, and it was his marriage to Elizabeth Woodville which brought about the first break in their relationship. Edward had found it useful abroad to be unmarried, and various potential brides had been canvassed for him in Europe in the hope of gaining allies. He had more or less pledged his troth to Isabella of Castile but had broken it off, and she was said to have nursed a grudge against him all her life even after her fruitful marriage to Ferdinand of Aragon. As the match with Isabella had come to nothing, Warwick was in France negotiating for a French princess, Bona of Savoy, when Edward calmly admitted that he was already married. Edward may possibly have done this to get away from Warwick's influence.

Edward could not have been more different in every way from the man to whose throne he succeeded. Tall, the best-looking king of his time, he was a good swordsman, rider and dancer. He loved rich clothes and comfortable living and was voluptuous rather than pious.

Elizabeth Woodville was a widow five years older than Edward, with two sons. By breeding and by marriage she was a Lancastrian. Her mother, a princess of Luxembourg, had first been married to Henry IV's brother, the Duke of Bedford, by whom she had no children, and then to Richard Woodville, who became Lord Rivers, by whom she had eleven. He had fought for the Lancastrians and at one time been Edward's prisoner. When she was twenty-one Elizabeth had married a rich Lancastrian knight, Sir John Grey, who had died of wounds in February 1461. His father had been Lord Ferrers and had died before him, but he had been so busy fighting that he had never claimed his title. She had also been one of Margaret of Anjou's maids of honour and had rejected a suitor, Sir Hugh Johns, a favourite of Edward's father pressed on her by Warwick.

After her husband's death she was deprived of his estates. The story goes that she waylaid Edward when he was hunting in the forest of Whittlebury near the Grafton estates, the home of her mother, threw herself at his feet and pleaded the cause of her little sons, who were with her. She was a beautiful woman full of feminine wiles and, ever susceptible, Edward fell. First he tried to seduce her but failed. 'My liege,' she said, 'I know I am not good enough to be your queen, but I am far too good to become your mistress.' He was even said to have threatened her with a dagger, but she managed to placate him and get her own way. They were married secretly on 1st May, 1464.

Her mother had been involved in the clandestine meetings all along and had encouraged the affair, but his mother was furious. Before her husband had been killed at Wakefield, when he had wished to assume the crown, she had taken to herself all the state of a queen and now, thwarted again, had to give place to the daughter of a man who had begun life as a squire of an almost unknown family. She had wanted Edward to marry Elinor, daughter of the Earl of Shrewsbury, to whom she said he had been formally betrothed. Both Edward and Elinor denied this, so then she tried to claim that he had had a marriage contract with Elizabeth Lucy, a mistress by whom he had two children—a son and a daughter. (The son, Arthur Plantagenet Viscount Lisle, lived on into the reign of Henry VIII, and when Henry made his illegitimate son, Henry Fitzroy, Admiral of the Fleet at the age of five, the little boy asked for Arthur to be his Vice-Admiral, which position he held until the boy died.)

When he denied that he had married Elizabeth Lucy his mother said that Elizabeth Woodville was unsuitable because she had two children, to which he replied that he had two also.

The witnesses at the marriage were Elizabeth's mother, a man who helped the priest who performed the ceremony, and two gentlewomen. Afterwards Edward rode back to Stony Stratford alone and Elizabeth used to ride over and visit him at nights. It was not until September that he publicly admitted that the wedding had taken place. Warwick was furious, but kept his feelings under control, as he and Edward still had to be united against Henry VI.

They celebrated the marriage once it was announced with fêtes and tournaments and she was crowned in March the next year, but he never made her a proper queen's settlement —the money went to his formidable old mother.

As soon as Elizabeth was acknowledged queen she set about advancing the Woodville family. Her five sisters she married well: Margaret to the heir of the Earl of Arundel; Elinor to the heir of the Earl of Kent; Mary to the heir of Lord Herbert; Katherine to the Duke of Buckingham; and Anne to a son of the Earl of Essex. Her eldest brother Anthony became Lord Scales, Governor of the Isle of Wight and Knight of the Garter; Lionel became Bishop of Salisbury; Edward was given a responsible position in the army; John was married off to the Duchess of Norfolk, one of the richest women in England, nearly eighty, and fifty years his senior.

This invasion of Lancastrian Woodvilles did not make her popular with the Yorkists, but for the greater part of their married life she kept her hold over Edward remarkably well. Almost from the moment they were married he was unfaithful to her and used to boast in after life that he had had three concubines, 'one the merriest, one the wiliest, and one the holiest whore in the realm'. Elizabeth never made scenes. Her words were always 'soft and caressing' and she accepted everything with gentleness and apparent humility. She was a very feminine woman, terrified of battles, bloodshed and wars and made no attempt to be any sort of Amazon, so much so that she appeared at times to be helpless to the point of stupidity. She was a great gourmet, kept a good table, and shared Edward's love of luxury.

During the seventeen years that they were married she produced ten children. The first, Elizabeth, was born to them on 11th February, 1466. The christening was as magnificent as if it had been for a son and heir, and Warwick was godfather. After this she had two more daughters in quick succession: Mary, who died when she was only fifteen, and Cicely.

Almost immediately after the christening Elizabeth upset Warwick's negotiations for another marriage. He wanted his nephew to marry the king's niece, Anne of York, but Elizabeth managed to get her for her eldest son by Sir John Gray instead. Not long afterwards Warwick and Clarence combined to defeat Edward at Edgecote, killing the queen's father and her eldest brother, the husband of the octogenarian duchess, and taking Edward prisoner. They detained him at Warwick Castle. There they tried to turn him against Elizabeth by accusing her mother of witchcraft. In evidence of this the Nevilles produced a lead figure which was meant to be

Edward and which they said had been found at Grafton Castle and used by Lady Rivers to cast spells against them.

Edward managed to escape from his imprisonment and reached France. Elizabeth, who had been left in the Tower, where Henry VI was still imprisoned, had fled from there to the sanctuary at Westminster—where Owen Tudor had taken shelter—and there her fourth child by Edward and first son—another Edward—was born on 1st November, 1470.

Once established on the throne after the battle of Tewkesbury and the murder of Henry VI, they lived chiefly at Windsor or Eltham, though they travelled about the country a good deal, and their second son Richard was born at Shrewsbury in 1472. Edward decided to pull down the old Chapel of St. George at Windsor and build another, hoping that it would outshine the chapel built by Henry VI across the river at Eton.

Their court was luxurious. The walls of their apartments were hung with tapestries. Feather beds had been in for some time, but the beds now became more elaborate and had hangings of velvet and silk, often richly embroidered, as were the counterpanes. The queen's ladies played at marbles and ninepins made of ivory. They had evening entertainments and at one the king danced with the little Princess Elizabeth, then aged seven. It was the age of elaborate jewellery, and the king had the figures of a milkmaid and of a ploughboy both set with diamonds, rubies and great pearls; he gave one of his guests a cup of gold with pearls in it, in the middle of which was a piece of unicorn's horn, and on the lid of the cup a great sapphire.

The queen had five more children: Anne, born in 1474, who married Thomas, the second Duke of Norfolk and Anne Boleyn's uncle; Katherine, born in 1479, who married the Earl of Devon; and Bridget, who became a nun and lived into the reign of Henry VIII. The other two, a son George and a daughter Margaret, died as babies. In 1477 she visited Oxford to preside over the marriage of her second son, Richard, aged five, and Anne Mowbray. They had an enormous banquet after the ceremony.

In about 1476 Edward met Jane Shore, the only mistress of his who became notorious. The wife of a London mercer, Thomas More wrote of her: 'This woman, born in London, worshipfully friended, honestly brought up, and well married, saving somewhat too soon, her husband a good citizen, young and goodly and of good substance. Proper she was and fair; nothing in her body that you would have changed, but if you would have wished her somewhat higher. Men took special delight in her pleasant behaviour. For a proper wit had she and could both read well and write, merry in company, ready and quick of answer, neither mute nor full of babble . . . where the King took pleasure she would mitigate and appease his mind; where men were out of favour she would bring them in his grace. For many she obtained pardon; of great forfeitures she got men remission. . . .'

Edward IV died unexpectedly after only ten days' illness, probably appendicitis, on 9th April, 1483. After his death the merry Jane became the mistress of the queen's son by her first marriage, the Marquess of Dorset, and of Lord Hastings, until Richard III had him executed. By about June she herself was in Ludgate prison, where Richard's own solicitor was said to have asked her to become his wife, but backed out of the proposal when Richard showed his severe displeasure. Richard had accused her amongst other things of withering his arm by witchcraft. He made her do public penance for her harlotry, whether because he was really morally shocked or because she was very much on the side of the Woodvilles, is open to doubt.

Poor Elizabeth lived through a series of tragedies. Her eldest son by Edward, who was at Ludlow Castle, fell into Richard III's hands when the latter passed through on his way to London on 29th April. She took her second son with her and her daughters to the Sanctuary, but meantime her son Dorset, who had been made Constable of the Tower, panicked and left it to join her. The whole thing was too much for Elizabeth and she went to pieces, so much so that instead of covering her head as was customary she let her beautiful fair hair, for which she had been renowned, flow to the ground, and instead of wearing a neat mourning dress, was untidy and unkempt. On 4th May she was forced to give up the younger prince and by July of that year the two little boys had been murdered. She then had to listen to arguments put forward that she and Edward had never been legally married because of his former engagement and also scandals repeated against his mother, saying that he was not his father's son, Richard, of course, claiming that he was.

She and her daughters had no money and were forced to leave the Sanctuary. Luckily for her this did not last long and after the battle of Bosworth and her daughter's marriage to the new king, Henry VII, she was better treated and took part in court life. All the same Elizabeth was never really given her due. Her mother-in-law, who outlived her was regarded as the dowager queen. She did not help Elizabeth with her daughters who had no position and at first were entirely dependent on their mother and then on their eldest sister after she became Henry VII's wife.

When she died in 1492 in the Convent of Bermondsey, she had few possessions and left no money at all. She was the first Englishwoman and the first commoner to become Queen of England.

16 - Richard III

Born 1452, killed 1485. Became king 1483. Married Anne Neville (born 1454, died 1485) in 1473.

RICHARD III is usually described as an unpleasant-looking man with an evil character. He has been accused of murdering Henry VI and his son, Edward Prince of Wales; his own brother Clarence; his nephews, the princes in the Tower; Lord Hastings; and a sentry. Hastings he had executed at a moment's notice, saying, 'For by St. Paul I will not to dinner till I see thy head off.' The sentry he stabbed because he found him asleep on duty and said afterwards, 'I found him asleep and left him so.' The little princes in the Tower must have been murdered at his command. That he took part in the other murders is not so certain. The death of Henry VI has always remained a mystery, and many historians say that Richard had nothing to do with the young Edward of Lancaster's death, keeping away on purpose because the boy was Anne's husband. He was almost certainly in the north of England when Clarence was found drowned in the butt of Malmsey wine.

Richard was born at Fotheringay, the eighth son and eleventh child of the Rose of Rouen and the Duke of York; four of the other sons died young and his second brother Edmund was killed fighting for his father, so that by the time Richard was grown up he, Edward and Clarence were the only ones left; after Clarence was murdered in 1478, he was heir to the throne after Edward's two little boys and Clarence's son, who was mentally retarded.

When he was twenty-one he married Anne Neville, who was nineteen, the second daughter of Warwick the King-maker and widow of Edward of Lancaster. They had spent a lot of their childhood together at Middleham Castle, the favourite home of her mother, Lady Warwick, in whose care he had been placed—he a small, hunchbacked, crooked little boy with a withered arm and not many prospects—she a great heiress.

When Anne was sixteen and her father had gone over to the side of Margaret of Anjou, she had been married to the young Prince of Wales, Edward. After he was killed at Tewkesbury she went into hiding in London for two years disguised as a servant. The circumstances of this were mysterious. Clarence, who had married her elder sister, Isabel, contrary to the express command of his brother Edward, was very much against his brother Richard marrying Anne, as he wished to have the Warwick fortune, which was considerable, all to himself. He may have persuaded her that she should disappear to get away from Edward's wrath, which she had incurred by marrying the Prince of Wales. Edward, in fact, was lenient towards her and did not seem to mind at all that she should marry Richard who was the brother that he trusted most. He had always fought with him rather than on the other side as had Clarence; and when Richard eventually found her, Edward allowed her to live first in sanctuary at St. Martin's-le-Grand, then with her uncle, the Archbishop of York, and even allowed her to visit her mother-in-law, Margaret of Anjou, while she was still in the Tower.

Some historians make out that Anne was reluctant to marry Richard because he had murdered her husband. Whether she was or not, they were married in 1473 and their son and only child, another Edward, was born in 1474. They then lived at Middleham together when Richard was not fighting in either Scotland or Wales on his brother Edward's behalf until Richard became king in 1483.

Once he became king she was constantly by his side and

showed no reluctance to accept her position as queen, nor to take her share of the spoils. They were crowned at Westminster on 6th July and again in York in August. Their little son paraded through the streets with them, although he had been so ill that he had had to be carried on a litter for most of the journey to York. After the York coronation Anne left the child, ill though he was, and went to London with her husband. She was said to have been heartbroken when he died on 31st March, 1484, and her sorrow hastened her own death.

Richard was desperate for an heir and there was talk of his divorcing Anne. As they were related this would not have been too difficult on the grounds of consanguinity if he had paid enough—but she was dying of tuberculosis and only outlived her son a year. Richard had then thought of marrying his niece Elizabeth, eldest sister of the princes he had murdered; but by this time rebellion had started in England and he was killed at the battle of Bosworth on 22nd August, 1485. Fighting was the thing that he did best, and he died bravely, king of England for a shorter time than any other king in our history since the Norman Conquest. Justifiably or not, he had a terrible reputation in his lifetime and after his death.

17 - Henry VII

Born 1457, died 1509. Became king 1485. Married Elizabeth of York (born 1466, died 1503) in 1486.

HENRY VII, the first of the Tudors, came to the throne through his mother, Margaret Beaufort. Her grandfather, John of Beaufort, was John of Gaunt's eldest son by Katherine Swynford. Born before his father and mother were married he was legitimized later by his cousin, Richard II.

Henry's father was of even more doubtful legitimacy, being the son of Owen Tudor and Catherine—Henry VI's widow—whose marriage, if any, remains wrapped in mystery.

Henry was born at Pembroke Castle on 28th January, 1457, two months after his father's death and when his mother was only thirteen years old. He was known as the Earl of Richmond. He had an unsettled childhood. His mother married again and he was left in the care of his father's brother Jasper. When he was four, Henry VI was dethroned and young Henry became Edward IV's prisoner. Later he was released from the siege of Harlech at the age of seven and put into the charge of the Earl and Countess of Pembroke. The earl was conscientious about his education and his countess was genuinely fond of the boy, who in his turn was very fond of one of their six daughters, Maud. This pleased the earl, who in his will said, 'I will that Maud my daughter be wedded to the Lord Henry of Richmond' . . . The Earl of Pembroke was put to death in 1469 when Edward was driven out by Henry, but the countess continued to have charge over him until Jasper took him over to Brittany, from where Edward IV tried to lure him back to England with promises of the hand of one of his daughters, usually the oldest, Elizabeth.

During Richard III's reign Henry spent his time plotting to gain the throne. At his first attempt he is believed to have landed in Wales to ask the hand of Katherine, Pembroke's daughter and younger sister to his first love Maud—who was now married. While there he was nearly captured by Richard's men and had to escape out of a window and go down a hole to avoid capture. It was also rumoured that he was in love with another Katherine, the daughter of one of his attendants, a man called Lee.

His mother was now married to her third husband, Lord Stanley, who had been Steward of the Royal Household to Edward IV, and had managed to retain that position under Richard III, although he was one of the chief plotters of his downfall. It was Lord Stanley who at the battle of Bosworth picked the Crown of England out of the bushes after it had rolled off Richard's head, and put it on Henry's.

Whoever was in power the Stanleys remained the friends of Elizabeth Woodville, and a betrothal was agreed upon by the two mothers between Henry and Elizabeth while Elizabeth was still in sanctuary after her father's death.

Henry was not an ardent wooer, probably because he did not wish for political reasons to appear too interested. Once it was certain that the little princes in the Tower were dead, many people considered that Elizabeth was the legitimate heir, and the marriage would certainly have been advantageous to him; but as conqueror he wanted it to appear that the Yorkists were taking the initiative in this match.

Born in 1466, the first child of her parents, Elizabeth's christening had been as magnificent as if she had been a boy. When she was four she spent some time in the Tower of London with her mother while her father was held prisoner by the Lancastrians. After he was free he used her to try and increase his influence in Europe and make his crown more secure in England. Apart from holding her out as bait to lure

Henry back to England or to keep him quiet when he was in England. They were betrothed first when she was seven years old. The young Prince of Wales had been thought of for her too, and she was later engaged to the Dauphin, Louis XI's son, taught to speak Spanish and French and addressed as Madame la Dauphine.

After Anne Neville's death there had been a public outcry when it was suspected that her uncle Richard wished Elizabeth to be his bride, particularly as he had been trying to prove that she was illegitimate and had tried to make her marry a commoner, Mr. Stillington, the natural son of a bishop.

Elizabeth was a very beautiful woman, tall and elegant like her father and with his brilliant colouring, fair hair and pink cheeks. She had perfect features and a great serenity. She was also affectionate and kind-hearted, and her chief handicaps were her delicate health—she suffered from 'agues' of malaria—and her penniless family. Her sisters were married without dowries and after her marriage she used to try and help them with her own money. She also tried to use this to help the poor, so much so that she pawned her plate and economized on her clothes, wearing much-mended shoes and dresses. Even so she was perpetually in debt and Henry had to come to her rescue.

After Henry had been crowned in October 1485, Elizabeth, prompted by the two mothers and Stanley, sent Henry a letter and a ring as a reminder of their engagement. Henry was supposed to have kissed the ring on receiving it but did not reply to the letter for three weeks.

On 10th December the Speaker of the House of Commons asked him if he would now deign to marry the Princess Elizabeth. The Lords joined in their supplications that he should do so and the marriage took place on 18th January, 1486.

He was the ablest king that England had had since Henry IV. Brought up in Wales he spoke Welsh as well as Latin and French, and had a hard-headed grasp of finance. Almost immediately he came to the throne he asked the City of London for a loan, but they, in view of the behaviour of former poverty-stricken kings, were pretty sceptical and only lent him half. He repaid this when he said he would and after that they had confidence enough to lend him more. His favourite punishment for any offence was a fine, and he was prepared to pardon anybody for more or less anything if they paid enough. He liked poetry, painting, architecture and hunting and had, for those days, a big royal library. He was always courteous. In appearance he was pale and slender and delicate-looking. There were no rumours that he ever had mistresses after he was married to Elizabeth, but he was reputed to be cold towards women in general and much more under the influence of his strong-charactered mother than his more gentle wife. The two women became friends and his married life seems to have been a happy one. There is plenty of evidence that Elizabeth was very fond of him. When he went to invade France in 1492 she wrote him such a loving letter that he was said to have raised the siege of Boulogne and come home to her at once. Another time when he was away from her fighting, she ornamented his basnet with jewels, with her own hands, a loving act even though he had to pay for the jewels. Possibly he did not mind this, as he had a fine collection, not from vanity because he wished to wear them, but because he looked upon them as a good investment and as easily portable treasure in a life full of emergencies.

Elizabeth's first child, Arthur, was born at Winchester unexpectedly early on 20th September, 1486. Her mother-in-law Margaret arranged all the elaborate lying-in ceremonies, the churching and the christening, and her mother was god-mother to the child. He was strong and lively although he had been premature and during her pregnancy Elizabeth had been continually suffering from ague.

The year after, on 25th November, she was crowned, and Henry went out of his way to make it her day and to present her to the people. Afterwards they had festivities which included a banquet and a dance. On St. George's Day, 1488, the queen took part in the St. George's Day ceremonies and appeared in the robes of the Order of the Garter. The ensuing year their daughter Margaret was born. During the next fourteen years she had another five children: Henry, born in 1491, Elizabeth in 1492 (she only lived three years), Mary in 1493, Edmund, who only lived a year, in 1499, and Katherine in 1503 who also died young.

During this century there had grown up an elaborate ceremony attendant on the queen's accouchement. She was allowed to choose in which room she would like to be and what hangings she would like to have. Ones with human figures on them were discouraged in case they were frightening, and she was meant to retire ceremonially to her chamber several weeks before the baby was expected. For her second child she retired in plenty of time on 1st November, and he was born on 29th November. First there was a church service, during which the queen received the sacrament, and the principal lords and office-holders attended. Then they went to her ante-room, where they had refreshments and her chamberlain desired all her people to pray that she had a good delivery. The chamberlain then led her into the room and drew the curtains that surrounded it, after which time no man was allowed in.

At her churching she reclined on a grand state bed. A duchess, or at least a countess, helped her down from the bed and led her to the church door, where two duchesses received her, and a duke led her to the chapel, where the ceremony took place. One of her lords carried a taper before her to the altar, where she and all her ladies offered money according to their degree. After that she went to the king's chamber, where she stood under the great canopy and had her largesse 'cried' to the court.

Henry and Elizabeth took trouble over the education of their children. Henry was naturally a studious man—he had learned Latin in Brittany because he had thought at one time that if he came back to England he might enter a monastery. Instead he had had to become a man of action. His mother was exceptionally well-educated for a woman of her century: she founded colleges, endowed professorships and was a patron of Caxton. His second son, Henry, was chiefly

educated by John Skelton—a poet and brilliant man but un-
orthodox; although a priest he had anti-clerical views and
later lived publicly with a woman to whom he was secretly
married.

In 1500 Henry sent the queen and her children to Calais
because the plague was ravaging England, but they were back
again well before November 1501, when their eldest son
Arthur was married to Catherine, daughter of Ferdinand of
Aragon and Isabella of Castile. They held great festivities
for this occasion and in the following January they had more
festivities when their daughter Margaret was betrothed to the
King of Scotland, James IV. Poor young Arthur died in
April and, when Henry's confessor broke the news to him
he sent for Elizabeth, saying to the friar that 'he and his wife
would take their painful sorrow together'. She consoled him
by saying: 'Remember that my lady, your mother, had never
more children but you only, yet God, by His grace, has ever
preserved you and brought you where you are now. Over
and above God has left you yet a fair prince and two fair
princesses; and God is still where he was, and we are both
young enough.' She almost immediately became pregnant again
and ten months later on her birthday, 11th February, had a
daughter, Catherine. At first the mother did well, but then
grew ill and died nine days later of puerperal fever. This came
upon her so suddenly that her doctor had gone to Gravesend
and had to travel all through the night to be at her bedside.

Henry was almost overcome by sorrow, but when he
recovered he made the most extraordinary attempts to re-
marry. His first thought was Catherine, Arthur's widow,
partly, one presumes, because he did not wish to pay her
dowry back to Spain. Her mother refused to allow the marriage but soon afterwards he entertained Catherine's sister,
Joanna 'the Mad', and her husband Philip at Windsor, and
when Philip died a few months afterwards he thought of
marrying her. This came to nothing but, still determined to
marry into the family, he tried the young widowed Queen
of Naples, another Joanna and a niece of Ferdinand. He even
went as far as to ask his ambassador there to describe her

looks, but he lost interest in her quickly when he discovered that her jointure in Naples was confiscated. He then tried Margaret of Savoy, who was twenty-seven years old and had already had two husbands.

None of his plans came to anything and he died on 5th April, 1509, aged fifty-two, after having been ill for several months with gout and infection of the lungs.

18 - Henry VIII

Born 1491, died 1547. Became king 1509. Married Catherine of Aragon (born 1485, divorced 1533, died 1536) in 1509. Anne Boleyn (date of birth uncertain, beheaded 1536) in 1533. Jane Seymour (born 1510, died 1537) in 1536. Anne of Cleves (born 1516, divorced 1540, died 1557) in 1540. Catherine Howard (born 1520, beheaded 1542) in 1540. Catherine Parr (born 1512, died 1548) in 1543.

WHEN HENRY VIII came to the throne at the age of eighteen in 1509 his grandmother, Margaret Beaufort, became Regent. She had lived through four reigns already and it was possibly from her that Henry inherited his enormous vitality and zest for life. Brought up to be scholarly, he loved hawking, hunting, hurling himself at ditches with a pole, wrestling and dancing. He would sometimes get up to hunt at four in the morning and not go to bed until late that night. He wrote poetry, composed music, could play the lute, recorder and harp. His lively mind was fascinated by architecture, the design of ships, and medicine. He was six feet two inches, auburn-haired and, except for a horrid little mouth, good-looking. He loved outward show and dressing-up and once, at the launching of a ship, dressed himself up in a sailor's coat over cloth of gold trousers and wore a whistle on a gold chain. On the whistle was inscribed 'Mon Dieu et Mon Droit'. He liked his own way and was supremely egotistical.

Soon after his elder brother Arthur died it was suggested that he should marry Catherine of Aragon, Arthur's widow. Her widowhood had been miserable. Brought up and carefully educated in the sunshine of Granada in a rich and formal court, she found herself penniless in England, where the climate did not agree with her and she was frequently ill. Her father had paid half her dowry on her marriage but refused to pay the other half after Arthur's death, and Henry VII would neither send her back to Spain nor give her any money, so much so that the poor girl and her attendants had almost literally no clothes to wear.

When Henry VII proposed that Catherine should marry him, she not surprisingly said that she had no inclination for a second marriage in England. All the same she never left these shores again and by 1504 was betrothed to his only surviving son, six years her junior. In 1508 Henry was told by his father to break off the engagement again because Ferdinand had not paid the rest of the dowry; but a week after his coronation in 1509 as Henry VIII he married her privately at Greenwich, on 11th June. After which they went in state through the streets of London and she was crowned at Westminster on 24th June. They started to have the usual celebrations but these had to be cut short because they proved too much for the doughty old Margaret Beaufort, who died.

Catherine was a dumpy little thing who grew fat and was never a beauty. She, like Henry, got up early, not to hunt—she hated field sports—but to pray. She spent a lot of her time fasting and, as she grew older, took less and less thought of what she wore, sometimes not changing her dress all day. Like most fat women she probably blew herself out between fasts. She was a little misery. One can be very sorry for her, but only with one's mind.

To begin with, Henry seems to have been a good enough husband, and so long as she perpetually told him how marvellous he was they got on well enough. Naturally their great desire and the purpose of their marriage was to have an heir. In November 1509 she was pregnant but produced a stillborn daughter in May 1510. On 1st January, 1512, she produced a son, Henry. There was great rejoicing at this, but the little boy died a few weeks later on 22nd February. Another son was born to them in November, 1513, but he died almost at once, and another was still-born in December 1514.

At last in 1516 they had a child that lived—a daughter Mary. After that Catherine had a miscarriage in 1518 and then no more children. As she and her husband had grown older they had grown more and more apart; she had aged more quickly than he had, and was quickly turning into an old woman. His temper was hot and quick, while hers was cold and distant, and they were both obstinate and imperious.

He also found other interests. In 1519 his illegitimate son, by Mary, the daughter of Sir John Blount, had been born, and he had also succumbed to the charms of the Howard family, something that he was going to do several times during the next twenty-odd years. He may even have succumbed before this date, as Elizabeth, the wife of Thomas Boleyn, daughter of the second Duke of Norfolk, had been a court beauty when he was a boy, and some historians have maintained that he had had an affair with her and that Anne Boleyn, his next queen, was his own daughter. Authorities differ about the date of Anne's birth—some say 1501, in which case Henry would have been only nine when she was conceived; others say that she was born in 1507, which would have made him fifteen. So it is just possible, not probable, that he could have been her father if she had been born on the later date.

It is certain, though, that he had an affair with Lady Boleyn's eldest daughter, Mary—who was pretty but insipid—before he met Anne. He got bored with her quickly and in 1521 she married William Carey. The next year Sir Thomas Boleyn had a family quarrel over money and, to settle the matter, wanted Anne to marry one of her relations. She refused to do so, as she was in love with Henry Percy, the eldest son of the Earl of Northumberland, who had chosen a quite different bride for him. Henry sent young Percy away from the court and he obediently married the bride of his father's choice. Anne's wedding plans came to nothing, but the course of her life changed: she had been brought to Henry's notice.

She was not insipid like her sister nor was she an actual beauty. She had a number of physical defects: the rudiments of a sixth finger on her left hand, an upper tooth that stuck out, and a sallow, even swarthy, complexion. Some descriptions of her say that she had strawberry-coloured mole on her neck, others that it was a protuberance, others that she had three nipples. She was also subject to asthma. These disadvantages made her more dangerous, as she had learnt how to attract and make the best of her assets, namely a good figure, jet-black hair, slanting eyes, and a sparkling wit. She dressed beautifully and was lively, but inclined to be neurotic. She had very definite ideas over trivial things, and a bad temper. She made many enemies on her way to the throne, among them Wolsey, who called her the 'night crow'. She in return helped bring about his downfall. She was well versed in court ways, as she had been attached to Catherine's court and a lady-in-waiting in France, from where she had had to return when her father died, to arrange her marriage.

In 1523 she was made one of Catherine's ladies-in-waiting. Her letter of thanks for this honour was provocative. She wrote:

'Sire, it belongs only to the august mind of a great king to whom nature has given a heart full of generosity towards the sex, to repay by favours so extraordinary an artless and short conversation with a girl. Inexhaustible to Your Majesties' bounties I pray to consider that it cannot be sufficient to your generosity; for if you recompense so slight a conversation by gifts so great, what will you be able to do for those who are ready to consecrate their entire obedience to your desires? How great soever may be the bounties I have received, the joy I feel in being loved by a king whom I adore, and to whom I would make a sacrifice of my heart if fortune had rendered it worthy of being offered to him, will ever be infinitely greater.

'The warrant of Maid of Honour to the Queen induces me to think that Your Majesty has some regard for me, since it gives me the means of seeing you oftener, and of assuring you by my own lips (which I shall do on the first opportunity) that I am Your Majesty's very obliged and very obedient servant without reserve.'

She then held him at bay until she was sure that he was completely infatuated. In 1524 she retired to Hever Castle, in Kent, one of the Boleyn properties, and when he chased down there after her, said that she was ill and could not see him. In 1525 her father was made Lord Rochford and, in answer to the king's passionate wooing, she said, 'I would rather lose my life than my honour.' In 1526 she went over to France again in the service of Margaret of Alençon and did not come back to England until 1527.

Catherine was fighting a losing battle. The more Henry grew to be irked by her the more she tried to insist on her rights. Her health was a handicap to her. During 1525 she was unwell with fevers and colds so was very little at court. Still she fought her hardest to remain queen—divorce, which was being talked about, was against her strong religious views and everything she held dear.

Anne danced with Henry at a masked ball at Greenwich in 1527 but left the court in the early part of 1528 when she had the 'sweating sickness' (influenza), and she and her brother went down to Hever Castle, where they both convalesced. Henry wrote her love letters there until she came back to court in August, by when she must have capitulated, as they lived in adjoining apartments. As a reward he gave her the revenues from the See of Durham and Durham House in the Strand, jewels, and items for her wardrobe, and her furs were paid for out of the privy purse; better still, he sent Bishop Gardner to Rome to plead for a divorce on the grounds that as Catherine had been married to his brother their marriage was not legal.

In 1530 he made Thomas Boleyn the Earl of Wiltshire and in 1532 Anne became Countess of Pembroke. She had an establishment grander than the sister and the nieces of the king; it included a train-bearer, three ladies of the bedchamber and four maids of honour, all of them daughters of barons or knights.

In that year the prior of a convent asked the Abbot of Whitby what news he had heard while he had been in York, and he replied, 'The King is ruled by a common whore.'

And the papal delegate wrote, 'He sees nothing, thinks of nothing but his Anne; he cannot be without her for an hour.' The French king, Francis I, was shocked when Henry brought her over with him to France, and Emperor Charles V, Catherine's nephew, wrote to his sister in Brussels: 'As to the report that the King of England means to take the opportunity of the meeting to marry Anne Boleyn, I can hardly believe that he will be so blind as to do so, or that the King of France will lend himself to the other's sensuality.'

It is difficult to understand how Anne held on to him for these years, but she did. She became increasingly petulant about her position and complained that she was wasting her youth, the chances of a good marriage and of bearing children. Between his two women Henry was in an unenviable position. Once, when he ran to Anne for comfort after he had been defeated in a battle of words with Catherine, all she said was that he had better not argue with the queen because he always got the worst of it.

Opposition always infuriated him and one day, after one of these arguments, he publicly insulted Catherine by riding out hunting with Anne and sending a message back to her not to join him.

The Pope had not granted Henry his divorce on the grounds he suggested, chiefly because it made Henry and Catherine's daughter Mary illegitimate. This would have upset the all-powerful Emperor Charles V, Catherine's nephew and Mary's cousin. Henry decided instead to alter the Religion of England; to break away from the Roman Catholic Church and make divorce in England legal, collecting the Church Revenue at the same time.

Henry did not marry Anne in France, he married her in England on 25th January, 1533, the Bishop of Lichfield performing the ceremony. The wedding was kept secret for a few weeks, but on 1st June she was crowned with all the usual public processions. Elizabeth, their daughter, was born at Greenwich on 7th September and Francis I was godfather. After the christening the latter wrote back to France 'the King's regard for the Queen is less and diminishes every day'. He added, 'He has a new fancy, you are aware.'

It is difficult to understand why, after all the trouble she had taken and the skill she had used to get Henry, Anne did not make more effort to keep him. Possibly the affair was on the wane after ten years; anyhow, once he had got what he wanted, Henry was not so attentive. If she had had a son it might have revived his interest, but she did not; she also seemed to stop using her brain. She frequently lost control of her temper and berated Henry when she was displeased, so much so that he became rather afraid of her. She made more and more enemies by her overbearing haughtiness. It did not help matters between her and Henry that her next attempt at having a child ended in a miscarriage.

The King of France was right. In 1535 Henry stayed at Wolf Hall on the fringe of Savernake Forest, where his host was the hereditary Ranger, Sir John Seymour. His daughter, Jane, was twenty-five, small, fair, shy and quiet. Henry found her soothing after Anne, made her lady-in-waiting to the queen, and laid siege to her. He offered her jewels and even bags of gold, but she played hard-to-get and said, 'I value so much my honour if the King's Grace wisheth to send me a present of money, I humbly ask him to reserve it for such time as God will be pleased to send me an advantageous marriage.' She was really rather old for such a marriage for those days, but it was a broad hint.

Jane did not hold out for long and soon Henry was writing to her: 'My dear Friend and Mistress, Advertising you that there is a ballad made lately of great derision against us, which if it go much abroad and is seen by you, I pray you to pay no manner of regard to it. For the things ye lacked I have minded my lord to supply them to you as soon as you can buy them. This hoping shortly to receive you in these arms, I end for the present. Your ever loving servant and sovereign.'

Anne was bitterly jealous, but to her reproaches Henry told her to 'shut her eyes as her betters had done', and added that he could 'humble her in a moment more than he had exalted her'. When she found Jane sitting on Henry's knee in her ante-chamber she made a terrible scene. She was again pregnant, and to placate her Henry said, 'Be at peace, sweetheart.' But she had hysterics, tore a locket from Jane's neck, cut her hand in doing so and then bore a dead son. Henry was furious and, standing over her bed, said grimly, 'You shall get no more boys by me,' adding meaningly that he would speak to her when she was well.

He did more than that. By April 1536 the Privy Council were receiving evidence that implicated the queen in adultery. Sir William Bereton, one of the household, was sent to the Tower on 27th April, and Mark Smeaton, a court musician, a few days later. Even so Anne appeared with Henry at a tournament at Greenwich on 1st May. Sir Henry Norris and Anne's brother, Lord Rochford, had just started to tilt against each other when the king got up and left for London. He left Anne to spend the night at Greenwich. The explanation for his sudden departure was that he had seen her drop her handkerchief and Sir Henry Norris pick it up.

By Saturday, 6th May, Rochford and Norris were in custody, and Anne in the same apartments in the Tower from which she had gone to her coronation. She was indicted of having had illicit intercourse with all four men and with Francis Weston as well. She and Norris were accused of it on 6th October, 1533, just one month after her daughter Elizabeth had been born, Bereton was accused for December of that year, Smeaton and Weston in 1534, and her own brother on 2nd November, 1535. One of the chief witnesses against her brother was his wife, Lady Rochford. (Later, when Mary was queen and Elizabeth was particularly in disfavour, possibly because Smeaton was the least aristocratic and Mary wanted to be really malicious, she used to say that Elizabeth looked like Smeaton, although he was not accused of misconduct with her mother until after her birth.)

Anne denied everything, but the men did not—they may not, of course, have had a chance. Smeaton was hanged and the rest executed, as was Anne too, on Friday, 19th May, 1536. Twenty-four hours later Henry married Jane Seymour. However strong the evidence against Anne may seem, it is difficult to see how a woman whose heart was ruled firmly by her head could have been so careless of her reputation.

Jane was never crowned. First the plague came back to England and then she became pregnant and Henry did not want to take any more chance of a miscarriage. He was now even more desperate for an heir, as Fitz-Henry, who at one time he thought he might appoint as his heir, had died—a few months after his marriage to the daughter of Lord Surrey, yet another Howard.

On 15th October, 1537, after having been in labour for thirty hours, Jane had a son, Edward, a fine baby who was christened three days after he was born. The excitement was tremendous and, although for once in his life Henry was considerate and did try to cut down on the deputations and crowds, Jane never recovered her strength and after sitting through a six-hour banquet she died on 25th October.

Henry was now a physical wreck of the man he had been. He was so fat that his small features had disappeared into flesh, he had an ulcer on his leg which caused him a great deal of pain, and high blood pressure. Some writers say that he had syphilis but this is not likely. Neither he nor his children showed real signs of the disease and it only reached Europe at the very end of the fifteenth century. His ailments did not stop him looking for a bride: he first made tentative offers to Christine of Milan, the widowed niece of Charles V, but she said that she would only marry him if she had two heads. Thomas Cromwell for political reasons wanted him to marry Anne of Cleves. Henry was not enthusiastic. His ambassador had sent back a report that he heard no great praise either of her personage or her beauty. Holbein did his best when he painted her portrait and left out the pockmarks, but even he could only make her personable.

However, Cromwell was insistent and Henry gave way and she arrived in Rochester on a bitter cold day in winter. Henry dutifully went to meet her with presents of sables, but he took against her so much that he could not bring himself to present them. The verdict of his court was that she was not only unsightly, but had displeasing airs about her. He promptly nicknamed her 'the Flanders mare' and studied the wedding treaty carefully to find a loophole. He also dropped hints to Anne about his feelings, which must have been difficult, as she did not speak a word of English and they had no language in common. It certainly wasn't effective, as they were married on Tuesday, 6th January, 1540.

Their married life was not a success. He complained to Cromwell that surely he would never have any more children for the comfort of the realm, but that he thought that he could still perform the act and had in fact done so twice with others. Anne's description of their married life was: 'When he comes to bed he kisseth me, and taketh me by the hand and biddeth me "good night, sweetheart"—and in the morning kisseth me and biddeth me "farewell, darling".'

Catherine Howard was appointed one of her ladies-in-waiting and Henry fell in love again. He set about getting a divorce from Anne, who was perfectly amenable to the idea. She was given £3,000 per annum and the rank and precedence of a princess of the blood, bought herself lots of dresses and settled down to enjoy life. There was one slight scandal when she was accused of becoming pregnant, but this died down and she remained friendly with Henry and Catherine and attended their court. The divorce was through by 9th July, 1540, and on the 28th of that month Henry, aged forty-nine, married Catherine, aged twenty, on the very same day that Cromwell was beheaded.

Catherine and Anne Boleyn shared the same grandfather, the Duke of Norfolk. Anne's mother was a child of his first marriage, and Catherine's father a child of his second. She was the prettiest of his queens, feather-brained and innocent-looking—he called her his 'rose without a thorn'. She had a small and plump but good figure, brown hair, very white skin and wide-apart, sparkling dark eyes.

Young as she was, she had had a past. One of ten children, she had been brought up by her grandmother, the old duchess, who had a number of young girls in her charge, and her chaperoning of them seems to have been casual. Catherine's first escapade was with her music master, Henry Manox. This probably did not go much further than clandestine kisses and love letters, but her next affair with Francis Dereham did. The girls used to sleep in a dormitory and men were often smuggled in, Catherine's Uncle William among them, as he was having an affair with one of the other girls, and Francis Dereham another. Francis and Catherine fell in love but were parted in 1539, when he went to Ireland.

Within a fortnight of the marriage a priest was arrested for speaking unfitting words of the queen, and on 27th August, less than a month after the ceremony, she had appointed Francis Dereham, now returned from Ireland, as her secretary.

The story of the pair did not get to Henry, or if it did he ignored it, and he appeared at first to be rejuvenated by his young wife and to regain some of his old vitality. He loaded her with jewels and presents, and hunted and danced until he became dangerously ill when the ulcer on his leg closed. He relapsed again into being an inactive old man and, because he could not enter into her activities, became bored with his young wife and 'shut his door against her'. In April 1541 it was rumoured that she was pregnant but it was found out that she was not so and another rumour started that she knew she could not have children. Worse still rumours accumulated about her past behaviour and got as far as the king. Manox was questioned and admitted that they had flirted but nothing more; Francis Dereham admitted making love to her but to try to save his own skin said that Culpeper had succeeded him in Catherine's affections. It was proved then that, with the help of Lady Rochford—the same who had given evidence against her husband and her sister-in-law, Anne Boleyn— Catherine had been arranging clandestine meetings with Culpeper. When Catherine was questioned she became silly and hysterical. She wrote to Henry and said that she had 'at the flattering and fair persuasions of Manox, being but a young girl, suffered him at times to handle and touch parts of my body which neither became me with honesty to permit him nor to require'. Also: 'Francis Dereham by many persuasions procured me to his vicious purpose and obtained first to lie upon my bed with his doublet and hose and after within the bed and finally he lay with me naked, and used me in such sort as a man doth his wife many and sundry times, but how often I know not, and our company ended almost a year before the King's Majesty was married to my lady Anne of Cleves.'

If she had said that she had pledged herself to Dereham, she might have got away with a divorce on the grounds that the marriage to Henry was not valid, but she denied this, so, married to the king, she was bound to have her head chopped off for treason over the Culpeper affair. Culpeper admitted that he had intended and meant to do ill with the queen and that likewise the queen had so intended to do with him.

She was sent first to Syon House and then to Hampton Court, where she tried to get to Henry to plead with him and was led away screaming through the now 'Haunted Gallery'. Henry left for London that evening and never saw her again.

She was taken to the Tower until 10th February and tried to resist her guards when she was being put on board the barge so that she had to be dragged there. She was executed in February 1542. Lady Rochford, who had intervened once too often, was executed on the same platform immediately afterwards.

Henry was heartbroken and his pride was hurt, but that did not deter him from marrying again, and he now chose to marry a woman of thirty who had been married twice before without having had any children. All the same in his will he said that any children of their marriage should take precedence over Mary and Elizabeth. His choice was Catherine Parr, the daughter of Sir John Parr of Westmorland, a Controller of the King's Household in the time of Henry VII. Her father had died when she was a child and her mother had brought her up to read and write Latin, Greek, Italian and French. After she became queen she used to write to the princesses, her stepdaughters, in Latin.

As a child a fortune-teller had told her that she would be royal and she believed this so much that, when her mother told her to get on with her sewing, she said, 'My hands are ordained to touch crowns and sceptres, not needles and spindles.' Her first husband was Lord Brough of Gainsborough, who had been years older than she was and had died in 1529. Her second, Lord Latimer of Snape Hall, Yorkshire. Both of them had left her money so that she was very rich. She was not a beauty but was full of intelligence and tact and she also shared the king's interest in theology.

Anne of Cleves had been complacent about Henry's wedding to Catherine Howard but was not pleased about this one. Catherine was older than she was and in her opinion no better looking. She stepped out of her frau-like bovine character to say 'A fine burden Madame has taken on herself'.

They were married on 12th July, 1543, in the queen's closet at Hampton Court. One cannot help feeling that even Henry, much as he liked his weddings garnished with executions, must have had some strange thoughts about this room. He was so fat that he could hardly stand, and ate as much as he had done when he was young and active. He also had gout as well as his other ailments. Catherine was good with him and was able to soothe him with words and help his pain; she used to let him use her lap as a footstool for his ulcerated leg.

They had one serious difference of opinion which nearly made her end in the Tower. Henry issued a proclamation forbidding the use of a translation of the scriptures, and she had protested. At the same time she had been accused of dealing with a heretic. The accusation was based on the fact that a friend of hers knew a woman who had been arraigned for heresy. They had a scene and she became hysterical. The king calmed her down with the words, 'Ye are become a Doctor Kate to instruct us.' After that she apologized and they made it up.

By the autumn of 1546 he could no longer sign his name and in January 1547, when he came up to Westminster, it was clear that he was a dying man. He died on 28th January and was buried by the side of Queen Jane.

Three months later Catherine Parr caused something of a scandal by marrying Thomas Seymour, the brother of Jane. He had proposed to her before she had married Henry. During the three months he had not only put himself forward as a husband for the young Princess Elizabeth but had also obviously been having an affair with Catherine. A letter she wrote to him went as follows:

'When it shall be your pleasure to repair hither, ye must take some pain to come early in the morning, that ye may be gone again by seven o'clock and so I suppose ye may come without suspect. I pray you to let me have knowledge overnight at what hour ye will come that your portress may wait at the fields for you. Then with my most hearty commendations, I take my leave of you for this time, giving you like thanks for your coming to court when I was there.

P.S. By her that is, and shall be your humble, true and loving wife during her life.'

Catherine became pregnant and soon afterwards found Elizabeth in Seymour's arms. At Whitsun Elizabeth was sent away from the household, and in September 1548, Catherine died of puerperal fever a week after giving birth to a daughter. After her death Seymour made wild plans not only to marry the Lady Jane Grey to the new king, but to kidnap the king and get the Bristol mint to produce gold coins for him with which to raise and pay an army. He was arrested in January 1549 and executed.

19 - Mary

Born 1516, died 1558. Became queen 1553. Married Philip of Spain (born 1527, died 1598) in 1554.

THE ONLY child of Catherine of Aragon and Henry VIII to survive, Mary was the first woman to inherit the throne of England and to be crowned. Born at Greenwich on 18th February, she had been brought up in great state for the first ten years of her life. During the time after her mother fell out of favour and before she herself came to the throne she was sometimes treated as the heir and sometimes as a bastard. The only certain thing in her life, once her mother was dead, was her religion, and because of her rigid determination to enforce it she went down in history as Bloody Mary.

When she was two years old she was betrothed to the Dauphin of France, and by the time she was four had been taught to speak of herself as his wife. Then Henry and Wolsey changed their plans and it was thought that she should marry her cousin, the Emperor Charles V, son of Philip 'the Handsome' and Joanna 'the Mad' of Spain.

Charles, a man of twenty-two, came to England in 1522 when Mary was six to arrange the marriage. He wanted her to be sent to Spain to be brought up to the etiquette of the Spanish court, but the match fell through because Henry refused to let her go, and Charles married another first cousin, Isabella of Portugal, whose mother was the sister of Catherine of Aragon; by her he had a son, Philip, born in 1527.

Other potential husbands suggested for Mary were Francis, the King of France, who was older than her father Henry; his second son, the Duke of Orleans; and Philip, the Palatine of Bavaria, who came over to woo her.

When she came to the throne at thirty-seven Mary was longing for love and a husband. She was said to have been romantically drawn to Reginald Pole, descended from Clarence of Malmesbury, and, after she became queen, to Edward Courtenay, who had been put into the Tower by Henry VIII for fifteen years because of his Catholic sympathies; but he put on so many airs and graces after she had taken notice of him that she did not consider him for long. Charles V, who needed help in subduing the Netherlands, then suggested his son Philip, and Mary, whose sympathies, because of her mother and her religion, were very Spanish, not only welcomed the idea but fell in love with Philip, although he was eleven years her junior and they had never met.

Philip had been married at the age of seventeen to his first cousin, Maria of Portugal, who had died seventeen months after the wedding after she had had a son, Don Carlos, a madman and an epileptic. He had mistresses, one a Spanish noblewoman, by whom he had several children, and another, a Flemish girl, by whom he had also had a child or two. Since his wife had died it had been suggested that he should marry her aunt, the King of Portugal's sister, and at another time Jean of Navarre, but the proposed matches had fallen through.

The English were against the marriage—they hated the power of Spain and they did not want to establish a Roman Catholic regime. But Mary was not a Tudor for nothing and was determined to get her own way. She announced that she was going to marry Philip, and Parliament was persuaded to accept this provided that Philip had no say in the government and only a few Spanish servants. The marriage was officially announced on 8th April.

Philip showed no signs of being in a hurry to get to the wedding. Before he left Madrid he sent her a 'great diamond' and his father sent her some beautiful tapestries. His ships were all waiting for him in June, but he did not actually set sail until the middle of July and landed at Southampton on the 20th. He made his way to Winchester in the pouring rain wearing a red cloak which covered his black velvet and white satin suit embroidered with diamonds and pearls. When he got there the rain must have stopped, because after supper he walked through a flower garden to visit her. She wore black velvet too, and lots of jewels, of which she was very fond.

Philip's and his suite's first impressions of Mary were not very favourable. One of his courtiers wrote home that she was 'older than we had been told' but that he believed that 'if she dressed in our fashions she would not look so old and flabby'. Another described her as 'a perfect saint and dresses badly'.

She was an energetic little reddish-haired woman, with a deep voice—deeper than her father's had been—and no eyebrows. She was shortsighted and had a habit of pursing her lips tightly. Like her mother she used to get up very early in the morning to say her prayers and hear Mass; and like her father, when she was young she used to take a lot of exercise. After she became queen she worked hard and conscientiously at her affairs, often staying up until midnight. She had a restless nervous energy and was scarcely ever still. She ate very little and suffered from ill-health all her life. She had amenorrhea, bad teeth, headaches and what she called her 'autumn sicknesses', which were fits of depression and low fevers which she got at the end of the summer. She was also nervously unstable, had crying fits and slept badly. She was intelligent and had been very well educated; and, like her father, was musical and played well upon the lute and upon the virginals.

Philip was a slow, patient man, secretive and crafty. He had a pale pink and white skin, pale blue lymphatic eyes, and the 'Hapsburg lip' inherited from his father. He brought with him ten of the highest nobles in Spain, and they were all told that they must be as charming as possible and take care not to offend the English.

The wedding took place on 25th July, 1544, and for a few weeks Mary was ecstatic. She had lots of new clothes, which she adored, and gave Philip presents of clothes, jewels, and elaborate saddles. Philip was not so ecstatic; another letter to Spain said: 'It would take God himself to drink this cup.' He seems, however, to have controlled himself and behaved well, although there is a story that he liked spying on her ladies through peepholes and that one of them, Lady Magdalen Dacre, caught him at it and hit him with a staff.

In 1555 Mary announced that she was pregnant and that the baby was expected for the following May. She went to Hampton Court, where everything was in readiness for her, and an elderly woman who had just been safely delivered of triplets was presented to her for encouragement. Nothing had happened by June, though she often lay crouched on cushions on the floor with her knees drawn up to her ears, surrounded by her woman attendants and nurses.

At last she had to admit that she had been mistaken and that she was not going to have a child. She moved her court to Oatlands and in August Philip, who had been longing to leave, went to Brussels. Here he made up for lost time and so enjoyed himself that he forgot to write to Mary. After Brussels he went back to Spain and she did not see him again until March 1557, nearly two years later. In January 1558, after the loss of Calais, she again said that she was pregnant. She was now forty and a very sick woman. By May they told her that she was not having a child, and Philip left in July. It seems as if she felt that she would never see him again, because she accompanied him to Dover, where she said fond farewells.

After that her health rapidly declined and again her autumn melancholy came upon her. She died on 17th November, 1558.

Philip lived another forty years and married twice more. His third wife was Elizabeth of France, his fourth Anne of Austria, by whom he had several daughters and also a son, who succeeded him as Philip III of Spain, Don Carlos having conveniently died. Although he was a cold, austere man, often cruel and occasionally given to fits of self-indulgence, he was devotedly loved by all his wives.

20 - James I

Born 1566, died 1625. Became king 1603. Married Anne of Denmark (born 1574, died 1619) in 1589.

OUR FIRST Stuart king inherited the throne of England through Princess Margaret, the eldest sister of Henry VIII. She had married James IV of Scotland, her son James V had married Mary de Guise, and their only child was Mary Queen of Scots, James's mother.

Margaret had also later married the Earl of Angus and it was through them that Mary's first husband, James's father, Darnley, was descended.

James's life was in danger three months before his birth, which took place on 9th June, 1566. His mother's favourite, Rizzio, had been murdered before her eyes, and to escape from her enemies who were holding her prisoner she pretended to have a miscarriage so that they thought she was ill. She had then got on a horse and ridden thirty miles to join Bothwell. Darnley was murdered eight months after James was born, and soon afterwards his mother married Bothwell. James was sent to Stirling Castle where he was put in the guardianship of the Earl of Mar. Lady Mar was a good woman and took an interest in him, which was lucky because until then he had been neglected, had been put in charge of a drunken wet-nurse and got rickets, which made him walk in an odd way for the rest of his life. He saw his mother for the last time when he was eleven months old, and officially became king of Scotland two months later.

He was given as tutor George Buchanan, a sour-tempered scholar who had once been an admirer of Mary Queen of Scots but had turned against her and had tried to nurture in the child hatred and distrust of his mother. He also had a second tutor, a younger and kinder man called Peter Young, who remained a friend all his life. The child was crammed with knowledge. He could speak Latin as well as he could speak Scotch, and he learnt astronomy as well as the more usual subjects. He was a willing pupil and loved reading—later he had six hundred books in his library—wrote poetry and a book about demonology, became a firm believer in witchcraft and took part in witch hunts. The Mars saw to it that he had companions of his own age, one of them their own son. When he was thirteen his kinsman, Sieur d'Aubigny, came over from France and at once, with his polish and sophistication—both of which were lacking in Scotland—became his favourite. James made him Earl of Lennox, Governor of Dumbarton, and later a duke, and tried to convert him to Calvinism. The Scots thought that the favourite had much too much power and, when James was eighteen, kidnapped him and insisted among other things as the terms of his release that d'Aubigny was sent back to France. James never saw him again, but after he died years later he left a son of ten years whom James had brought up in his court.

In his early twenties he started to think about marriage. Elizabeth wanted him to marry Henry of Navarre's sister, Elizabeth, but James heard that she was 'old, crocked and somewhat worse if all were known', and decided to marry the younger of the King of Denmark's two eligible daughters, Anne. He was married to her by proxy in September 1589, and, because her ship was driven back by storms, he went over to fetch her himself.

He had grown into a heavy, ruddy-faced man, with a shambling gait, who had not inherited either of his parents' good looks or their height. He ate and drank much too much and was slovenly in his habits. He was never strong, but suffered from catarrh, and would spit and hawk and blow his nose on his sleeve or between his finger and thumb. He also suffered from gravel and piles, and had a stutter.

Anne was a straight-forward character. Blonde and blue-eyed and pretty rather than a beauty, she liked hunting, dressing up and acting and, as long as she was enjoying a round of gaiety, she was fairly happy.

They were married again in October and celebrated with a month of festivities, after which they travelled round hunting, eating and drinking, the last of which James did to excess. His own court was so poor that the Danish court must have seemed like paradise, and it was only in April that he reluctantly dragged himself and his bride back to Scotland. She was crowned in Edinburgh in May, in a ceremony that lasted for seven hours.

James had been idealistic in his approach to the marriage and had written her poems. He had also written an extraordinary document which explained that it had been his own idea and nobody else's to go and fetch his bride without telling anybody, and adding: 'My long delay bred in the breasts of many a great jealousy of my inability as if I were a barrenstock. These reasons and innumerable others hourly objected moved me to hasten the treaty of my marriage, for as to my own nature, God is my witness, I could have abstained longer.'

What Anne who was only fifteen, thought of his ungraceful and sombre Scottish court is difficult to imagine. She was never on the same intellectual plane as he was, but to begin with, except for an occasional quarrel, they got on quite well. She tried to join in his pastimes and even went shooting with him, but accidentally shot his favourite hound Jewel, which cannot have pleased him much.

James was occupied with the continual plots and intrigues of the Scots. He became jealous because Anne admired the Earl of Moray, and also became very friendly with two of the Ruthvens, Alexander and his sister Beatrice. Moray was a distant relation of James's and an ally, and he was killed in 1592, when he was having a quarrel with the Earl of Huntly. Many people said that James plotted the whole thing to get rid of him.

JAMES I

A ballad of the time said:

> He was a braw gallant
> And he played at the Gluve;
> And the bonny Earl of Moray,
> He was the Queen's luve.

In 1594 Anne became a Roman Catholic, which was to cause trouble when she became Queen of England. In February of that year she had her first child, Henry, who was handed over to the Earl of Mar, son of James's guardian, and his mother, the old countess, as soon as he was baptized. Anne was furious and she and James quarrelled. Whenever she went to Stirling Castle to see the child she made a scene, and she refused to speak to either the earl or his mother. On 15th August, 1596, she had a daughter, Elizabeth, who became Elizabeth of Bohemia and from whom the Hanoverians are descended. On 24th December, 1598, she had another daughter, Margaret, who died in infancy.

In 1600 she was the central figure in another scandal. She saw Alexander Ruthven asleep under a tree and tied round his neck a silver ribbon that James had given her. James walked past later and recognized the ribbon. Beatrice, Alexander's sister, saw all this and quickly took the ribbon to Anne before James reached her, so that in answer to James's questioning she was able to produce it from a drawer. Soon afterwards James went hunting and, with only a few attendants, went to Gowrie House at the invitation of Alexander Ruthven, who told him that they held a Jesuit priest there who had been caught carrying a bag of gold. After dinner he went with Alexander to see the priest and said later that he was then attacked by Alexander, who accused him of causing the death of his father. He yelled for his attendants, who killed not only Alexander but his brother too. Anne was very upset about Alexander's death and showed her feelings to James so that there was a coolness between them, until four months later she presented him with a second son, Charles, on 19th November, 1600. She had another son, Robert, the next year but he died almost immediately.

In March 1603, Queen Elizabeth of England died and, after a tearful farewell with Anne, James departed for the South on 5th April. As soon as he was gone Anne dried her tears, went to Stirling Castle and demanded the young Prince Henry. Lady Mar refused to hand him over and Anne, who was pregnant again, became so hysterical that her son was stillborn. However, she won her point with James and left Scotland at the beginning of July with Henry. She also had with her the stillborn child in a casket. When she got to Windsor she found six thousand dresses left by Queen Elizabeth, and she and James plunged into an orgy of spending. In the next four years he managed to spend £92,000 and she £40,000 on jewels alone.

They were not crowned until July because of an outbreak of the plague in London, and when they were, Anne, the first queen to be crowned since Anne Boleyn refused, because she was a Roman Catholic, to take the sacrament according to the rite of the Anglican church.

She had another daughter, Mary, in 1605, and her last child, Sophia, who died twenty-four hours after she was born in 1606. How much she cared for her children when she had them in her charge is doubtful. When Mary died, aged two, she shocked the court by taking part in a masque a fortnight after her death. The length of mourning for the court for a royal child was one month and, one would have imagined, might have been longer for a fond mother.

She and James had been married now for seventeen years and were getting on badly. They had frequent open quarrels and, although there were never any more hints that she had affairs, he had his favourites. They continued to share a good deal of court life together but had separate establishments. James gave her a beautiful house, Theobalds, to which she could retire when she wished.

His court was free and easy to the point of being disreputable, and the young Prince Henry disapproved so much that he set up his own establishment on austere lines. When the queen's brother came over to England in 1607 the Masque of *Solomon and Sheba* was performed for him, but the Queen of Sheba was so drunk that she fell over when she tried to offer King Christian a present and 'deluged him in wine, cream, jelly, cake and spices'. King Christian seemed to bear her no grudge for this because, after they had cleaned him up, he danced with her and they both fell over and were so drunk that they had to be put to bed. Then Faith, Hope and Charity appeared, but Faith staggered off at once and was sick in the Lower Hall, where Hope joined her when she found that she could not speak. Charity managed to curtsey before she too left and joined them. James liked this sort of rough and tumble and also liked practical jokes, even if they were played on him. He once put a frog down the Earl of Pembroke's neck, and the Earl in retaliation put a pig in James's bed.

His first favourite after he was king was Robert Carr. On the journey from Scotland to England Carr had been his page runner, his job being to run beside the king's carriage. They did not have page runners at the English court, so he was given a new suit of clothes, £50 and dismissed. He went over to France and did not come back until 1607, when James recognized him when he broke his leg tilting. James made him a gentleman of the bedchamber, gave him the title Lord Rochester, petted him in front of the whole court and, it was said, 'leaneth on his arm, pinches his cheek, smooths his ruffled garment.' He also thought that Carr needed to be educated and taught him Latin every morning; but, as one of the courtiers remarked, Carr had such a broad Scottish accent that it would have been better if he had taught him English. As James also had a strong Scottish accent this was a double-edged criticism.

Anne very much disliked Rochester, who was a conceited, clumsy, good-looking athlete, who behaved as badly as he possibly could and preferred the society of his friend Overbury to the king's. Overbury saw some letters about the queen's debts and gossiped about them, so that Anne had him arrested. Rochester then fell in love with Lady Essex, who used to drug her husband so that she could be unfaithful to him. After three years of this Lady Essex thought that it would be better if they got married, and James, who took a vicarious delight in his favourites having sexual relations with women, but was jealous if they had them with men, helped her get a divorce. The marriage took place in 1613; James gave her £10,000 worth of jewels and made Rochester the Duke of Somerset so that she should not lose rank. Rochester by way of showing his gratitude treated James cavalierly and said openly that he preferred Overbury. James tried to separate the two men by giving Overbury an appointment away from the court and Somerset. He refused to accept it, so James put him in the Tower. There the duchess tried to have him poisoned, but she was found out. Both she and her husband were implicated and they were sentenced to death. The sentence was not carried out, but they were never seen at court again.

James had other minor favourites. One of them got married and James showed his usual enthusiasm by allowing the bride and groom to spend their first night in his council chamber, where he visited them early the next morning in his nightgown and spent a long time with them in or on the bed.

The court, who had for some time been trying to take James's attention off Robert Carr by producing pretty boys for him, eventually managed to attract his attention with George Villiers. The latter was well-educated, charming and civilized and had an uncontrollable passion for women.

He was made Earl of Buckingham in 1617 and six years later a duke, and he and Anne agreed to reform James's habits, which had deteriorated sadly. James was now a gouty and arthritic fifty. Although he liked his favourites to be splendidly dressed, he himself scarcely ever washed, wore dirty old clothes which he had made too large for him because he sweated so hard, and, as his unsympathetic courtiers said, 'suffered from a terrible looseness as the result of cramming himself all day with every soft fruit washed down with vast quantities of sweet wines'.

Anne and James nicknamed Buckingham 'Steenie' because he looked like a beautiful head of St. Stephen that they had at Whitehall. Anne also addressed him as 'dog'. As early as

1614 she wrote to him: 'My dear, kind Dog, I have received your letter, which is very welcome to me. You do very well lugging the sow's ear, and I thank you for it; and would have you do so still upon condition that you continue a watchful dog to him and always true to him. So wishing you all happiness, Anna R.'

And to James at the same time she wrote: 'I am glad . . . that my dog Steenie does well, for I did command him that he should make your ear hang like a sows lug, and when he comes home I will treat him better than any other dog.'

In 1617 James announced to his council that 'I James am neither a god nor an angel, but a man like any other. Therefore I act like a man and confess to loving those dear to me more than other men. You may be sure that I love the Earl of Buckingham more than anybody else and more than you who are here assembled. I wish to speak on my own behalf and not have it thought to be a defect, for Jesus Christ did the same and therefore I cannot be blamed. Christ had his John, I have my George'.

Anne had not been really well since 1614: she had dropsy, which got progressively worse, was melancholy and in the summer of 1618 developed a bad cough and spat blood. She stayed at Oatlands mostly until near the end, when she moved up to Hampton Court. The king went and saw her twice a week and she corresponded with Steenie, writing to him to get him to intercede with James for Sir Walter Raleigh, who was then in the Tower. She died on 2nd March, 1619, but could not be buried for a month because James had spent so much money doing a royal tour of the north and Scotland and on Buckingham that he could not pay for the funeral. She had seven children, only two of whom, Elizabeth and Charles, survived her. James also was very ill that year with stone in the kidney.

Buckingham had married some time before this, but James did not let this disturb their relationship and even went further and encouraged him to become friends with his son Charles, for whom he felt a sort of maudlin affection. When the two of them went off to Spain together in 1623 he wrote letters to them to 'His only sweet and dear child', 'sweetheart', 'Sweet Steenie gossip' and 'Sweet child and wife', signing them 'Thy dear dad and steward' and 'Thy dear dad and purveyor'. He also wrote and assured Steenie that he was wearing his picture on a blue silk ribbon next to his heart.

He grew more and more bad-tempered and seldom went to bed sober. He was terrified of dying and sat for hours alone, weeping and muttering to himself. In March 1625 he got the tertian ague, and against his physician's advice drank vast quantities of beer to cool himself. This brought on convulsions and fainting fits. He then had a slight stroke, followed by a violent attack of dysentery, and died on 25th March. His heart was found to be enormously enlarged, and he had two stones in his left kidney, which had shrunk.

21 - Charles I

Born 1600, beheaded 1649. Became king 1625. Married Henrietta Maria of France (born 1609, died 1669) in 1625.

CHARLES I WAS the second son of his father. For the first few years of his life his legs had to be put into irons and he was considered the weakling of the family. However, it was the tall, fair, good-looking Henry, his eldest brother, who died—so Charles became heir to the throne.

As he had no surviving brothers around his own age James tried to get Charles to like his favourite, Buckingham. At first he did not succeed; Charles tried on a ring of Buckingham's, did not give it back and said that it had been lost; he also squirted water from a fountain into his face. James took the favourite's side in both cases and boxed Charles's ear for him after the second episode. He then called the two young men to him and commanded them on their allegiance to love each other. This worked and they became practically inseparable, so much so that, on James's death, Buckingham became Charles's favourite until he was assassinated by a madman in 1628.

Charles grew into a healthy, good-looking young man. He was only five feet six inches but was well-proportioned and elegant. He liked tilting, vaulting, running in the ring, and shooting with crossbow and musket. He was as well educated as his father, spoke French and Italian, liked the classics, mathematics, architecture, music and painting; and his collection of pictures was so fine that Rubens called him the best judge of art of any prince of his time. He was dignified and well-mannered, had no small talk, a high voice and a Scots accent, and like his father a stutterer. He was fearless, but hated making up his mind and broke his promises. He was exceptionally moral with both women and men and, in contrast to his father, there were never any rumours that Buckingham was anything but a friend.

The first marriage suggested for him was to Queen Christina of Sweden. Nothing came of this and, encouraged by James, he determined to marry one of the Infantas of Spain. As part of their terms for the marriage the Spanish wanted religious tolerance for the Infanta and all the other Roman Catholics in England.

Charles promised this but the Spanish, who knew the feelings of the English people, did not believe him. Charles, who was twenty-three and impetuous, thought that some personal wooing would help his cause, so, with James's blessing and against the wishes of the English Parliament, he and Buckingham set out for Spain disguised as Mr. Smith and Mr. Brown.

The Spanish were horrified with Buckingham's familiar behaviour towards Charles and the Spanish ladies, and Charles was never allowed to talk to the Infanta alone. The most successful thing about the expedition was that the Queen of Spain suggested that Charles should marry her sister, Henrietta Maria of France, rather than the Infanta. He took this advice after the failure of his wooing, and a marriage was arranged between him and Henrietta Maria, which took place by proxy on 1st May, 1625, two months after his father's death.

Henrietta was the youngest child of Henry of Navarre and Marie de Medici. A beautiful little thing, sixteen years old, with a lovely skin and jet-black hair and large eyes, good delicate features, but slightly too big a mouth. She was musical, could sing well and was a graceful dancer, but she had a fiery temper and could be very tactless and temperamentally difficult.

Her father, who had thought Paris 'worth a Mass', had been assassinated just after her birth and she had been brought up and influenced by her bigotedly Roman Catholic mother, Marie de Medici, whose parting instructions to her in a long letter were: 'You are a descendant of St. Louis. Be after his example, firm and jealous for the Christian religion which you have been taught, for the defence of which he, your royal and holy ancestor, exposed his life and died faithful to him amongst the infidels'.

She arrived in England after a journey which took twenty-four days. Her ship had been held up by storms and also by Buckingham, who had started a flirtation with the young Queen of France, Anne of Austria, and when he saw that the weather was bad, rushed back to Paris from Boulogne to see her again. Henrietta had to wait for him and was furious, and this episode did not predispose him in her favour. She disliked him from the first.

When she first met Charles she burst into tears. He comforted her kindly and then showed surprise because she was so tall—she only reached to his shoulders even so—and she lifted up her skirts to show she had not got on high heels.

The first night of their marriage Charles locked the doors of their bedroom to prevent the mummers coming into the bridal chamber, which was then the custom in England.

One of the first things she had said to Charles when she arrived was that she was very young and would need his guidance, but this humble attitude did not last for long and they had many disagreements. Charles thought that her attendants thrust themselves forward too much and that she encouraged them to do so. Madame St. George, her favourite, who claimed that she should ride in their carriage with them, was turned out by Charles, who pointed out that there were many higher-ranking women who should have priority. Charles then became annoyed because he did not think that Henrietta was bothering to learn English.

When she first went to Hampton Court they had a real quarrel. Charles sent some of his council to her with instructions for running it as his mother had done. She sent back a message that she hoped he would give her leave to order her house as she wished herself. He said, 'Now if she had said that she would speak with me, not doubting to give me satisfaction in it, I could have found no fault with her, whatsoever she would have of this to myself, for I could only impute it to ignorance. But I could not have imagined that she would affront me with such a thing publicly.'

In another of his complaints he said, 'Many little neglects I will not take pains to set down, as her eschewing to be in my company; when I have anything to speak to her I must means be use a mediator, her servants first, else I am sure to be denied.'

They had other disagreements about who should be in attendance on her, and once he sharply told her to remember to whom she was speaking. Like most marital quarrels there was more behind these seemingly trivial matters. In the marriage treaty Charles had promised that prosecutions of Roman Catholics should cease, but as he had promised Parliament when he came to the throne that they should not have special privileges, he went back on his word. On religious grounds Henrietta refused to appear at his coronation in 1626. Soon after this Charles could stand her French retinue no longer and ordered them to leave. They refused to go and put up a fight with the soldiers sent to enforce his command. Henrietta was so cross that she smashed several panes of glass in her room in Somerset House, from which she had been watching the scene.

Louis XIII heard about their quarrels and was so concerned that he sent over an ambassador to make peace between them. When the ambassador saw the queen deliberately pick a quarrel with her husband, he told her that she must behave herself. After that they got on better and eventually became a devoted couple, even though her temper got the better of her at the oddest times; once when Charles bought her a diamond brooch as a present, in trying to pin it on he scratched her and she threw it on the floor.

In 1627 Henrietta lost her first child, a boy, born on 8th May, who died the same day. Just before the birth she had been badly frightened by two large dogs who had been fighting in a corridor of the palace; she had also made one of her scenes when she had longed for a dish of mussels but could not get them. Both incidents were thought to have accounted for the baby's death. On 29th May, 1630, they had another child, who lived to become Charles II. He was a dark, ugly baby and Henrietta wrote to her confidante, the now-exiled Madame St. George, apologizing for his looks, but saying that his size and fatness made up for his want of beauty. In 1631 a daughter, Mary, was born to them, and in 1633 a son, James, who became James II; in 1635 another daughter, Elizabeth, was born, and in 1636 yet another, Anne.

The queen had blossomed and was now the acknowledged beauty of the English court. She had mastered the English language and had become absorbed in her young family, spending a lot of time in the royal nurseries. Charles too was an attentive father. Young Charles inherited the family weakness in the legs, and he ordered that the child should wear steel boots, but they were taken away and hidden by one of the people in charge of him, who, when taken to task by Charles, said, 'It was I, Sire, who had the honour some thirty years since to attend on your Royal Highness in your infancy, when you had the same infirmity wherewith now the prince your very own son is troubled—and then the Lady Carey commanded your steel boots to be taken off and your legs got better.'

The Queen had her own chapel, monks and priests, which was bad enough in English eyes, but when it was found out that Charles worshipped there too, there was a public outcry, and her persistent attempts to get Roman Catholicism recognized helped Charles to lose his throne.

By 1638 France, and in particular Richelieu, could bear Marie de Medici and her meddling no longer and she was banished. She came to England with six hundred more Roman Catholics and was given a royal welcome, but even Henrietta had to admit that they were a nuisance.

In 1640 the Duke of Gloucester was born and the little Princess Anne, then four years old, died.

In 1641 Marie de Medici left for Holland because she was

frightened of the state of affairs in England. Charles had betrayed Strafford, the one man who might have been able to help him and who had served him loyally since Buckingham's death; and he had been trying to rule without a parliament. When he was forced to have one he tried to seize five members of the Commons in violation of their parliamentary rights. This put many more people against him and the Civil War started at the end of 1642.

Henrietta rushed to Holland, taking with her Mary, who had at the age of ten been married to William of Orange, aged fifteen. She sold some of the crown jewels and her own, and in all raised £2,000,000. She came back to England at the end of 1643 and when she landed slept in a house on land at Burlington Bay while they loaded her stores. Five Roundhead ships fired on the house where she was and she had to dress quickly and leave. Finding that she had left a favourite old dog, Mitte, behind her, she went back and rescued it.

She joined up with Charles near Edgehill and they entered Oxford together. Here she became pregnant again and then caught rheumatic fever. Because of her poor health Charles wished her to try the waters at Bath. He escorted her to Abingdon, where they said goodbye. They never saw each other again.

From Bath she moved on to Exeter, where on 16th June Henrietta was born, and less than a fortnight later she had to flee to France with the baby from there because the Roundhead troops were upon her. Poor Charles tried to reach her and succeeded in fighting his way to Exeter but only got there ten days after she had left. Henrietta was smuggled out to her two years later. Her eldest son joined her soon afterwards and in 1648 James, her second son, made his escape from England disguised as a woman. Only the Princess Elizabeth and the young Duke of Gloucester were left in England.

Charles lived for six years after their parting. In 1647 he was in the custody of the Army and Cromwell. He moved about the country with them and was able to see the Princess Elizabeth and the Duke of Gloucester. The princess had tuberculosis and fell into a fever not long after she had bade farewell to Charles the day before he was beheaded. She died in her prison on the Isle of Wight on 24th September, 1650. In 1652 Cromwell sent the young Duke of Gloucester to join his mother in France.

Once a prisoner Charles occupied himself in reading the Bible, Spenser's *Faerie Queene* and Shakespeare. He wrote letters to Henrietta and to a Mrs. Whorwood, a woman of thirty-seven to whom he had given a casket of jewels for safe keeping. The letters to Mrs. Whorwood were very loving, but it is doubtful whether she was ever his mistress. Henrietta was his real love and in one of the letters he sent to her he wrote, 'Dear Hearte, I love thee above earthly things.' One of the last things he did before he was executed was to take off a medallion he was wearing in the form of the Order of the Garter; it had a secret spring which disclosed her miniature. He was executed on 30th January, 1649.

When Henrietta arrived in France she was in a very bad state mentally and physically and became very thin and lost her looks. Her chief counsellor and prop was Jermyn, who some said was her lover. She certainly insisted that his apartments should be next to hers and James II when he was only eighteen burst out, 'She cares for him more than for all her children.' He had always been a loyal servant to Charles and was trusted by both of them and she must have felt the need of somebody on whom she could rely. She wrote long, loving letters to her husband until his death. Jermyn was a rough and ready character, so fond of gambling that in his old age, when he could no longer see, he employed a young boy to stand by his side and tell him what cards turned up. He was a great opportunist and was reputed to have lived far better than any of the other exiles in France—even than the queen herself. There were one or two court scandals about his relationships with women but he never married. After the Restoration he was made Earl of St. Albans.

Henrietta was always trying to convert her children to Roman Catholicism, and although Charles II resisted her and told his brothers to do so too, she succeeded so well that all her children except for Mary, who had got out of her sphere of influence, died Catholics.

This ardent crusading spirit did not help Charles II's cause, neither did Henrietta's matrimonial plans for her sons. Early in life he learnt to treat her with deference but to ignore her protests and outbursts. What she thought of Charles's mistresses and indecorous court one wonders. She tried to be nice to his wife, but, as they could not speak each other's language when they met, they cannot have got very far together. Two more of her children died, the young Duke of Gloucester a few weeks before the Restoration, and Mary of Orange in 1660. She crossed the Channel nine times altogether, the last time in 1665 in June, when her health was beginning to fail. In the spring of 1669 she had a chest complaint and a terrible cough and she could not sleep; one night her doctor gave her a sleeping draught and she never woke again.

22 - Charles II

*Born 1630, died 1685. Became king 1660. Married Catherine of Braganza
(born 1638, died 1705) in 1662.*

CHARLES II SPENT fourteen years in exile before he became
king. In 1646 he went to the Scilly Isles and then on to
Jersey. While there he had his first amorous adventure and
rumours started later that his paramour had had an illegitimate
child 'James de la Cloche'. When he was eighteen he had
reached the continent and had his first notorious mistress,
Lucy Walters, who came of a good Yorkshire family but
who had been living with a colonel of Cromwell's Army in
The Hague. He had handed her on to his own brother, who
was a Groom of the Bedchamber to Charles, and that is how
they met. In 1649 she had a boy by him, James, later the
Duke of Monmouth. Although it was said to have been a
great love affair, Lady Shannon had a daughter by him the
next year, and by 1551 he was trying to keep James and get
rid of Lucy.

Charles's mother Henrietta was busily plotting to marry
him to her niece, Mlle. de Montpensier, 'the Grande Mademoiselle', and was furious when Lucy Walters arrived in Paris
with her son James and a new lover, and the three of them
moved into the Louvre where Charles was living. Charles,
who was really a sultan at heart, thought that it was an
excellent idea because he could see his son. The situation
changed when she went off with another man, taking the

young James with her. She then had a series of other affairs, and Charles did not get the boy away from her until just before she died. In the meantime he had been living with a woman called Catherine Pegge, by whom he had another son, who became the Earl of Plymouth after the Restoration. He never had any intention of marrying the 'Grande Mademoiselle'; it would have harmed his cause with the English to marry a French wife. He also disliked her large blonde looks, her big nose and determined chin. He liked his women to be feminine and well-dressed; she was not interested in fashion and did not take trouble with her clothes. Worse still, he did like, and showed it, the beautiful Duchess de Chatillon, which annoyed Mademoiselle very much indeed.

He had flirted with the idea of marrying Sophia, one of the many children of his Aunt Elizabeth of Bohemia, but she disapproved of Lucy Walters and also thought, probably rightly, that his reasons for thinking of the marriage were because he hoped that her rich relations would give him money. He also thought of marrying Mazarin's niece, Hortense, but Mazarin would not allow it and married her to a madman, from whom she ran away after they had had several children. By the time Charles was thirty he was still unmarried, but might be called an approved Sire. The nickname given him by his courtiers in England was 'Old Rowley', from a stallion in the royal stables.

He arrived in England at the Restoration with his newest mistress, the beautiful Barbara Palmer—a Villiers and cousin of the second Duke of Buckingham. He first made her Lady Castlemaine—the title to be handed down through her heirs rather than Mr. Palmer's, to whom she was still married— and later the Duchess of Cleveland. She had plenty of heirs by Charles—three dukes (Southampton, Grafton and Northumberland), three daughters and several more children, whom Charles would not acknowledge as his. She was very unfaithful, bad-tempered, avaricious and extravagant, but she remained his chief favourite for fifteen years and her jewels were finer than the queen's.

He had grown up from the dark, hideous baby described by

his mother to a tall, six feet two inches, dark, cadaverous-looking man. He had a good, graceful figure. He always looked after his health and was devoted to sport and physical exercise. He played tennis, rowed, danced well and liked walking at such a speed that his courtiers had difficulty in keeping up with him. He loved animals, and besides the little dogs—'King Charles spaniels'—that he made famous he liked to have deer and antelope in his parks. He liked talking, astronomy and beauty of any sort: women, beautifully-bound books, flowers, brocades and furniture. He was fond of music, especially violin and light instrumental music; he played the guitar himself. Like his father he liked pictures and collected clocks and watches. He had his own laboratory and grew herbs to use in it. He was indolent mentally with all these interests and his great physical energy. He got up early and went to bed late but spent most of the day and night on pleasure. He had a sardonic sense of humour and was extremely good-natured and kind.

It was essential for him to find a queen and his choice of brides seemed to be between two women. He had made tentative offers before he came to the throne to Henrietta, the daughter of the Prince of Orange and sister-in-law to his sister Mary, but as they had not thought much of his prospects of coming to the throne they had made difficulties. When he was fifteen and his father was still king a marriage between him and Catherine of Braganza, then aged seven, had been considered. At the Restoration she was twenty-two and still unmarried, and the Portuguese promised her a magnificent dowry, the biggest ever offered with a queen of England. She was to have £50,000 in ready money, and Tangiers, also free trade with Brazil and the West Indies and Bombay. The Orange contingent tried to spread rumours about her that she was very ugly and that it was well known in Portugal that she would not be able to have children; but Charles did not believe them and she was sent over in 1662 without there having been any form of proxy wedding first.

Charles was not at Portsmouth to meet her when she arrived. Barbara Castlemaine was about to have a baby and

Charles stayed with her until the last minute. Like most of our queens, Catherine had had a terrible crossing and, when he arrived, had a cough and a fever so that she had to receive him in bed. It was perhaps fortunate that she was not well, as Charles wrote back to London to Hyde, the Earl of Clarendon, 'It was happy for the honour of England that I was not put to the consummation of the marriage last night, for I was so sleepy, my having slept but two hours in my journey, that I was afraid that matters would have gone very sleepily.' They were married at Portsmouth the next day.

About his first impression of her Charles was reputed to have said, 'They have brought me a bat instead of a woman.' But he wrote: 'Her face is not so exact as to be called a beauty, though her eyes are excellent good, and not anything in her face that in the least degree can shock one. On the contrary, she has as much agreeableness in her looks altogether as I ever saw; and if I have any skill in physiognomy, which I think I have, she must be as good a woman as ever was born. Her conversation, as much as I can perceive (she did not speak English), is very good, for she has wit enough and a very agreeable voice. I think myself very happy, but am confident our two humours will agree very well together.'

Whether it was true that she had a physical defect, so that she could not have children, seems doubtful. The conditions under which she was expected to produce them were appalling, and the most naturaly fertile woman might have failed. She loved her husband, who was surrounded by his mistresses, most of whom produced children but were under no obligation to do so—in fact, Charles might very well have wished that they were not quite so prolific. She had both anxiety and neglect to put up with and, with the example of Catherine of Aragon ever before her, she must have expected divorce; but Charles had a kindlier nature than Henry and he was also in sympathy with the Roman Catholic religion, although he had fought against his mother's and others' Catholicism to regain his throne.

As she showed no signs of becoming pregnant she went to Bath to take the waters in 1663, and Charles went with her.

In October she became desperately ill with spotted fever. In her delirium she thought that she had had children. Charles, who was attentive to her all through her illness, humoured her in this, and when she seemed to be worried because the boy was so ugly, reassured her and said that it was pretty. At another time she imagined that she had had three, one of them a daughter who looked like Charles, and she kept asking after them in her semi-conscious moments.

She had recovered by 1664 and the next year went to Oxford with Charles to avoid the plague which had broken out in London. Here she became pregnant. Charles wanted her to stay in Oxford and not attempt the journey to London because of her condition; but she disobeyed him, made preparations to follow and had a miscarriage the evening before she started. She was said to have had another in 1668 when she hurriedly had to leave a dinner party, but many of her ladies said that this was just an indisposition.

She was as ill-equipped as she possibly could have been to become the bride of such a man. Brought up in strict seclusion, taught chiefly by religious teachers—she arrived with a number of particularly dirty priests in her retinue—she had no idea of court life nor of the immorality that existed in the English court, where gambling, drinking, flirting and more were allowed. During a court ball a new-born baby was found on the floor and was picked up and wrapped in a handkerchief. Catherine soon learnt to pause before she entered her own apartments in case Charles had a woman there. At Windsor she once saw a woman's shoe in his bedroom and left quickly lest the 'pretty little fool' who was hiding should catch cold. In looks she was no match for Charles's beauties either; she was small and very dark and had prominent teeth. She was also thought to have permanent leukorrhea and to be careless in her personal habits. She and her attendants wore such old-fashioned clothes that they were the laughing-stock of the court. Charles gave her another wardrobe which at first she would not wear, but did so when she found out that he was seriously displeased at her appearance.

They spent their honeymoon together at Hampton Court

and Charles was discreet for a week or two, possibly because the gorgeous Castlemaine was still having her baby; she produced a son in June and as soon as possible Charles took her and presented her to the queen. The queen had heard of her but did not recognize her at first. When she did she burst into tears, her nose bled, and then she fainted. Later she and Charles had a terrible quarrel which was heard throughout Hampton Court. During one of their arguments she said that she would go back to Portugal and he replied, 'that she would do well first to know whether her mother would receive her; and he would give her fit opportunity to know that, by sending to their home all her Portuguese servants; and that he would forthwith give orders for the discharge of them all, since they behaved themselves so ill, for to them and their counsels he imputed all her perverseness.' He was determined to get his own way and flirted and carried on his own life, ignoring her, until she gave way.

Catherine could not hold out for long. She made pathetic attempts to be friendly with Castlemaine and even joked with her. Castlemaine was appointed a lady-in-waiting, and Charles's idea of domestic felicity was to drive in the park with the two women and Lucy Walters's son James, always his favourite child.

Soon Castlemaine too was called upon to be tolerant, because in 1663 Charles fell in love with La Belle Stuart, another lady-in-waiting of the queen's. She had a beautiful face, figure and legs and, although stupid, resisted him so that he became completely infatuated with her. Castlemaine, having been forced to accept her, became so friendly that, one day when Charles called on Castlemaine, he found the two girls in bed together and got in too. All the same Frances hung on to her virtue and, to Charles's fury, married the drunken Duke of Richmond. Charles for once lost his temper and banished her from the court. Soon after this she got smallpox, which somewhat ruined her looks but weakened her resistance to Charles, who was allowed to climb over her garden wall so as not to disturb the gate-keeper. She never had any children.

He had many lesser mistresses. 'The most impertinent slut in the world,' Moll Davis, an actress, had a daughter by him, Mary Tudor, later Countess of Derwentwater. Others were Margaret Hughes, the daughter of a clergyman; Jane Roberts, a singer; Mary Knight, another Maid of Honour; and Winifred Wells, with whom he had an affair for ten years. He took up with the buxom Nell Gwynn in 1668; she was then eighteen and because she had already been kept by two other men whose christian names were Charles—Lord Buckhurst and Hart, the actor—she called Charles 'Charles the Third' to his face. She was frankly a whore and he never ennobled her but made her little boy the Earl of Burford and then the Duke of St. Albans after she had addressed him one day as 'you little bastard'. She had another son by him who died. She was the least grasping and most good-humoured of his mistresses, but she did not take kindly to Louise de Quérouilles when she became favourite in 1670, and nicknamed her 'weeping willow' or 'squinterella' because she had a cast in her eye.

Louise had been deliberately sent over to England by the French in the train of Henrietta, Duchess of Orleans, Charles's sister, in the hope that she would catch his eye, become his mistress and spy on him. He made her the Duchess of Portsmouth and she was the chief favourite until his death. She only had one son, whom he made Duke of Richmond. The Londoners hated her because she meddled in public affairs and once they mobbed Nell Gwynn's carriage thinking that it was Louise's, until Nell put her head out of the window and said with engaging frankness, 'I am the English whore, not the French one.'

In 1676 Hortense Mancini, Charles's former love arrived, having escaped from the madman to whom she had been married. She had a splendid welcome, but her temper was so bad that even Charles could not put up with it, nor with her relationship with the Prince of Monaco, whom she brought with her. Because of him Charles cut off her allowance but gave some of it back later, and she lived respectably at Chiswick.

For the last sixteen years or so of her marriage, after she

realized that she would never produce an heir, Catherine made her own pattern of living. She stayed a lot at Somerset House, prayed a lot and encouraged Italian opera. Her English had improved and she had turned into a fat, dumpy little woman with a complexion so sallow that it looked green. She travelled about the country with Charles whenever he would take her. She liked to live simply, so that her private apartments seemed bare compared to the other ones in the palace. She kept her accounts in good order and did not overspend, but was often short of money because she was not paid her proper allowance. Although Charles treated her badly he was amiable towards her so long as she did not interfere with his plans and let him have his own way. When she was accused of being involved in the Titus Oates plot, he would have none of it and stood by her.

Charles probably had a mild stroke in 1680. In 1684 he had another which left him lame. He could no longer stride along with his courtiers as quickly as he used to, and he accounted for this by saying that he had gout.

In 1685 he started to feel ill on Sunday evening, 1st February, but had gone to the Duchess of Portsmouth's that night. At supper there he asked for soup but did not like the taste of it. He spent a restless night and when he got up he was unsteady on his feet and his speech was blurred. At eight in the morning he had an attack of apoplexy and was bled at once; as the doctor did not have a lancet with him, he opened the vein with a penknife. They put a hot iron on Charles's head and gave him strong stimulants. He came round after a couple of hours and asked for the queen. She had just left his bedside and sent an apology for not being there. 'Alas, poor lady,' he said. 'She beg my pardon? I beg hers with all my heart.'

As the hours went by the queen became so tired and overwrought that she had to be taken away from his bedside and bled too. He died on 6th February, and before he did so a Roman Catholic priest, John Huddleston, heard his confession and gave him the sacrament of extreme unction. His Father John had hidden Charles in the Boscobel Oak after the battle of Worcester, and Charles said to him before he died, 'You have saved me twice, first my body at Worcester and now my soul.'

James II treated Catherine with consideration and let her stay on at Whitehall for two months before she moved into Somerset House. After James lost the throne she went to Holland and stayed with William of Orange for a short time. She then went back to Portugal where she was given a warm welcome by her brother and treated with great respect. She acted as Regent in 1705 when her brother was ill. She died of colic at the end of that year on 31st December.

23 - James II

Born 1633, died 1701. Became king 1685. Married Anne Hyde (born 1637, died 1671) 1660. Married Mary of Modena (born 1658, died 1718) in 1673.

JAMES II HAD many similar tastes to those of his elder brother Charles but was always overshadowed by him. Even with women this was so, although he had better natural looks; but he had less brain and charm and was a bore. His idea of wooing was to play to a woman on a guitar or talk for hours about hunting; as he had inherited his father's stutter this must have made him doubly tedious. Some of his mistresses were so ugly that Charles said that he thought that the priests had imposed them upon him as a penance.

While he was in France he had contemplated marrying a great heiress, the daughter of the Duc de Langueville, but Charles for political reasons had been against the marriage. He then met his first wife, Anne Hyde, the daughter of the Chancellor, the Earl of Clarendon, who was lady-in-waiting to his sister, Mary of Orange. She was in Paris with his sister, who was on a visit to see their mother. He did not see her again until three years later when at Breda they became secretly engaged, and an agreement of marriage dated 24th December was signed by James. Anne was then a plump twenty-two, with flashing, bulbous eyes, a large mouth, a white skin and large bosom.

After the Restoration things moved rapidly. In February she became pregnant, and in September 1660 they were married secretly in the middle of the night. Henrietta was furious that her son should marry a Protestant and a commoner, and stormed at him when, in his capacity as Admiral of the Fleet, he had to meet her when she came over from France. Mary of Orange was also furious that her erstwhile lady-in-waiting was now her sister-in-law, and Clarendon bellowed out that he would rather his daughter should be the king's whore than his wife, and that the king should 'immediately order the woman to be cast into the Tower, and be cast into a dungeon under strict guard'. As an added complication a man called Sir Charles Berkely said that he was the father of the child that Anne was carrying. Later he refuted the story and said that he had said so as he thought that to marry her would ruin James.

The only people who seemed to take the matter calmly were Charles II and Anne's mother who helped the two lovers meet after Clarendon had locked Anne in her room. In November Anne produced a boy, the Duke of Cambridge, who died within a year; the Queen Mother forgave her and accepted her at Court; and Mary of Orange, before her sudden and early death, repented of her harshness.

James was genuinely fond of her, but this did not stop him from being unfaithful and even Charles was amazed by the number and variety of his mistresses. His first notorious affair was with Lady Southesk. This came to an end after a narrow escape when Lord Southesk returned to his house unexpectedly and found one of James's courtiers waiting outside her bedroom. Not knowing who Lord Southesk was, the courtier jokingly told him to seek another mistress as this one was already engaged. Southesk tactfully retired, but James thought the situation was too dangerous and took up with Lady Robarts, aged eighteen and married to a man of nearly eighty. He then fell in love with Lady Chesterfield, but her husband packed her off to the country before the affair really got going. After this he tried Miss Hamilton, a lady-in-waiting of his wife's, and Frances Jennings; but does not seem to have had a great deal of success with either.

Lady Denham then became his acknowledged mistress and

said openly that she would not be like Miss Price (another) going up and down the privy staircase, but would be owned publicly. She died in 1667 and some people said that Anne had had her poisoned. The mistress he loved the best was Arabella Churchill, sister of John, later the Duke of Marlborough, by whom he had two sons, James, Duke of Berwick, and Henry, Duke of Albemarle, and a daughter, Henrietta. Arabella was plain and skinny but had beautiful legs, which James only discovered when she fell off her horse and her skirts went over her head. It was after that that she became his mistress.

Anne knew about his mistresses and suffered accordingly. She was even said to have tried retaliation and to have looked twice at their Master of the Horse, so much so that James was furious and banished him from court. How she could have had time or energy for such an affair it is difficult to understand, for she had eight children in eleven years and died of cancer of the breast in great agony in 1671, crying out, 'Duke, Duke, it is a terrible thing to die!' On her deathbed she became a Roman Catholic.

Four children survived her—a boy and a girl who died almost immediately, and two little girls, Mary and Anne, both of whom in turn became Queens of England. Possibly because she was unhappy she was a compulsive eater. She became enormously fat and passed on her bad eating habits to her youngest daughter Anne, with whom she used to sup on 'chocolate and sweetmeats' till Anne too grew as round as a barrel and was made so ill that she had to be sent away for a holiday.

As soon as Anne died, James thought about remarrying, and wished to have as his bride Lady Bellasis, a plain but witty widow, but Charles II refused to let him do this, saying that no man should be allowed to make a fool of himself twice. Everybody by now had given up hoping that Charles would have any children by Catherine, so as James was the next heir it was essential that he should marry suitably.

The ban on French women seemed to have been lifted and a widow Mary de Guise was considered. She had been pregnant three times in two years, so they thought that she was likely to produce an heir. She was also very rich but very ugly, and James seemed to look for beauty in his wives if not in his mistresses. Another rich woman, Mademoiselle de Retz, was also hideous, so he settled on Mary Beatrice, the daughter of Alfonso d'Este, the Duke of Modena, a state in Northern Italy.

Mary was only fourteen when she was told of these plans. She had never heard of England and when she was told she was to marry a man of forty, she suggested that her aunt of thirty might be more suitable and said that she would like to enter a convent. Nobody would listen to her suggestions and they were married by proxy at Modena in September 1673; she left there on 5th October, her fifteenth birthday. She arrived with her mother at Dover, where they held another ceremony of marriage, in November. The marriage was extremely unpopular in England. James had refused to sign the Test Act and had had to give up his position as Admiral of the Fleet because of this, and Mary of Modena was, of course, another Roman Catholic.

From the point of view of looks he had been lucky. She is described as being beautiful, with jet-black hair, eyebrows and eyes, an oval face, tall and graceful, a good figure and a sweet expression. English court life amazed her. She fell in love with her elderly husband, and was extremely jealous of his mistresses. Far from suffering them as most queens had in her position, she would pine, refuse to eat, and make scenes. She started to do her duty in providing an heir at once. By May she had already had a miscarriage and by January 1675 a daughter, Catherine Laura, who died in October of the same year from convulsions. In the same month she had another miscarriage. In 1676 she had the Princess Isabella, a beautiful but delicate-looking child who died when she was five. At last, on 6th November, 1677, she had a fine, strong baby boy, another Duke of Cambridge, christened Charles. He was born just after the wedding of James's daughter Mary to William of Orange. Princess Anne had felt ill, so stayed away from the wedding; her illness was then diagnosed as smallpox. James, a good father, went to see her every day, and it is thought that it was he who carried the infection to the baby, who died of it on 12th December.

Mary was only four years older than her eldest stepdaughter with whom she became quite friendly. At first she was quite friendly too with Anne, but later Anne spied on her and James and helped turn the tide of public opinion against them before they fled. She and Anne had one or two violent quarrels and during one Mary threw a brush at her.

By 1677 James had a new mistress, Catherine Sedley, a witty woman but skinny and haggard and puzzled by James's infatuation for her. 'It cannot be my beauty,' she said, 'for he must see that I have none; and it cannot be my wits, for he has not enough to know that I have any.' She became one of Mary's ladies-in-waiting and had a daughter by James.

In March 1678 Mary and Anne went over to see Mary of Orange in The Hague. Mary of Orange was homesick, had had a miscarriage and was pregnant again, and Mary went to see that she took more care. The next year, in March, she and James were exiled to Brussels after the Titus Oates plot. They were allowed to come back to England at the end of the year but had such a terrible crossing that Mary was really ill, and when James was sent immediately up to Scotland Charles tried to persuade her to stay at Whitehall with Anne and little Isabella, but she was firm and insisted that she should be with her husband. In February 1680 they got back from Scotland but returned there in October of that year and were not allowed to take Anne or Isabella with them. While they were still there in 1681 they heard that little Isabella had died. Later in the year Mary fell off her horse and was dragged by her clothes but miraculously was only scratched and bruised.

After five years of not having any children Mary became pregnant again. She travelled by boat to England in May and had the baby, Charlotte Mary, in August, but it died of convulsions in October. The next year she had another miscarriage and another in 1684.

When he became king James made a good resolution and decided that he would give up Catherine Sedley. As a parting present he wished to make her Countess of Dorchester; this was too much for Mary, who cried out to him, 'Let me go, you have made your woman a countess; make her a queen. Put my crown on her head. Only let me hide myself in some convent, where I may never see her more . . . You are ready to put your kingdom at hazard for the sake of your soul; yet you throw away your soul for the sake of that creature.'

James compromised by sending Sedley to Ireland, but she did not like it there and soon came back again and became Countess of Dorchester but was no longer his acknowledged mistress.

On June 12th, 1688, Mary produced a son that lived, an incident largely responsible for making James lose his crown. There were tremendous rumours spread about the birth, many of them fostered by Anne, who said that the baby had been smuggled in. This seems quite impossible. Catherine of Braganza was with her all the time she was in labour and there were sixty-seven people in her apartments in all. The Lord Chancellor and the Privy Council were brought up to her bed, the curtains pulled aside so that they could watch the birth, and the queen asked the king to hide her face with his periwig because she 'could not bear to be brought to bed and have so many men look on her'.

Astonishingly enough, in view of their unpopularity as Roman Catholics and in spite of all that had happened before, the royal couple had the child baptized in public on 15th October with full Roman Catholic rites. The Pope himself was godfather by proxy.

Only three weeks later William III landed at Brixham in Devon on 5th November, and James left London on the 17th with his army to do battle with him.

The Prince of Wales was taken to Windsor and then to Portsmouth—the queen remaining in London where James rejoined her on Monday the 26th. He had had a series of nose bleeds that were more like haemorrhages; the people were deserting to William, and Anne had run away from him too. On 9th December James and Mary dined in public as usual, and after dinner she pretended to retire to bed but reluctantly parted from the king and went to Gravesend, where the little prince was brought to her. They reached France together two days later—on the same day that James left Whitehall by a secret passage. He had to return to London, as a crowd of people recognized him and he also had another violent nose bleed. On the evening of the 23rd, helped by his bastard son by Arabella Churchill, the Duke of Berwick, he got away to France, which was his home for the rest of his life.

He made occasional and unsuccessful attempts to get his kingdom back. After one of these in 1692 when Mary had her last child, Marie Louise, he was nursing a defeat at The Hague and was so depressed about the failure of this attempt that he could not even raise the energy to travel to St. Germaine to be with her. They never had enough money and now James, who had always been poor, became melancholy as well. In 1699 they thought he had gout and his stutter got appreciably worse; but more probably, like Charles, he had had a stroke. In March 1701 he fainted in church and a week later had a stroke which left him paralysed down his right side. He got back partial use of his muscles but dragged his leg and his speech was worse than ever. The French king gave them money to go to the thermal springs at Bourbon, but he did not benefit much from his visit and when they got back to Paris in June he had another stroke and yet another on 16th September, which killed him.

After his death Mary, who had nursed him devotedly, tried unsuccessfully to have him recognized as a saint and always went into retreat for the anniversary of his death. Her son, James, grew into a big dull boy; but Marie Louise was pretty and vivacious. Both of them got smallpox in 1712, and Marie Louise died. After he recovered, James, the only child out of her eight pregnancies to grow up, was pockmarked and more lethargic than ever. Mary herself had been ill for years; as far back as 1701 she had had an abscess of the breast—she also had gout and in 1718 got a chill which developed into a fever and she died on 7th May. She was one of our most unhappy queens—her life had been a long tragedy.

Entrée de l'impératrice Mathilde à Winchester.

V. THE EMPRESS MATILDA ARRIVES AT WINCHESTER

VI. 14TH CENTURY BED AND CRADLE

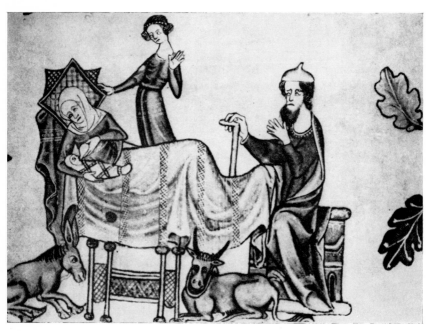

VII. 14TH CENTURY NATIVITY SCENE
From the Luttrell Psalter, c. 1340.

VIII. A LADY'S BEDROOM—15TH CENTURY

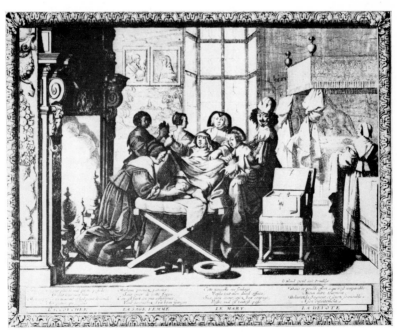

IX. A WOMAN GIVING BIRTH—17TH CENTURY
From a print by A. Bosse (1602–1672).

X. RICHARD II AND ANNE
OF BOHEMIA
From the 14th century *Liber
Regalis*, or Coronation Order
of Service.

XI. MARRIAGE OF HENRY
VI AND MARGARET OF
ANJOU.

XII. HENRY VIII TILTING AT THE JOUSTS
Catherine of Aragon, who has just borne him a son, looks on.
From the Royal College of Arms Westminster Roll.

XIII. MARY I AND PHILIP II OF SPAIN
From a gold medallion by Jacopo da Trezzo, dated 1555 and now in the British Museum.

XIV. CHARLES I AND HENRIETTA MARIA
From a painting by Van Dyck in the Pitti Gallery, Florence.

XV. JAMES II AND MARY OF MODENA
From the painting by E. M. Ward. They are hearing the news that William III has landed in Devor

XVI. CORONATION OF WILLIAM III AND MARY
From a contemporary Dutch engraving.

XVII. WILLIAM III AND MARY PROCEED TO WESTMINSTER
From a contemporary Dutch engraving.

XVIII. GEORGE II AND HIS FAMILY
Engraved from a painting by William Hogarth.

XIX. QUEEN CHARLOTTE
From the painting by Benjamin West (1738–1820).

XX. GEORGE IV AT HOME
A cartoon from *The English Spy*, by R. Cruickshank.

XXI. MARRIAGE OF GEORGE IV AND MRS. FITZHERBERT
Contemporary caricature. Charles James Fox holds Mrs. Fitzherbert's left hand.
Lord North is seated, fast asleep.

XXII. MRS. FITZHERBERT

Illustration from *European Magazine*, 1786. Artist unknown.

XXIII. WILLIAM IV AND ADELAIDE

24 - William and Mary

William of Orange, born 1650, died 1702. Became king jointly with Mary 1789.
Married Mary (born 1662, died 1694) in 1677.

WHEN MARY was told by her father, James II, that she was to marry her cousin William of Orange she wept for twenty-four hours. William's mother, who was her father's sister, had always hated Holland and she was prepared to hate it too. The marriage was arranged for political reasons between Charles and William, and Mary was given only a fortnight's notice of the event. Her father James did not want this union because, he said, he wanted her to marry for love as he had done. He may also have seen the danger to his own chances of succession if his daughter married a Protestant.

William had been born eight days after his father had died of smallpox. After his death the office of Statholder which he held had been abolished, and William, a delicate boy, had grown up among enemies. This had taught him to hide his feelings, so that he was seldom ever able to show them afterwards. Self-disciplined and austere, he had not at all cared for the way of life of the English court where he had paid an eleven-day visit eight years before. The English did not like him much either and found him dull, except for one evening when they managed to get him so drunk that he broke the windows of the maids of honour's room and had to be restrained from going further. Between that visit and his marriage he had proved himself to be a statesman and a general.

When he came over for the wedding he insisted on seeing Mary before the actual ceremony. She must have passed inspection, because the wedding took place in her apartments at nine o'clock at night on Sunday, 4th November, 1677. Afterwards they had to go through the ordeal which Charles I had so skilfully avoided of being seen into bed by the court. Charles II closed the curtains round it with his own hand, saying, 'Now, nephew, to your work. Hey! St. George for England!'

Mary left for Holland in tears, and when Mary of Modena tried to comfort her by saying that she had felt the same when she had left her own country, Mary replied like a true Briton, 'But, Madame, you were coming to England—I am leaving it.'

Mary was sixteen, slim, dark and lively. A possible successor to the throne, no great care had been taken with her education. She could embroider and play on a spinet, and liked reading and flowers. She liked riding, walking, dancing and gambling and card games, and was apt to be over-emotional and garrulous. As the Tudors were haunted by the Howards so the Stuarts were by the Villiers. At an early age she and Anne were handed over to the care of Lady Frances Villiers, who was the daughter of the Earl of Suffolk and married to a cousin of Barbara Castlemaine's. Lady Frances brought the two girls up with her own daughters. One of them, Elizabeth, a plain woman with a squint, became Mary's lady-in-waiting and William's mistress, and another, governess to Anne's son. Lady Frances brought in other companions too, one of them, Sarah Jennings, became Anne's favourite; and another, Frances Apsley, Mary's. Mary became so emotionally attached to her that she wrote letters to her as 'Dear, dear husband', and signed them, 'Your dog on a string, your fish in a net, your bird in a cage, your humbel trout, Mary Clorinne.'

William was twelve years older than she was and looked older still, with his slim, fragile body, large forehead, hooked nose and hard, peevish mouth. He was highly intelligent, a good linguist, and his conversation was chiefly about public affairs. He was never interested in literature or science, except for the latest developments in war, and was bored by the theatre. He could be extremely bad-tempered and had a chilling manner. He was never strong and was always subject to asthma, so much so that after he became King of England he preferred to be at Hampton Court or Windsor, as he could not stand the dirt and fog in London. He often had a racking cough so could not go to sleep unless he was propped up by pillows, had severe headaches and, although he led his army in the field, could not bear too much physical exertion.

The February after they were married Mary had a miscarriage. James wrote that he hoped that she would take more care of herself next time. She had another miscarriage in 1681. After that she did not become pregnant again.

William paid little attention to her but he did add on some rooms to his 'Palace in the Wood' outside The Hague, where she liked to stay when he was away making war. Their court was the dullest in Europe, only once livened up when Monmouth visited them. Then they gave a state ball in his honour and he tried to teach Mary to skate, for which she 'wore a skirt shorter than usual'. Early in her married life she took to religion and to intriguing against her father, in which cause she wrote to his ex-love, Lady Bellasis, with her left hand so that her father would not recognize her writing. Although William was an absent and a frigid husband, and in spite of all her early tears, she had fallen in love with him.

William landed in Torbay on 5th November, 1688. He and Mary were proclaimed joint sovereigns on 13th February, 1689; and crowned together on 11th April of that year. He had always been determined that she should not be queen with himself only consort, to which Mary had been perfectly agreeable but he had been suspicious of her intentions. Once he had been crowned he treated her with much more respect and consideration.

The English never liked him, and he not only made no attempt to court popularity but quite plainly showed that he preferred Dutchmen. Mary was not popular either to begin with, but became so later because of her gentleness and charitable works. She made a bad impression on the court when she first arrived by talking too much and 'running round the palace looking into every closet and conveniency, and turning up the quilts of the beds just as people do at an inn, with no sort of concern in her appearance.'

Many people who had not liked James and did not want him as king were against her because they thought she had behaved disloyally. They were in sympathy with the Countess of Dorchester, James's ex-mistress who, when she approached Mary and Mary turned away her head publicly snubbed her by saying that she had not sinned more in breaking the Seventh Commandment than Mary had in breaking the Fifth.

In 1689 a fire broke out in St. James's Palace; being a heavy sleeper, Mary did not wake up and would have been burnt if she had not been dragged semi-conscious in her nightdress into St. James's Park.

William was the real ruler and had the last say in everything, even to the disposal of her own father's private estates in Ireland, which she wished to be used for schools 'to instruct the poor Irish', but which he made over to his mistress, Elizabeth Villiers, whom he had made Countess of Orkney.

He had to defend his throne against James's attempts to get it back, and while he was away from her she wrote him long and loving letters pouring out all her thoughts on paper. On 29th June, 1690, she wrote: 'You will be weary of seeing every day a letter from me, it may be; yet being apt to flatter myself, I will hope you will be as willing to read as I to write. And indeed it is the only comfort I have in this world beside that of trust in God.'

She did show some concern over her father after the Battle of the Boyne, and wrote to William: 'I know I need not beg of you to let him be taken care of, for I am confident you will for your own sake; yet add that to all your kindness and for my sake let people know you would have no hurt come to his person. Forgive me this.'

William in one of his next letters ticked her off because Kensington Palace would not be ready for his return, and she had 'a million fears in consequence', as she admitted she had 'not been pressing enough until it was too late'. She then goes on to explain to him that she thinks she can arrange things so that he will be comfortable, and adds, 'For it is no matter what inconveniences anyone else suffers for your dear sake.'

In 1694 she got smallpox. She had often been ailing before and frequently in letters to William mentioned her swollen face, caught, she thought, from standing in a draught, but 'not so bad as the time she had the same thing in Holland'. At first they did not realize it was smallpox; she was not well for a few days and they thought that it might be measles, scarlet fever, spotted fever or erysipelas. When she realized it was smallpox she sent away from her any of her attendants who had not already had the disease. William stayed near her night and day, and tears poured down his cheeks when he was told that there was no hope and she was going to die.

He lived for another eight years and, curiously enough, died like the two Williams before him after an accident on horseback. He had been having fevers, headaches and shivering fits for some weeks before, probably consumption. On 20th February, 1702, he was galloping on his favourite horse Sorrel at Hampton Court when it stumbled over a molehill and fell to its knees. He fell off and broke his collar-bone; in his bad state of health this was too much for him and he died on 8th March. Round his neck was hung a little black silk bag and in it was a gold ring and a lock of Mary's hair.

25 - Queen Anne

Born 1665, died 1714. Became Queen 1702. Married Prince George of Denmark (born 1653, died 1708) in 1683.

'I HAVE tried him drunk and I have tried him sober, but there is nothing in him,' was Charles II's summing-up of George of Denmark, the man who was going to marry his niece Anne; and when George, who was too stout, asked him how he could control his weight, Charles replied, 'Walk with me and hunt with my brother and do justice by my niece.'

They were married on the evening of 28th July, 1683, when he was thirty and she eighteen. He was tall, fair and handsome, if rather large, and, like his brother-in-law William, subject to asthma. Like him, too, he was a brave soldier; when fighting with his brother, King Christian, who had become surrounded by the enemy, he had hacked a way through to him and saved his life. Unlike William he was stupid and unambitious and had no pretensions about wanting to be king if Anne became queen, neither did one ever hear of his taking a mistress. He ate enormously and she joined him in this; he may possibly too have taught her to drink.

Anne was more of a Hyde than a Stuart. She was dark and high-coloured and blushed easily and, although she was too fat, had had smallpox and was short-sighted, her looks were quite pleasing. Like her husband, she was mentally limited; she never read, her writing was poor and ungrammatical and, although her reign gave its name to some of the most beautiful houses and furniture England ever produced, she had little interest in the arts. Considering her weight she had rather surprisingly inherited her father's love of hunting and, when she got too fat to ride a horse, followed in a narrow, one-seated, one-horsed calesh with high wheels, in which she used to charge round the countryside. She used to go to the races at Newmarket, though it was not customary for women to do so in those days. After she became queen she started Ascot and gave prizes for some of the races.

She liked making up nicknames. Her brother-in-law William was Caliban, or the Monster; her father and Mary of Modena, Mr. and Mrs. Mansell—this may have been advisable for political reasons when she mentioned them in her letters; she and Sarah Jennings were Mrs. Morley and Mrs. Freeman; and after they were married Prince George was Mr. Morley, and John Churchill, Mr. Freeman. Sarah Jennings her girlhood friend, her governess, and her husband, the Duke of Marlborough, ruled her for years, without any objection being made by George.

Prince George of Hanover, who later became George I, had been over to see her with a possible view to matrimony in 1680, but had decided against her because she was the daughter of a commoner. Possibly she took umbrage at this for she always hated the Hanoverians and, even when it became certain that they would succeed her, had as little to do with them as possible. She did have a slight romance with John Sheffield, the Earl of Mulgrave, whom she made the Duke of Buckingham when she came to the throne. He was a dashing Groom of the Bedchamber to Charles II, with a reputation with the ladies, and had almost certainly had an affair with Barbara Castlemaine. He wrote letters and songs to her, until Charles II found out what was going on, when he sent him off to Tangiers.

The first months of Anne's marriage were spent travelling round the country. In August they were hunting at Windsor and in September at Winchester, and at Newmarket in October. Charles II gave them £20,000 per annum, which he later increased to £50,000, and for their London house the Cockpit, originally built by Henry VIII as such, then turned into a theatre and then into a house for Anne. Her flight from there in 1688 certainly helped to turn more of the English against her father.

She did not come to the throne until nineteen years after her marriage, and two months after her poor little eleven-year-old son the Duke of Gloucester had died. The nineteen years had been full of tragedy and turned her from a strong-looking, motherly type of girl into a fat invalid. By 1689, when the Duke of Gloucester was born, she had had three mis-carriages and three daughters; the first was stillborn, the second lived for a year and a half and the third for seven months. The young prince was a worry from the first; his wet nurse had to be changed because her nipples were too big; he had convulsions; and when he was three a swelling appeared on his head which was drained off and was the start of his hydrocephalus. After the little duke she had a girl, born in 1690, who lived a few hours, and a boy in 1692, who died at once, and six more miscarriages.

George had certainly done his best to follow Charles's advice and do justice by his niece. In all she had nine mis-carriages and six children, all the children dying in infancy, except the poor little Duke of Gloucester, who died when he was eleven of hydrocephalus. Two of them died on the same day within a few hours of each other.

George tried to look after her. He mourned with her and comforted her, and he was one of the few people near her with whom she never quarrelled. She had done so with her father and Mary of Modena; she had goaded Mary of Modena into throwing a hair brush at her when she was carrying her last son, and Anne wanted to feel her stomach because she did not believe that Mary was really pregnant. She quarrelled with her sister and William, having spied against her father for them, and later she quarrelled with the Marlboroughs. The tragedy and strain of watching the poor little Duke of Gloucester, her only surviving son, fight a brave but losing battle for his life, was a blow from which she never recovered.

Her own health deteriorated rapidly. She had to be carried to her coronation, as she had gout and had grown to be so enormously fat. Even before she came to the throne she had virtually withdrawn from public life. She only ate in public on Sundays and, when she did appear in public, always wore black and lots of diamonds. As a result of all this her court was terribly dull.

George died in 1708 and, after she got rid of the Marlboroughs in 1710, she took on another favourite, Lady Masham, a poor relation of Sarah's, who was with her to the end. She became very ill in 1712 and was never really well again, so that there were repeated rumours of her death until she did die in 1714 of an apoplectic fit on 30th June.

26 - George I

Born 1660, died 1727. Became king 1714. Married Sophia Dorothea, only daughter of the Duke of Zell (born 1666, died 1726) in 1682.

WHEN QUEEN ANNE, the last of the Stuarts acceptable to the English people, died, the Hanoverians reigned in England. The first of them to do so was George Lewis of Brunswick-Luneburg, a descendant of the ancient Guelph family. His claim to the throne was through his grandmother Elizabeth, the eldest daughter of James I, and he became George I.

The Guelphs liked women but did not like marriage. The law of primogeniture did not exist in their Duchy, so to stop their inheritance from being split up among seven of them, George's great-uncles drew lots as to which of them should marry and inherit the dukedom. The sixth uncle won—or lost, depending on how you look at it—and later, when his heir came to the throne, he in his turn had to choose whether he would rather rule Hanover or Celle. He chose Celle, so his younger brother inherited Hanover and was betrothed to Sophia, the daughter of Elizabeth, daughter of James I. He was so allergic to marriage that he handed over both his potential bride and his dukedom to another brother, Ernest Augustus, who was the father of George I. He himself became the Duke of Zell, a Duchy a few hundred miles away from Hanover and Celle, morganatically married a French-woman, and their daughter, Sophia Dorothea, married his nephew George.

They were married in November 1682, when Sophia was sixteen and George was twenty-two. She was a romantically-minded girl who had been engaged when a child to Augustus Frederick of Brunswick-Wolfenbüttel, who died when she was ten years old. When she was told the news of his death she fainted.

She grew up to be pretty and graceful, had a lively wit, and was accomplished and agreeable. George had inherited the family reluctance to marry, and had the bulging eyes and lugubrious looks of the Guelphs; he was pale and short and ate too much. He liked soldiering, hunting, shooting and the theatre. He spoke French but, although heir to the English throne, never bothered to learn English well. He already had mistresses, one of them being the daughter of his father's mistress, Countess von Platen.

Sophia soon found out about his mistress, complained to the Electress Sophia and asked to go home. The Electress merely told her to ignore the whole thing. Her own marriage had been very unhappy; she had been much more fond of the fiancé who had jilted her than the brother she had to marry, and was indifferent whether her husband had mistresses or not. She composedly received any he had at court.

George went off to the wars in 1683, and on 10th November of that year Sophia had a son, later George II. After this George was a more attentive husband for a short time until he went off to the wars again. She did not have her next child until 1688. This time it was a girl, also called Sophia Dorothea, who lived to marry Frederick of Prussia and become the mother of Frederick the Great.

It was in this year that Count Philip von Königsmark came to Hanover and was appointed a colonel in the Dragoons. He was descended from a noble family which was already notorious. His sister Aurora was the mistress of Augustus of Saxony. His brother Philip had been accused of murdering an Englishman, had bribed the jury to get him off, then married the rich widow and retired to Greece. He died there and left Philip all his money.

Philip was a born adventurer, more because he liked the

excitement than because he needed to be. As a boy he had been a page at the court of Zell, and some people said that he and Sophia had been in love with each other as children. Whether this was true or not, he laid siege to her now and she, pining for love, reciprocated. At first it was a flirtation, but they were indiscreet and were warned to behave themselves by one of George's younger brothers, by the Electress Sophia and by George Augustus himself, who sent Königsmark away from Hanover for a short time on a diplomatic mission. This did not stop the love affair and soon they were writing indiscreet love letters. In one he writes: 'Adorable, I will love thee to the tomb! Tonight thou shalt be mine—yea, though I perish!'

In another he scolded her for flirting with 'that violinist' and said in it: 'For mercy's sake cannot you alter your ways for the sake of a lover who adores you so tenderly? Think of all the trouble you have caused me, of all the risks I have run.'

She became his mistress round about 1692, after he had threatened to volunteer for service abroad if she resisted him any longer. In June 1693 letters that had passed between them were handed to Ernest Augustus. Königsmark seems to have been out of Hanover then and to have kept out until 1st July, 1694, when he went to Sophia's apartments. As he left them he was seized and never seen again. His sister Aurora tried to find out what happened to him, but she was not allowed into Hanover, and when the Duke of Saxony made inquiries he never got a satisfactory reply. When George II succeeded to the throne he had alterations made to the palace, and Königsmark's skeleton was found under the floor of Sophia Dorothea's dressing-room. Whether they were going to elope or whether he just came to say goodbye is not certain, or even if she arranged their meeting or if it was a plot of Countess von Platen's, who hated Sophia and wanted to forward her daughter's interests; or if, as some people said, the Countess had also favoured Philip herself and had been snubbed.

Sophia was sent to the Castle of Ahlden in Zell and was

kept prisoner there for thirty-two years until her death in
1726. She was treated with respect and allowed a certain
amount of freedom, but she never saw her husband or her
children again. George had no regrets about the failure of his
married life.

His father died in 1698. The rule of primogeniture was
established and he became Elector of Hanover and, in 1714,
King of England. He wept when he left Hanover and so did
his subjects. He had ruled them well and lived there the life
of a country gentleman on a large scale. The English considered it a great privilege for anyone to be their king and
looked upon Hanover as unimportant, so could not understand why he was always longing to get back there. He brought
his mistress, Baroness von Kielmansegg, over with him. She
was very fat, and the English nicknamed her 'the Elephant
and Castle'. He made her Lady Darlington and her daughter
by him married in England and became Lady Howe, mother
of the famous admiral. His other mistress, Countess von
Platen's daughter, Fraülein von der Schulenberg, would not
come over at first because she thought that the barbarous
English were sure to cut off George's head. She took courage
later and he made her the Duchess of Kendal. She was tall
and scrawny, and the English nicknamed her 'the Maypole'.
He also had a daughter by her who became Lady Walsingham.
Both these good ladies had been his mistresses for many years
and were elderly, but he remained faithful to their ageing
charms, though he added an Englishwoman, Anne Brett, also
to his harem.

His court was full of old mistresses. At his coronation he
had the Duchess of Portsmouth, Charles II's; Lady Orkney,
William III's; and Lady Dorchester, James II's. When they
all met Lady Dorchester said with engaging frankness, 'Good
God! Who would have thought that we three whores would
have met together here!' Their presence did not enliven the
court, which was extremely dull; sometimes not more than
six ladies attended it. George's English was always appalling
and, when one of his courtiers tried to talk to him about the
arts, he said that he hated 'boets and bainters'.

During the thirteen years of his reign he went back to Hanover seven times, and he died on his way there in 1727 after eating a large dinner and several water melons. It had been prophesied to him that he would die soon after Sophia Dorothea, and he did, seven months later.

The Duchess of Kendal was with him when he died and he promised that he would visit her after he was dead. Not long afterwards a raven flapped at a window of her house at Twickenham; she was convinced that it was his spirit and kept it in a cage until her death.

27 - George II

Born 1683, died 1760. Became king 1727. Married Caroline of Anspach
(born 1683, died 1737) in 1705.

CAROLINE OF ANSPACH, the wife of George II, was the
most remarkable Queen Consort that we ever had. With the
help of Walpole she virtually ruled the country for ten years
and the English knew it. A lampoon of the time went:

> *You may strut, dapper George, but 'twill all be in vain,*
> *We know 'tis Queen Caroline, not you, that reign—*
> *You govern no more than Don Philip of Spain.*
> *Then if you would have us fall down and adore you,*
> *Lock up your fat spouse, as your dad did before you.*

George seems to have been impervious to this. He once
said:

> 'England was ruled by Elizabeth;
> James I by his gross appetites;
> Charles I by his wife;
> Charles II by his whores;
> James II by his priests;
> Mary II by William III;
> And Anne by her woman favourites;'

But he asked, 'Who rules me?'

Caroline was born in the tiny state of Anspach. Her father,

the Margrave, had married for his second wife Eleanor
Erdmuth Louise of Saxe-Eisenach, who, with her fair hair
and blue eyes, was 'the most beautiful princess in Germany'
and was Caroline's mother. He died three years later of smallpox, and six years later Eleanor married as her second husband
the Elector of Saxony, where Caroline and her brother went to
live. Two years later the Elector also died of smallpox, which
he caught from nursing his mistress, who had that disease. In
1696 Eleanor also died.

The new Elector of Saxony had so many illegitimate children
and mistresses that he could not be bothered with the two
children, and they were sent back to Anspach, where their
stepbrother was Margrave. He could not be bothered with
them either, but fortunately for Caroline the Elector of
Brandenburg, her guardian, suggested that she went to live
with them.

The Elector's wife, Sophia Charlotte, believed in the education of women and that they should have interests other than
their children and gossip. She loved music and the arts generally and liked to have intelligent and lively people round her.
At her court Caroline met Leibnitz, the German philosopher
and mathematician, who had a great influence on her and
begged her to study and read. This she had always done,
though until she reached Sophia Charlotte's court, her education had been neglected. She had always longed to learn, but
had had to teach herself to read and write, with the result
that her writing was always bad and she could not spell.

In 1704 the Archduke Charles, second son of the Emperor,
courted her, but she turned him down on religious grounds.
This made her something of a heroine in the Protestant world,
because she had relatively no position or importance and the
match would have been very advantageous. The Electress
Sophia of Hanover met and approved of her, and George,
spurred on by her approval and his father's, and travelling
incognito as Monsieur Busche, arrived to pay her court.

To the German taste Caroline was as beautiful as her mother
had been. She was large, plump and blonde, with fine features
and well-shaped hands; she was charming, vivacious and

friendly and, more important still, when dealing with the Hanoverians, had plenty of tact.

George was only five feet eight inches, had the delicate features of his mother but the unfortunate lugubrious expression of the Guelphs. He was dapper, polite and attentive. He arrived in Anspach in early June 1705 and asked for her hand officially on the 22nd of that month. The engagement was made public in July and the wedding took place in August.

During the month that they were parted he wrote her formal little letters. In one he said, 'You have conferred so great a favour upon me expressing no aversion to the proposal with which Baron d'Eltz was charged . . . I found that all I had heard about your charms did not nearly equal what I saw.'

Later he warmed up and, when she announced the date of her departure for Hanover, wrote: 'I desire nothing so much as to throw myself at my Princess's feet and promise her eternal devotion.'

Almost immediately she thought that she was going to have a baby, which she expected would be born in the autumn. It was a false pregnancy, but she did produce a son, Frederick Louis, on 31st January, 1707. Nobody of importance was present at the birth; the English envoy did not see the baby until it was a month old, and the English court heard about it through one of her ladies-in-waiting. As the Electress Sophia said: 'If Duke Maximilian (her second son) had as much power as the English Parliament he would declare his nephew a spurious child, for no one from here was present at his birth.'

In 1707 Sophia had smallpox and George worried and fretted and fumed at her bedside. She got better, but then caught a chill and nearly died. After she recovered from this George himself caught smallpox, and also recovered. Neither of them seem to have been much disfigured.

George I, who hated his eldest son, was just about as nasty to the young couple as he could be. They had to share a communal house with him, his brother, the Electress Sophia and his daughter, Sophia Dorothea. He gave Caroline £950 per annum and paid her servants, which meant that he rather than she had authority over them. He gave George £2,000 per annum, out of which he had to pay for her horses and carriages and put aside money for her in case he died. He grew increasingly jealous of their popularity and for a brief spell they fell out of favour with the Electress Sophia too, chiefly because Caroline and George had been afraid to push themselves forward enough and the Electress thought that they were being rude and casual. After the smallpox, touched by their obvious devotion to each other, she took them back into favour.

In 1708 George, who now had an heir, was at last allowed to fulfil his other ambition and go into battle, and went on his first campaign under the command of Marlborough. He fought in the battle of Oudenarde and his horse was shot under him. This was the high point of his life, and until he died he liked to wear the uniform of the regiment he fought with on every possible occasion. While he was away Caroline wrote him frequent twenty-five-page long letters.

It was nine years between their marriage and George I's accession. She had three more children, all daughters: Anne, born in 1709, Amelia in 1711, and Caroline in 1713. Frederick was a worry. He was a backward child and had rickets and later glandular trouble. Apart from this worry and George I's jealousy, the years passed happily enough. They were tremendously physically attracted to each other, although they did not have many tastes in common. While he hunted, shot or went to war, she studied and had children. They both took the trouble to learn English.

They followed George I over to England in 1714. George made them leave Frederick behind, and they left the baby Caroline with him until a few months later, when they thought that she was old enough to travel. When she did join them Frederick was again left behind.

Caroline took care to be as English as possible. Her language was free and surprising to their ears, but she was friendly and approachable, dressed well and with care, and tried to adapt herself to their customs. She noticed that the English ladies went regularly to church, so, although she was not religious, she went regularly too; she soothed over her husband's tactlessness and his worst outbursts of temper. It was said that the only man she could never manage was George I, who disliked them even more in England because of their comparative popularity there also. He again insisted that they should live with him, and allowed George as little responsibility as possible, giving him the minimum amount of authority when, on his frequent visits to Hanover, he left him as Regent.

In November 1716, she had a son who was born dead, and in November 1717, another, George William, who died in infancy but lived long enough for them to have another quarrel about him with George I. After the birth George sent a messenger to his father to tell him the news but did not bother to write a letter. George I took umbrage and, when he called on Caroline to see the child, ignored his son. The young couple asked the king to be a godfather and he accepted, but insisted that the Duke of Newcastle, a man whom both Caroline and George particularly disliked, should be a co-godfather. After the christening, which took place in Caroline's bedroom, George could no longer control himself and, rushing up to Newcastle, said in his guttural voice, 'You rascal, I will find you!' Newcastle thought he said 'fight'. News of George's behaviour got to the king, who promptly put his son under arrest and then sent him away from court. Caroline was told that she could stay in the palace in strict seclusion until her strength had come back, but she declined and left with George. They were ordered to leave their children behind, even the newly-born prince. He was a delicate child and died three months later.

Parliament had voted them £100,000 per annum, so they now had money. They bought Leicester House in London for their town house and Richmond Lodge for their country home. Caroline was pregnant again when they first went there in 1718, but a tree crashed down outside her window during a thunderstorm which frightened her so much that she had a miscarriage. At Richmond Lodge George used to like shooting wild turkeys which had been fattened on acorns and barley until they weighed about thirty pounds. To flush them they were chased by hounds. He used to hunt stags twice a week but did not like foxhunting.

Caroline now became friendly with Walpole. At first she had distrusted him but, after knowing him for about three years, she grew to realize his political astuteness and he to appreciate her qualities. Together they tried to patch up a peace between the old king and the prince, and made matters so much better that they at least appeared together in public and young George took his place at court. Her children were not handed back to her but she was allowed to see more of them and they were allowed to see their father.

Anne, the eldest of the children and the most like her mother, was now eight and remarked one day in public, 'We have a good father and a good mother, yet we are like charity children.' When she was asked if the king did not visit the nurseries, she replied, 'Oh, he does not love us enough for that.' George I heard about this and afterwards was more attentive. Later the same child said of her father: 'When great points go as he would not have them he frets and is bad to himself; but when he is in his worst humours and the devil to everybody . . . it is always because one of his pages has powdered his periwig ill, or a housemaid set a chair where it does not use to stand.' A courtier described him as 'too stupid for clever men and too dull for rakes'.

In 1721 their eighth child and second son to live to manhood, William, Duke of Cumberland, was born; after that there were two more daughters: Mary, born in 1723, and Louise in 1724.

Walpole broke the news to George of his father's death on 14th June, 1727. He had to wake him up from his after-lunch sleep and all George said was, 'That is a lie.' When he was persuaded that it wasn't and Walpole asked him for instructions, he told him to go and take them from Sir Spencer Compton, the Speaker of the House of Commons, looking at Caroline sidelong as he did so to see her reaction. But she did not look up from her embroidery.

Gradually with patience and with tact Caroline made her husband like Walpole, and the two of them ruled for George until her death. She was the first Queen Consort of England to be crowned since Anne of Denmark, in 1603.

George loved Caroline but, as a Hanoverian, he felt it incumbent upon him to have mistresses. His first choice was Mrs. Bellenden, one of Caroline's ladies-in-waiting, who was so discreet that she insisted that another lady-in-waiting, Mrs. Howard, chaperoned their meetings and, playing for safety, married a Colonel Campbell. Disappointed in her, George turned his attention to Mrs. Howard, who had been with them in Hanover. She was deaf and three years older than him. She was also short of money, as she had no private means, and pleased with any little extras that came her way. Another of his mistresses was a governess to his daughters, Lady Deloraine, married to a Mr. Wyndham. She was pretty, amoral and brainless. Once when she was standing in the hall at Richmond with a baby in her arms, Walpole said to her, 'That's a very pretty boy, who got it?' To which she replied without rancour: 'Mr. Wyndham, upon my honour, but I will not promise who the next will be.'

Caroline was upset but, encouraged by Walpole, was clever enough not to make a fuss, continued to enjoy the marriage bed and became George's confidante over his affairs, which he used to discuss with her in detail. In one of his letters from Hanover he asked Caroline if she could invite the Prince of Modena and his wife to England, as he had heard that Her Highness was pretty free of her person and he had the greatest inclination imaginable to pay his addresses to a daughter of the late Regent of France, the Duke of Orleans. Another time he consulted Caroline about his mistress in Hanover, Madame Walmoden, whom he suspected of having another lover. Another of his mistresses was Madame d'Eltz; another Schulenberg. Her great aunt Countess von Platen, had been mistress to George I's father, and her aunt the Duchess of Kendal to George II. She excelled them both as she was reputed to have been the mistress of George I, George II, and of Frederick, George II's son.

As he got older George became more and more critical of the English and their way of life. He said that they did not know how to cook, and that the women did not know how to dress or bring up their children and that was the reason why the English had no manners. His own children were chastised regularly and once, when the Duchess of Marlborough (Sarah, who was still at court) visited the royal family, the queen was beating one of the children, who was bellowing so loudly that they could not hear themselves speak. Later in life when he was at Hampton Court he lost his temper with the little George III and boxed his ears so soundly that young George hated the place for ever after. Caroline had to bear the brunt of his irritability. A description of one of his morning visits to her said that as soon as he arrived he reprimanded her for drinking chocolate and 'always stuffing'. He then scolded his daughter Caroline for growing fat, his daughter Amelia for not hearing what he said, and his son William for standing awkwardly. He then took Caroline off to the garden to grumble to and at her there.

Their chief source of worry was their son Frederick. They had both professed a loving, and Caroline even a yearning, interest in him while he was in Hanover but, now that there was nothing to stop their bringing him to England, they seemed in no hurry to do so and he did not arrive until eighteen months after his father had succeeded. For the first few months the family reunion went moderately well but, when George went to Hanover in 1729, he left Caroline as sole Regent and Frederick with no responsibility. It was the same story all over again, father and son disliked each other, and Frederick, without enough to do, made as much trouble as he could. It was decided that he should marry and the Princess Augusta of Saxe-Gotha became his wife. Saxe-Gotha was such a small state that the ambassador who was sent over to bring her to England said that, to find it, he had to wander all over Europe.

Caroline, who at that time still got on quite well with her son, advised Frederick to give up his mistress before the princess arrived, which he did. Augusta could speak no

English, and when it was suggested she might learn, her mother said it would not be necessary, as England was governed by Hanoverians. Soon after the marriage she said that she could not go to communion in the Church of England, it would have to be in a Lutheran church; but she was persuaded to change her mind. Next there was a row about the birth of their eldest child, a daughter.

Caroline had always been worried that Frederick might not be able to function as a father, as he had had glandular trouble, and frequently discussed the matter with her confidants. When the princess did become pregnant Caroline was not told until June, although the ladies-in-waiting had known in March and the baby was born in July. They had all been at Hampton Court, from where Frederick had smuggled his wife to St. James's Palace, where she had the baby, a girl. This was bad enough, and the king and queen cannot have been mollified when they hurried from Hampton Court in the middle of the night and arrived at four in the morning, to be told that the baby had been born at ten o'clock the evening before. Like his father before him, Frederick was then banished from court.

Caroline had only ten years as queen and her health was not good. She had gout after her coronation but explained it away by saying that she had been kicked. She used to try and nurse her feet so that she could walk with George in the garden. She had a horror of physical defects and was surprisingly prudish about her body. In 1716, when she had had a stillborn son, it had taken several days to be born and she had been so ill that George, who was acting as Regent, and his council, had tried to make her have a doctor instead of her German midwife, but she had refused. When her last child was born she had had an umbilical rupture. She had made light of it and told George that it was quite a common complaint for a woman who had had several children; she had made him promise not to tell anybody.

In November 1737 she became dangerously ill. She had had fits of sickness and colic during the summer and had them again, complaining of pains in her stomach. These became suddenly worse and she had a fever. The next day she was blooded and her temperature went down, but she kept saying, 'I have an ill which nobody knows of.' They tried every remedy, put blisters on her legs, gave her snake root, and blisters and purgings, to no effect. Then George whispered to her that he thought her illness was caused from the rupture about which he had promised never to speak again. Her surgeon examined her and then went and spoke quietly to the king, whereupon Caroline said to him, 'You lying fool, you are telling the king I have a rupture.' The surgeon admitted that he was and that another surgeon must be called in. This was too much for Caroline, who turned away her head and wept. George said that it was the only time he had ever seen her cry. The new surgeon said he would operate, but the first one said that if they did so her guts would come out all over the bed, and suggested putting hot fomentations on a large swelling that had suddenly developed on her stomach. They then lanced this, the wound mortified and they thought she would die immediately; but the mortification didn't spread and they went on with their treatments, while she was in agony. She only took morphia one night and lived for ten days from the beginning of her illness until she died on 20th November.

Even on her deathbed she would not see and forgive Frederick. George cannot have been much of a comfort. Mad with grief and worry, he managed to do and say all the wrong things. He would insist on lying on her bed all night, so that neither of them could sleep. When she was in great agony he told her that her fixed stare made her look like a cow that was going to have its throat cut; and when she told him to marry again after her death he said, 'No, I will have mistresses,' to which she replied, 'My God! That would not stop you.'

She was survived by two sons: Frederick, who died in 1751 before his father, and William, Duke of Cumberland, who only outlived his father by five years; and four daughters: Anne, who married the hunchbacked Prince of Orange; Caroline, who never married; Mary, who married Frederick of Hesse-Cassel; and Louise, who married the King of Denmark.

After Caroline's death George's court was terribly dull. Walpole was getting old and needed somebody to replace Caroline to influence George. First he tried Lady Deloraine but she was too frivolous, so he suggested that the king should bring Madame Walmoden over from Hanover; but she would not meddle in politics and did not like Walpole. George made her the Countess of Yarmouth and she kept him happy. Her son by him was called General Walmoden. Before he died he handed her a wad of banknotes and signed a certificate to say that he had done so.

In 1743 he commanded his army at the battle of Dettingen, the last English king to fight in the field. He died in 1760 sitting in his lavatory, where he had a stroke, and was buried next to Caroline in Westminster Abbey. One of the panels in her coffin had been made to slide out so that he could be put beside her.

28 - George III

Born 1738, died 1820. Became king 1760. Married Charlotte Mecklenburgh-Strelitz (born 1743, died 1818) in 1761.

GEORGE III WAS a dull, good man who for fifty-seven years was faithful to one of the plainest women ever to become Queen Consort of England.

He was the second child and eldest son of George II's son, Frederick, and his unpopular wife, Princess Augusta of Saxe-Gotha, who had been chosen as his bride partly because George II had met her when he was in Hanover and thought that she would be suitable, and partly because she was one of the few Protestant princesses unmarried in Europe who did not have madness in her family. They had eight children and, after she became a widow in 1751, she was suspicious of everybody and kept them away from the outside world as much as possible, but had the foresight to bring George up as an Englishman; he never during the whole of his life set foot in Hanover. She also brought him up to be religious.

He was a seven-month baby, which made him delicate at first, after that he was backward; he could not read until he was eleven. With all his affection for England, he never mastered the language, its spelling or its grammar, but he was a conscientious plodder and, once he became king, applied himself to the job. He grew up to be tall and healthy-looking and handsome in the bulgy-eyed family way. He was essentially middle-class rather than aristocratic and liked walk-

ing round the countryside near Windsor, shooting questions
at his tenants punctuating them with 'What, what?' He knew
a lot about farming and used to write letters about it to the
Annals of Agriculture, using an assumed name. He was very
inquisitive and liked to know the names of all his servants
and to hear details about their families. He was considerate
to them and, because he liked to get up at five in the morning,
he had an alarm clock to wake him and made his own tea.
Because he was afraid of getting fat like the rest of his family,
he ate very little and very simple food, preferring vegetables
to meat; and he used to ride for hours on end whatever
the weather. He was fond of music, especially church music,
but found Shakespeare 'sad stuff'. He was a great stickler for
etiquette.

His sheltered life did not stop him falling in love twice
before his marriage. Once with Hannah Lightfoot a Quaker—
there was a rumour that they were actually married—and the
other time with Sarah Lennox the beautiful daughter of the
Duke of Richmond. George proposed to Sarah through a girl
friend and because of his proposal she broke off her engagement to the Duke of Newbottle. His mother did not approve
of the prospective marriage and produced another bride, the
eighteen-year-old Charlotte, second daughter of the Duke of
Mecklenburgh-Strelitz.

Charlotte was pale and thin, with too broad a nose and
a big mouth but good teeth; she came from a poor, dull
German court. She brought no dowry to England, and the
English people always thought that George might have done
better. She had a rough crossing over to England, during
which she played the harpsichord while the rest of her suite
was sick. At her official reception she saw a cushion in front
of the old Duke of Grafton and thought that she was meant to
kneel on it; she was prevented from doing this, but then
threw herself in front of George as if he were an eastern poten-
tate, and he had to pick her up. The large formal procedures
must have been confusing to her but she did not lose her self-
possession and must have been well-informed about the court,
because when the Duchess of Hamilton smiled at her she said,

'You may laugh. You have been married twice, but it is no joke for me.' They were married at night at St. James's Palace and Sarah Lennox was bridesmaid.

A limited woman insomuch as she had little charm or personality, she was quite well-educated and splendidly fulfilled her duties as a queen by producing fifteen children in twenty-two years. Most of them were healthy until they became dissipated: two of them lived to be over eighty.

George bought Buckingham House (now Buckingham Palace) for her, but they seemed at first to be happiest at Kew, where their increasing family were housed in different houses on the green with their own staff, tutors and nurses. They lived frugally and liked simple pleasures. They liked to invite a few friends to take part in country dancing, which George would do for hours on end. She also liked to play cards and George would join her in this; the stakes, one imagines, were very low. Otherwise they delighted in domesticity. He would read to her while she embroidered, or she would play the spinet; and there were the children, whom they liked to watch having their dinner. They brought them as much as possible into court life. When the Prince of Wales was twelve days old he was on view to the ladies, railed off so that they could not touch him. This was a great success, and entertaining them with wine and cake cost £40 a day. At the age of three he received a deputation on St. David's Day; and the Duke of York was made Bishop of Osnaburgh at the age of seven months. At the same time George gave instructions that they were to be treated as 'ordinary boys', which meant that they were flogged regularly.

From her letters Charlotte sounds as if she would have liked some more sophisticated pleasures. She wrote: 'You may apply our style of life to this,

> *They ate, they drank, they slept, what then?*
> *They slept, they ate, they drank again!*

Yet after I have said this, though we are not La Bande Joyeuse, we are La Bande Contente, et c'est beaucoup dire en peu de mots.'

That she had a sense of humour is certain; in another letter she gives a description of one of her courts: 'I have seen several ladies just returned from Paris, some very much improved in looks, and others far otherwise. Mrs. Goldburn is made quite formidable by three immense feathers, which so directly ran into my eyes when she was presented, I was under the necessity of drawing myself back in order to avoid mischief, and I rejoiced a little in Lady Claremont's distress who presented her . . .'

When she wanted a footman dismissed she was amusing about that too and wrote to her Chamberlain: 'My Lord, I want you to exert your authority in dismissing my footman Oby as soon as possible, as his unquenchable thirst is now become so interfering that neither our absence nor presence can subdue it any more.'

She was fond of jewellery, and on official occasions appeared covered in diamonds, some of them given by the Nabob of Arcot, some by George, and some which she bought for herself.

The precautions about madness taken by his family had not worked, and George had his first attack of nervous instability in 1765. He had all the symptoms of porphyria, a hereditary disease which to a lesser degree his sons, William and Adolphus, inherited too. In those days it could lead to permanent insanity. This first attack lasted for three months. On top of this the family troubles with which they had to deal for the rest of their lives had started to accumulate. His favourite brother, Gloucester, married the illegitimate granddaughter of Sir Robert Walpole. Another brother, the Duke of Cumberland, was first cited in a divorce case, in which George had to pay the £10,000 damages awarded to the husband, and then married a widow, Anne Horton, who came from a family called Luttrell, notorious for their disreputable way of living. This prompted George to bring in the Royal Marriage Act in 1772, which provided that: 'No descendant of his late Majesty George II (other than the issue of princesses married or who may marry into foreign families) shall be capable of contracting matrimony without the previous consent of His Majesty, his heirs and successors, signified under Great Seal. But in case any descendant of George II, being above twenty-five years old, shall persist to contract a marriage disapproved of by His Majesty, such descendant, after giving twelve months' notice to the Privy Council, may contract such a marriage, and the same be duly solemnized without the consent of His Majesty, etc., and shall be good except both Houses of Parliament shall declare their disapprobation thereto.'

As if the men of the family were not enough worry to him, his youngest sister, Caroline, Queen of Denmark, was caught having an affair with the court physician. The physician was executed and she was sent to Celle, where she died six months later. George I's wife was buried there too so it was quite a place for unfaithful Hanoverian queens. George's mother, who had cancer of the throat, died just after this, to the undisguised delight of the English, who had always disliked her, and who stole some of the black carpets and draperies at her funeral.

The one certain thing in George's life was that the queen would continue to supply him with children. She had fifteen: the Prince of Wales, later George IV, 1762; Frederick, Duke of York and Albany, in 1763; the Duke of Clarence, later William IV, in 1765; Charlotte in 1766; Edward Augustus, Duke of Kent, in 1767; Augusta in 1767; Elizabeth in 1770; Ernest Augustus, Duke of Cumberland, later King of Hanover, in 1771; Augustus Frederick in 1773; Adolphus Frederick, Duke of Cambridge, in 1774; Mary in 1776; Sophia in 1777; Octavius, who only lived four years, in 1779; Alfred, who only lived two, in 1780; and Amelia in 1783.

These children, too, gave trouble as soon as they were old enough. When the Prince of Wales was still in his teens he wrote letters to one of his lady loves and George had to buy them back for £5,000. He then got into debt pretty well continuously, and set up his own household more or less in opposition to his father's, as all the Hanoverian Princes of Wales had done before him. His marriages to Mrs. FitzHerbert and later to Caroline of Brunswick, and the scandals that surrounded both of these, caused his father more anxiety. The Duke of York had a childless marriage with the niece of Frederick the Great and was unfaithful to her for thirty years; in 1809, when he was Commander-in-Chief, his mistress, Mrs. Clarke, was accused of selling promotions in the Army. The Duke of Clarence fell in love with unsuitable women from the age of sixteen and then settled down for years of unwedded domestic bliss with an actress. The Duke of Kent, the father of Queen Victoria, did the same thing with a French-Canadian woman until he married late in life. He had military ambitions and had constantly to be moved to different posts abroad because of his inhuman treatment of the men under him; he was also constantly in debt. The Duke of Cumberland was strongly suspected of murdering his valet, and had to give evidence at the inquest when a verdict of suicide was brought in. He was also, almost certainly wrongly, suspected of an incestuous relationship with his sister Sophia. She had an illegitimate baby but it was the son of Captain Garth, an equerry of the court. The Duke of Cumberland then married his cousin Frederica of Solme-Braunfels, who had been married first to a son of the King of Prussia, by whom she had had two children. She had divorced him and then married the Prince of Solme, by whom she had four children. He was divorcing her when he suddenly died, and many suspected that she had had a hand in his death. Queen Charlotte disapproved of her so much that she would never speak to her or receive her at court. The Duke of Sussex married morganatically and was honest enough to consider it binding. The youngest son to reach manhood, the Duke of Cambridge, was the most normal and married happily and suitably. His bride was the daughter of the Landgrave of Hesse-Cassel; they lived in Hanover because it was cheaper than England, and their granddaughter Mary was the wife of George V.

Charlotte bore the brunt of her daughter Sophia's misdemeanour. George was told that she had dropsy when she was pregnant and he used to prattle away about her miraculous cure. Later Charlotte helped keep from him Amelia's love for another of his equerries, General Fitzroy, to whom she left all her possessions when she died. Three of their daughters, Charlotte, Elizabeth and Mary, married but none of them had children. Their second daughter, Augusta, was the most biddable, although there was even a rumour that she had secretly married an Irishman called Sir Brent Spencer. She helped both her parents when they needed her and tried to keep the family together by writing friendly letters to smooth over their quarrels.

George had a return of his illness in the summer of 1788. This was a bad attack from which he did not recover until February 1789. When it started he talked for sixteen hours without stopping. He was sent off in his carriage with the queen to go for a drive which they thought might soothe his nerves, but he got out of it to talk to a tree which he thought was the King of Prussia.

The poor man knew that he was on the borderline of insanity and said to his wife and daughters, 'You know what it is to be nervous, but was you ever as bad as this?' He also developed an embarrassing passion for the very respectable Lady Pembroke, 'which', as the court said, 'was more than Lord Pembroke did'. The most terrible cures were tried for him and he was often in a straitjacket. In 1804 he had another attack, from which he recovered his senses but not his health, and he started to go blind. 1809 was the year of the Duke of York scandal; as he was George's favourite son this upset him. Princess Amelia's death at the age of twenty-seven in 1810 was even more of a blow. She was his favourite daughter and when she knew that she was dying, put one of her rings on his finger for him to wear in remembrance. After 1811 he remained an imbecile for the rest of his life, and at the end he was also totally blind.

During the 1788 attack Queen Charlotte spent a lot of the time in tears. By the time of his later attacks her own health was going into decline and, as he frequently took an aversion to her, she retired from his life as much as possible, spending a lot of time at Frogmore, where she made a beautiful garden. She was criticized because she would only go and see him if accompanied by one of her daughters, and because she adopted an unfortunate and unsympathetic attitude towards him. None of her family seem to have liked her very much except possibly her dutiful daughter Augusta. Sophia, when she wrote from her mother's address, used to head the writing paper 'The Nunnery'. Charlotte did not like her daughters-in-law, quarrelled with the Prince of Wales when he was Regent, and saw little of her other sons, who did not visit her if they could avoid it. She neither liked the English nor they her. When she was being carried in a sedan chair from Buckingham Palace to St. James's Palace towards the end of her life, they crowded round her, booing and jeering, only to disperse when she put down the window and shouted at them, 'I am seventy-two years of age. I have been fifty-two years Queen of England. I was never yet spit at.'

She died at Kew in November 1818. George outlived her by fourteen months.

29 - George IV

Born 1762, died 1830. Became king 1820. Married Caroline of Brunswick-
Wolfenbüttel (born 1768, died 1821) in 1795.

GEORGE IV LOATHED his parents in a hearty, Hanoverian
way, and he reacted strongly against the domesticated atmosphere of their dull home life. Unlike his ancestors he was
not averse to marrying, so much so that he married the
Roman Catholic Mrs. FitzHerbert in secret and morganatically
and, without bothering about a divorce, then married Caroline
of Brunswick.

He had his first love affair when he was sixteen, with Mary
Hamilton, one of his sister's governesses; he was sixteen and
she was twenty-three. After this he had an affair with an
actress, Betty Robinson, and his father had to buy back the
letters that he wrote to her. When he was eighteen a Mrs.
Elliott had a child which she said was by him and gave it the
royal christian names of Georgina Frederica Augusta; some
people thought that in fact its father was Lord Cholmondeley.
By the time he was twenty-two he had fallen madly in love
with Mrs. FitzHerbert. She was twenty-eight and had already
been twice widowed. Her first husband, who was twenty-six
years older than she, died after a fall from his horse, and her
second was killed when helping to quell the Gordon riots.

Her terms were marriage or nothing. George tried everything to get her without this: he stabbed himself in the side—
or said he did; some people believed that he was only blooded

by his physician—and staged a gory scene. He lured her to Carlton House on the pretext that he was dying and would only live if she promised to marry him. She did, but on reflection decided she had been duped and went to France to get away from him. He tried to persuade his father to allow him to go there too, pretending that he wanted to economize, and when this plan did not succeed pestered her with letters. She stayed away for a year and came back in December 1785, when Robert Burke, a young priest, was paid £500 to marry them on the 15th. Her uncle and her brother signed the register.

George already used the Pavilion at Brighton as his country residence, and Mrs. FitzHerbert had a house nearby. She tried to control his eating and drinking and did not approve of many of his friends, who included prize-fighters and toughs. She had a fierce temper and they had quarrels because he was not always faithful. George and his friends were fond of practical jokes. One man even tried to ride a horse up the stairs of Mrs. FitzHerbert's house, where it got stuck and they had difficulty in getting it down. Another time Sheridan dressed himself up as a policeman and pretended that he had come to arrest the respectable Dowager Lady Sefton for unlawful gaming.

After nine years of marriage George grew tired of Mrs. FitzHerbert and fell in love with the beautiful and well-preserved Lady Jersey, a grandmother of forty-two, the daughter of a bishop and wife of George's Master of the Horse. By way of breaking off his alliance with Mrs. Fitz-Herbert he wrote casually one evening and said that he never wanted to see her again; he had been with her only that afternoon. His debts by now were enormous—he had failed to clear them either by honest or dishonest means—so he agreed to marry Caroline of Brunswick if they were paid. Under the Royal Marriage Act 'Any union of heirs-apparent or presumptive to the throne were rendered null and void if they had been contracted without Royal Consent'. The FitzHerbert marriage had never been publicly accepted, though everybody knew that it had taken place and cartoons had been published about them in the newspapers. In one George and Mrs. FitzHerbert were depicted dancing a reel while Burke the priest watched.

Caroline was his first cousin, the daughter of his father's sister Augusta, whom his mother loathed. It was a surprising marriage in view of his father's madness, when one would have thought that they would want to inbreed as little as possible; even more surprising, as both her father and brother had fits of insanity.

Her father was sane when Lord Malmesbury was sent to fetch her, for he said of her, 'She is no fool, but she lacks judgment.' Malmesbury's description of her said that she 'had a pretty face, not expressive of softness, fine eyes, good hands, tolerable teeth but going, and a figure that was not graceful', but that she had 'les épaules impertinents'. On the journey over he told her that she should be more careful about dress and that she did not wash enough. She asked him about Lady Jersey because she had been sent an anonymous letter about her affair with George, and he found it necessary to warn her that any man who made approaches to her, as the wife of the King of England, would be guilty of treason. Her English was not good. She was badly educated, neither had her manners any polish; she was (according to Malmesbury) often too familiar with the English ladies who had been sent over with him to bring her back, calling them, 'ma chère, ma petite.'

She was said to have had one or two offers of marriage before George's and to have been in love with one of her father's officers, who was sent away from court because of this. As she was by this time twenty-seven, high-spirited and healthy, it would have been surprising if no sort of romance had ever come her way.

George was six years older than she was. He had been good-looking as a boy but had always had a puffy look about him which had now turned to fat. He drank too much and now weighed seventeen stone. He had inherited a skin complaint from his grandmother Augustus which made him come out in blotches and was aggravated if he did himself too well.

He was dissipated, dishonest over money, wildly extravagant, and extremely vain. As he got older he painted his face and padded his suits—some of which he designed himself—so that his whole appearance was grotesque.

Lady Jersey did everything she could to make Caroline's life hell and influenced George to do the same. She was appointed one of Caroline's ladies-in-waiting and delayed things so much when they were going to meet her on arrival that they were an hour late. She then said that she could not sit with her back to the carriage and must sit facing; but Lord Jersey, who must have been used to her little ways, told her that she should not have become a lady-in-waiting if she did not like travel and suggested that she should sit in another coach.

The first meeting between George and Caroline was disastrous. After she had curtsied to him he turned aside and said, 'I am not well, pray get me a glass of brandy.' Her impressions of him were not good either, because she asked Lord Malmesbury 'Is he always like that?' and complained that he was too fat. The dinner they had later was as bad; Caroline talked too loud and too long, made references to his relationship to Lady Jersey, and because she had heard that he liked a good head of hair let hers down.

He arrived at the Chapel Royal for the wedding on 8th April full of brandy. Caroline said later that he was so drunk that he spent their wedding night in the grate where he had fallen and she had let him lie. Two days after the wedding they went to Kempshott, the house that George had bought to live in with Mrs. FitzHerbert where she had laid out the gardens. After that they spent their time between Carlton House and the Pavilion at Brighton.

Lady Jersey's and George's behaviour became more and more audacious. He used to drink out of her glass when sitting at the same table as Caroline, and once took away a bracelet that he had given to Caroline and gave it to Lady Jersey, who wore it in public. Lady Jersey was said to have seen that Caroline was always supplied with horses that were too fresh for her. Queen Charlotte was no help; but George III, when

Caroline appealed to him, told his son that Lady Jersey was no longer to be lady-in-waiting.

Their daughter Charlotte was born on 7th January, 1796, at Carlton House. Immediately after her birth George moved out of Carlton House and wrote to Caroline, 'Nature has not made us suitable to each other . . . in the event of any accident happening to my daughter, which I trust Providence in his mercy will avert, I shall not infringe the terms of the restriction by proposing, at any period, a connexion of a more particular nature.'

Caroline again appealed to George III but he was not prepared to interfere further, and she moved into the Old Rectory at Charlton, near Blackheath, where she was continually spied on by her husband and ignored by the court. George had promised that the little Princess Charlotte should join her and should be in her charge until she was eight years old, but he broke his promise and she was kept at Carlton House and then at Shrewsbury until 1805, when she came back to Carlton House and divided her time between living there with her father and in Windsor with her grandparents.

Caroline's behaviour became eccentric in the extreme. She delighted in shocking people, dressed in the most extraordinary way, left off her stays, although through eating and drinking too much she had grown fat, and painted her face like a prostitute. She would sit at table for five or six hours at a time and liked to stay up until the early hours of the morning.

In 1805 the 'delicate investigation' against her started. In 1802 she had adopted a baby boy called William Austin, the son of a dockyard worker. It was rumoured that the baby was really hers. It was also rumoured that she had had affairs with Captain Manby, a naval officer, and with Sir Thomas Lawrence, the painter; and she was accused of sending pornographic drawings to a Lady Douglas. At dinner parties she had often put Manby next to her, although his rank did not warrant it, and after dinner would call him over to sit with her. She had written loving letters to Manby in which she had mentioned the little boy, and given them to Admiral

Nugent to deliver. The admiral had left them in a coach. The coachman read the letters and then sold them to the highest bidder, Caroline, who paid £2,000, George having stopped at £1,500.

In May 1805, the king gave a warrant for an inquiry to be held. The charge was drawn up in July 1806, and sent to her on 11th August; it said that the slanders against her and Captain Manby must be credited until they received some decisive contradiction. She was given no chance to defend herself, which was the usual treatment for English Queen Consorts, but she was luckier than the others because it was only proved that she had been indiscreet.

After the inquiry she was given apartments at Kensington Palace until she moved to a house in Connaught Square. She came to court occasionally, where she found Queen Charlotte stiff but civil. She did not make a good impression at the court and was described as an over-dressed, bare-bosomed and painted-eyebrowed figure who tottered to the throne.

She saw her daughter once a week, and insisted that at the age of nineteen she presented her at court rather than the Duchess of York. George did not want his daughter to become fond of her mother and laid down that they were only to meet once a fortnight, and later not at all. When Caroline wrote to him complaining about this he sent back her letters unopened, so she sent them to the *Morning Chronicle*, where they were published. Young Charlotte grew into a great hoyden of a girl who had a will of her own and did not get on well with her father. Once when they had a quarrel he threatened to declare her illegitimate.

In 1814 Caroline went abroad for seven years, taking with her the adopted boy William Austin and a couple of Italian singers whom she had patronized and entertained in her house in London. The household was ruled by a handsome chamberlain called Peregami who was reputed to be her lover, and who had his daughter with him, and whose sister was Caroline's lady-in-waiting. They all sat at meals together and William Austin slept in her room until he was fourteen. Her behaviour deteriorated further, her clothes became more and more revealing and bizarre and, with her bright red face and eccentric behaviour, she caused a sensation wherever she went.

When Princess Charlotte died in childbirth in 1817, George did not even bother to write and tell Caroline, but in 1818 sent a commission to Geneva to collect evidence against her so that he could get a divorce. In 1819 she was offered a considerable sum of money if she would renounce the title of Queen when he came to the throne. When he became King in 1820, he had her name taken out of the liturgy and told his ambassadors in foreign countries that she was not to be recognized as queen abroad.

She came to England in June 1820, and in July a bill to dissolve her marriage went to the House of Lords. It was passed by a small majority in November, but popular feeling was on her side and it never became law. She was not allowed into Westminster Abbey for George's coronation in July 1821 and died three weeks later. About the charge of adultery against her she said, rightly or wrongly, 'I only committed adultery once with Mrs. FitzHerbert's husband.'

Soon after Caroline had been banished to Blackheath after the birth of Princess Charlotte, George had grown tired of Lady Jersey and her machinations; he had even grown frightened of her and the scenes she made and eventually forbade her to approach him and went back to Mrs. FitzHerbert, who in 1799 got a papal dispensation to resume their relationship. Again she tried to reform his eating and drinking habits, and cannot have approved of some of the parties that he gave. He once had a target put up at the end of the room and shot quite accurately at it. He then asked the ladies to try. One shot hit a passing fiddler, another a door and another the ceiling.

By 1805 he was tired of Mrs. FitzHerbert again and had fallen for the charms of Lady Hertford, a haughty, bad-tempered but intelligent grandmother of forty-seven. To begin with he used to visit Mrs. FitzHerbert during the day and Lady Hertford in the evenings. Even this was not enough for him and it was said that he 'could not remain faithful even to Lady Hertford, particularly if left alone with somebody's grandmother'. Otherwise, although only in his early forties, George lived the life of an old man. He stayed in bed writing letters and dealing with business matters; he would then ride out in his carriage and spend the rest of the afternoon with Lady Hertford. Dinner was at six-thirty and at midnight there were sandwiches and wine. He drank a great deal too much and had also taken to laudanum. By 1811, when he became Regent for George III, his speech was slow and his brain confused. He had had several severe illnesses and believed in bleeding so much that he used to ask a succession of different doctors to do it for him without telling them that it had just been done. Sometimes he had as many as seventeen leeches on him at a time.

It is doubtful whether he had affairs with these elderly women in the accepted sense of the word; they were probably mere petting parties and flirtations. Like many cruel and egotistical men he was sentimental and would treasure locks of hair, gloves and dried flowers. He liked the outward trappings of romance years after he could perform the act of love. When he met a new mistress, Lady Conyngham, he was in an advanced state of decay and she was the usual grandmother—but fatter and more avaricious than most—who always had with her her husband and some of their grown-up family. George was as jealous of her as if she had been a tempting young girl, and lost thirty pounds in an attempt to make himself more attractive. He loaded her with jewels, some of them crown jewels, and it was said that she shared his taste for cherry brandy and laudanum. During his coronation he winked and nodded at her, and at one moment looked at her and pressed a diamond brooch to his lips.

He heard of Caroline's death when he was in Ireland with Lady Conyngham, and celebrated the occasion by appearing on his yacht in a bright blue coat with yellow buttons. He himself had only nine more years to live and became more and more moribund and, whether from drink, drugs or senile decay, was prone to hallucinations, one of them being that he had led the army at the Battle of Waterloo. He did not get up until six in the evening and, not surprisingly, could not sleep at night, so would ring the bell by his bedside sometimes as much as forty times rather than put out his hand to get himself a glass of water or to look at his watch to tell the time. He had got his dose up to two hundred drops of laudanum a day. By 1827 he had to be carried up and down stairs, and in 1828 had such bad gout in his hand that he could not hold a pen. He also developed inflammation of the lungs and kidney trouble. He died on 25th June, 1830. Around his neck was hung a picture of Mrs. FitzHerbert.

Lady Conyngham is reputed to have helped herself to as much in the way of jewellery as she could, and money and trinkets were found scattered around his room in disorder. Mrs. FitzHerbert lived until 1837. William IV always treated her with great respect and recognizing her as the legal widow ordered her to put her servants into mourning after George's death.

30 - William IV

Born 1765, died 1837. Became king, 1830. Married Adelaide of Saxe-Coburg-Meiningen (born 1793, died 1849) in 1818.

ACTING ON the principle in which he firmly believed, that his boys should be brought up as ordinary children, George III sent William, his third son, into the Navy at the age of fourteen as 'William Guelph'. His ten years in that service turned out to be anything but ordinary. He arrived as a midshipman with a clergyman tutor to teach him classics; he was best man at Nelson's wedding; there was a plan to kidnap him when he was in America with a view to forcing his father to come to terms; for two of the ten years he was sent on a grand tour with his brother Frederick; and at times he stepped out of character as William Guelph and as the king's son made the most extraordinary speeches; and when he did not like Nelson's successor and did not want to serve under him, up-anchored and sailed his ship away. The most ordinary thing that he did was to fall in love frequently. He did this first at the age of sixteen on leave in London, when his affections fastened on a Miss Fortescue, a child of about the same age as himself. His leave was stopped and he was sent back to his ship. In Havana he fell in love with the sixteen-year-old and much-chaperoned daughter of a Spanish admiral, which almost caused an international incident, so that Nelson had to step in and hush the matter up. He then acquired a coloured girl called Wowski, who was nicknamed 'the Mole' by his ship-mates because when anybody came on board she used to dive below decks. He next went to Ireland and fell in love there, and when he was twenty asked his parents if he might marry Sarah Martin, the beautiful daughter of an admiral. Years later a German woman claimed that he had married her in Hanover in 1790. He was not there in that year but he did acknowledge an illegitimate child, born in that country in about 1785.

In 1790, when he was twenty-five, the Navy made it clear that it did not require his services any longer. He was made the Duke of Clarence and Ranger of Bushey Park, where he settled with Mrs. Jordan, the actress, with whom he was to live for twenty years and by whom he had ten children; as well as these they had living with them several other children whom she had had by her former lovers.

During the time that this liaison lasted he lived a useless, ramshackle life and took little part in public affairs except occasionally to make speeches in the House of Lords, some of which convinced a lot of people that he was as mad as his father. He had inherited his father's nervous symptoms and would very easily become over-excited as he talked; and at these times, although he did not normally like writing, he would cover sheets of paper with his view on diverse subjects. All this time he was short of money and frequently had to borrow from Mrs. Jordan who to earn it had to go back to work on the stage between babies.

In 1811 he had a bad attack of asthma while paying a duty visit to his mother. While she had him in her power she persuaded him that he ought to marry somebody suitable, and the usual bribe was offered that his debts would be paid and his children supported. Mrs. Jordan, who was to be given £4,000 per annum, left the country and went to live in Paris, where she died five years later.

William tried hard and conscientiously to find a bride. Several English heiresses turned him down, one six times. Another said that she would marry him, but the Prince Regent stepped in and forbade the match, as he did not think it suitable. Abroad he tried Princess Anne of Denmark and the sister of the Czar of Russia, and he asked the Duke of Cambridge to keep an eye open for a prospective bride for him in Hanover. Nothing came of any of this so, discouraged, he retired to Bushey.

Princess Charlotte's death in 1817 made the matter more urgent and he renewed his efforts. She had been the only child born in lawful royal wedlock which the seven surviving sons had managed to produce. An heir or even an heiress to the throne was needed. At last, on 19th April, 1818, his betrothal was announced to Amelia Adelaide Thérèse Caroline, daughter of the Duke of the tiny duchy of Saxe-Coburg-Meiningen. Three of his younger brothers were galvanized into action too and also married. One of them was the Duke of Kent, the father of Queen Victoria.

Nobody in England took much notice of William's engagement. They hardly knew what he looked like and it never occurred to them that he might be of any importance. Adelaide arrived with her mother in July and they were sent to Grillon's Hotel off Bond Street, where rooms had been booked for them at the Crown's expense. The Prince Regent came to visit them the same evening, before Adelaide had had time to change out of her travelling clothes, and hard on his heels came William.

William was fifty-three, bluff to the point of eccentricity, red-faced, the fat father of an illegitimate family, a man who had never had enough money and who hated foreigners. Adelaide was twenty-six, the same age as his eldest daughter, slight, neatly built and quietly dressed. They were married on 11th July, four days after they first met, but not before Adelaide had promised William that she would look after his youngest daughters. The first night of their honeymoon William took the young bride and her mother to his bachelor flat in St. James's Palace which had been decorated for him nine years before in rather theatrical taste by Mrs. Jordan. Otherwise they only had Bushey to live in, as the Government, which had kept its word about paying his debts, had otherwise not been generous. To economize they went to live in Hanover.

Adelaide became pregnant almost at once. William, used to Mrs. Jordan, who had children with the greatest ease, took no special care of Adelaide and made her go visiting round Germany with him. The joint effect of the bumpy German roads and her being bled because she had pleurisy, was to bring on the baby, Princess Charlotte Augusta Louise, prematurely and it only lived a few hours.

Adelaide became pregnant again, but William had not learnt his lesson and decided that they should go back to England for his eldest son's wedding and that she should have the baby there; but first he drove her all over the bumpy German roads again to visit his various married sisters. This time she collapsed and had a miscarriage at Dunkirk while they were waiting to embark for England. Once in England she became pregnant again and this time produced a daughter, Elizabeth Georgina Adelaide, born a week after they had attended the wedding of William's third daughter by Mrs. Jordan. The baby weighed eleven pounds, although she was born six weeks early. Her arrival nearly killed Adelaide.

They decided they would stay in England at Bushey. Adelaide had settled down to married life intelligently. She was devoted to William and made patient efforts to reform him. She made him study more and talk less and generally tried to stop him making a fool of himself—he used to read *The Times* and the *Morning Post* every day, interjecting out loud at various bits of news, 'That's a damned lie!' She reorganized the domestic arrangements at Bushey so that he was much more comfortable than he had ever been before, and yet she managed to save money. She kept her word about bringing up his daughters, and was kind and tolerant to his sons and grandchildren as well. When she found that he had put away a picture of Mrs. Jordan for fear that it might hurt her feelings, she had it hung up again, saying sensibly that it was only right to do so as they had been fond of each other for twenty years.

For a few months after the little princess was born Adelaide was blissfully happy. She wanted to nurse her child, but had too many public duties to perform since both the Queen and the Duchess of York had recently died, and she, the Princess

Augusta and Sophia and the Duchess of Kent were the only royal ladies in England. Conscientious as usual, she bought new clothes and prepared to play her part. In March 1821, the little baby died in great agony after convulsions, followed by other complications.

One year later she had a miscarriage of twins. That was her last attempt at having a baby. She liked to see other people's children, enjoyed giving children's parties and would have liked to see more of their little niece Victoria; but the Duchess of Kent was unfriendly and refused to let her children mix with the bastard FitzClarences.

Clarence House was built for them in London, and Adelaide entertained there, chiefly for William's daughters. She went over to Germany several times without William, and once took two of his daughters with her when she visited Meiningen.

When the Duke of York died in 1827, William became heir to the throne. His income was increased by Parliament and he was also made Lord High Admiral, an office from which he resigned the next year when it was brought home to him that the title was only honorary and did not mean that he could travel round promoting officers. He was now determined not to die before George IV. He ate sparingly and did not drink until dinner time, when he had a bottle of sherry—presumably unfortified—and as he believed in gargling salt water as a preventive for asthma, he did so religiously every day, sometimes getting through as much as two gallons of water at a time.

William was still personally almost unknown to the British public and when he became king in 1820 they found his behaviour strange in the extreme. He was at Bushey when George IV died and was woken in the morning by the news, upon hearing which he said he was going back to bed, as he had never before had relations with a queen. When he did get up he put a long piece of black crepe round his hat and drove to London, bowing and waving all the way to people by the roadside, most of whom had no idea who he was or that George was dead. At the funeral he nodded and smiled at people as he walked up the aisle and stopped to shake hands with a friend. As king, until Adelaide stopped him, he insisted on walking round the streets of London on his own. There was one incident when he had to be rescued from a too-friendly mob in the streets by the members of White's Club, who then escorted him back to St. James's Palace. When the King of Württemberg came to visit him, he took him, Adelaide and the Princess Augusta round London in an open carriage to show him the sights and then dropped the German king back at his hotel, which although it sounds perfectly sensible, was too informal to please his ambassadors and courtiers. In 1828 he had had to be put in a straitjacket for a while. He recovered, but his excitability had increased during the last months of George's illness so that Adelaide had had difficulty in keeping him calm. His nervous energy was enormous and his ministers had difficulty trying to keep up with him. He rushed down to Windsor, which was being extravagantly run, and raced round the place reorganizing it; then he would rush back to London and do the same there. One of the things that he did at Windsor was to have gas installed but Adelaide did not trust it, so it was turned off. He hated Buckingham Palace and wanted to live in Marlborough House, using the Palace as a Ministry and building an underground passage between the two. If he did have to live in it, he said, he hoped it would be plain and have no gilding, which he disliked.

Adelaide watched him with loving care. Because he had gout in his fingers it hurt him to hold a pen, so when he had to sign a lot of documents she would stand by him with a basin, which she kept full of hot water so that he could dip his fingers in it to soothe them. Every spring his nervous symptoms returned, and she did her best to keep him quiet and calm and away from the crowds.

Their coronation was not until 18th September, 1821. William did not want a ceremony because he thought it a waste of money, nor did he want to be William IV but Henry IX; but it was said that he was persuaded against this because of an old rhyme which went:

Henry VIII pulled down monks and cells;
Henry IX would pull down bishops and bells.

Why he should be particularly affected by this is difficult to
follow, as he was in no way a religious man; but he was
crowned William IV, and Adelaide wore a gold gauze dress
over a white satin petticoat, a diamond stomacher and a
purple velvet train lined with white satin. Prince George,
son of the Duke of Cambridge, came to live with them and
was a great comfort to Adelaide who was extremely fond of
him. She wrote on 27th March, 1831, 'The Birthday and
death of my first child were much softened for me by the
possession of Georgy, for he is a consolation for my loss in
this world'.

The English sometimes found William IV lovable, he at
least seemed to be human; but the monarchy was not popular,
his court was dull and his courtiers were put out by his bluff-
ness, his bad language—it was colourful and he had a simple
delight in dirty stories—and his lack of polish generally. By
way of getting rid of his guests one night he said, 'Now you can
go to your own amusements. I am going to mine, which is in
bed with the queen.'

They were plagued by his children, the FitzClarences, who
thought that now he was king they ought to be treated in the
same way as the illegitimate children of Charles II. Times had
changed and, even if he had wished to give them enormous
allowances and make them dukes, Parliament would not have
allowed it. His eldest son, who committed suicide five years
after his father's death, was made the Earl of Munster, and
the others were given the rank and title of the younger children
of a marquis. One son became a captain in the army, another
a major-general, another a rear-admiral and was an A.D.C.
to Queen Victoria despite her mother's horror of the family,
and another a clergyman. All the daughters married advan-
tageously. The widowed Duchess of Kent was a trial as well.
Unhampered by a husband and with the prospect of being
Regent if William should die before Victoria was twenty-
one, she was uncooperative, near-insolent in her behaviour

towards Adelaide, and made every excuse to keep Victoria away from court. William disliked her so much that in the same way as it had been his ambition to live to become king, it now became his ambition to live until Victoria obtained her majority. In a speech after a dinner party for a hundred people at which the Duchess of Kent was sitting next to him, he openly said he trusted in God that his life would be spared for nine months longer: 'I should then have the satisfaction of leaving the royal authority to the person of that young lady'—here he pointed to Victoria—'and not to a person now near me.' At this Victoria wept, Adelaide looked perturbed, and the Duchess of Kent ordered her carriage.

Like William the Conqueror his last wish was granted. Early in the year 1837 he had had exceptionally bad asthma and he had developed a weak heart as well. In May he held a levée in London and then drove to Windsor, where he arrived so weak that he could not walk upstairs. He insisted on going back to London the next day for a court drawing-room. A few days later he collapsed, but two days after that on 24th May, Victoria's birthday, he gave a ball for her coming-of-age. After this his pulse rate went down to thirty. All the same they gave the usual Ascot house party, but half-way through the queen decided that it was too much for him and asked their guests to leave. She hoped to take him to Brighton to rest but he was too ill to be moved. He would not go to bed but sat in a chair. He died on 20th June, 1837.

After William's death Adelaide's one idea seemed to be to efface herself as much as possible. Victoria told her that she could take anything that she wished to keep away from Windsor Castle, but the only two things that she took were a silver cup out of which William had drunk during his illness, and a family picture. Her own health had been bad for several years, with rheumatism and a persistent bad cough, but she had been too busy looking after William to pander to her own troubles. Now she travelled about in search of health and visited Malta and Madeira among other places to try and find the right climate. She died twelve years later in England at Bentley Priory near Stanmore, on 2nd December 1849.

William IV died seven hundred and fifty years after William I. It is doubtful if any of the Hanoverian kings would have been able to hold his throne in the eleventh century, and if William I would have had it all his own way in the nineteenth. William IV was such a simple man that he was on the verge of being below average intelligence. He could not have been more in contrast to the first William, nor could the truly gentle Adelaide have been more in contrast to the reputedly gentle Matilda. Their courtships could not have been more different either. William I made up his own mind that he would marry Matilda and after seven years she made up her own mind that she would accept him. William IV and Adelaide met after they had been betrothed and only four days before their marriage.

Between these two kings England had twenty-eight sovereigns who married. Three of them were women who treated their spouses with loving respect and affection. The same cannot be said for the majority of the twenty five men. Henry VIII, who had six wives, beheaded two and divorced two. George I imprisoned his wife for thirty-two years and divorced her as well; Henry II imprisoned his for thirteen years; and John imprisoned his for one. Edward III imprisoned his mother when she was Queen Mother; and Henry V imprisoned his stepmother, when she was the dowager Queen, for witchcraft. George IV married his second wife without bothering to get divorced from his first. Most of the kings were unfaithful and publicly acknowledged their bastards and lavished honours on their favourites.

The twenty-five kings married in all twenty-seven foreign women, most of whom, like Adelaide, met their bridegrooms only a few days or even hours before their weddings when they were feeling at their lowest ebb after a channel crossing which for some reason was always the worst on record. On arrival they and their retinues were scrutinized by the attendant court ladies who were for the most part beady-eyed and ready to be malicious. All of them—except the wives of Richard I and George I, Berengaria and Sophia, who never came to England— had to adapt themselves to new customs. Many of them had to learn a new language; often they had to change their loyalties. Several of them never saw their countries again.

It is true that ruling families were brought up in the knowledge that love and marriage were not synonymous and that it would be necessary for their marriages to be political rather than romantic. Even so, many of the little brides had hardly had time to be brought up at all, and it must have been a rude shock to them to be torn away from their homes and married to a complete stranger—sometimes a middle-aged old warrior—by whom they were expected to produce sons. The breeding methods were quite extraordinary as no account was taken of poor physical or mental health however bad the prognosis. So far as eugenic suitability was concerned, they took far more care over the provision of the parish heifers for their town bulls. A succession of miscarriages and children dying in infancy cannot have made the lot of these unfortunate girls easier to bear.

With so much against them it is natural to find that these alliances were some of the least successful and most anguished in the history of our social life. What is surprising and sometimes touching is the occasional glimpse of a union which, against all the odds, led to love and even to happiness.

BIBLIOGRAPHY

W. Gore Allen	*William IV*
John T. Appleby (ed.)	*The Chronicles of Richard of Devizes*
R. D. Arkell	*Caroline of Anspach*
S. Armitage Smith	*John of Gaunt*
J. J. Bagley	*Life in Medieval England*
J. J. Bagley	*Margaret of Anjou*
Tufton Beamish	*Battle Royal*
Mary S. Beard	*Woman as a force in History*
H. Belloc	*James II*
H. Belloc	*William the Conqueror*
	Betham's Genealogical Tables
	Lair's Chronological Tables
Elizabeth Bowen	*Mary II*
M. Bowen	*Famous Love Letters*
John Bowle	*Henry VIII*
G. Brooks	*The Dukes of York*
Sir Arthur Bryant	*The Age of Chivalry*
Sir Arthur Bryant	*Memoirs of James II*
Sir Arthur Bryant	*The Story of England*
Mary Nancy Brysson	*Private Life of Henry VIII*
J. B. Bury (ed.)	*The Cambridge Medieval History*
Cecil and Loeb	*Textbook of the practice of medicine*
E. B. Chancellor	*Old Rowley*
H. C. Chapman	*Queen Anne's son*
H. C. Chapman	*The tragedy of Charles II*
Charles Chevenix Trench	*The Royal Malady*
R. Chiswell	*Short review of the unfortunate reigns of William II, Henry II, Edward II, Richard II, Charles II, and James II*
Winston S. Churchill	*History of the English-speaking Peoples*
G. N. Clerk	*The later Stuarts*
G. G. Coulton	*Medieval Panorama*
Eyrton R. Court	*Household and Itinerary of Henry II*
Thomas Creevey	*The Creevey Papers*
E. Curll	*Memoirs of the lives of Edward IV and Jane Shore extracted from the best historians*
H. W. C. Davies	*England under the Normans and the Angevins*
J. D. G. Davies	*Henry IV*
J. D. G. Davies	*Henry V*
Gordon Daviot	*Richard of Bordeaux*
M. M. Davy	*Extracts from Peter de Blois*
	Debrett Dictionary of National Biography
P. W. Dillon	*Remarks on the manner of the death of Richard II*

Maurice Droun	*The She-Wolf of France*
William Dugdale	*The Baronage of England*
H. P. Dunster (ed.)	*Sir John Froissart; the Chronicles of England, France and Spain*
	Eloge de la Glorieuse Matilda Reine D'Angleterre
	Encyclopedia Britannica
Lilian Eichler	*The Customs of Mankind*
Nina Epton	*Love and the English*
H. A. L. Fisher	*A history of Europe*
Percy FitzGerald	*The good Queen Charlotte*
T. Forrester (trans. and ed.)	*The Chronicles of the Earl of Huntingdon*
E. A. Freeman	*History of the Norman Conquest*
J. A. Froude	*The Divorce of Catherine of Aragon*
J. A. Froude	*History of England from the fall of Wolsey to the death of Elizabeth*
Roger Fulford	*Royal Dukes*
Roger Fulford	*George IV*
J. Gairdner	*Henry VII*
Cardinal Gasquet	*Religious life of Henry VI*
Compiled by William Geoffrey	*The Complete Lover*
J. A. Giles (trans.)	*Odericus Vitalis by Geoffrey of Monmouth*
J. A. Giles (trans.)	*William of Malmesbury Chronicles*
Charles Graves	*Palace extraordinary*
Cecil and Margery Gray	*The Bed*
A. S. Green	*Henry II*
John Richard Greene	*A short History of the English People*
J. O. Halliwell Philips	*Letters of the Kings of England*
F. Harrison	*Oliver Cromwell*
J. Harvey	*The Plantagenets*
W. C. Hassall	*How they lived, 55 B.C.–1485*
Philip Henderson	*Richard Coeur de Lion*
Christopher Hibbert	*The Court at Windsor*
Christina Hole	*English Home Life 1500–1800*
Raphael Holinshed	*Chronicles of England, Scotland and Ireland*
M. R. Hopkinson	*Anne of England*
Frances Mary Hopkirk	*Queen Adelaide*
G. Huens	*Selections from Clarendon*
A. S. Hume	*Philip II of Spain*
Morton M. Hunt	*The Natural History of Love*
Brian Inglis	*History of Medicine*
E. F. Jacob	*Fifteenth Century*
Elizabeth Jenkins	*Elizabeth the Great*
Edward Jenks	*Edward Plantagenet*
Capt. Jesse	*The Life of Beau Brummell*
A. Kelly	*Eleanore of Aquitaine and her courts of love*
Paul Murray Kendall	*Richard III*
Paul Murray Kendall	*The Yorkist Age*
Charles Knight (ed.)	*London*

BIBLIOGRAPHY

Margaret Wade Labarge	*A Baronial Household of the Thirteenth Century*
Margaret Wade Labarge	*Simon de Montfort*
W. E. H. Lecky	*History of England*
Hilda Lewis	*Wife to Henry V*
Eric Linklater	*Mary Queen of Scots*
P. Lindsay	*Loves of Florizel*
P. Lindsay	*Kings of Merry England*
P. Lindsay	*The Queenmaker*
Sir S. L. and F. S. Pulling	*A Dictionary of English History*
Lord Lyttleton	*Henry II*
J. D. Mackie	*The Earlier Tudors*
Lord Macaulay	*History of England*
	Diaries of correspondence of James Harris 1st Earl of Malmesbury
W. McElwee	*The Wisest Fool in Christendom*
May McIsack	*Fourteenth Century*
Lewis Melville	*The First George*
Lewis Melville	*Farmer George*
Lord Mersey	*King of England*
J. H. R. Moorman (ed.)	*Edward 1st (An account of the money spent on Queen Eleanore's illness)*
Morris Marples	*Princes in the Making*
Clifford Musgrove	*Royal Pavilion*
A. R. Myers (ed.)	*The Black Book of Edward IV*
J. E. Neale	*Queen Elizabeth*
K. Norgate	*History under the Angevins*
K. Norgate	*John Lackland*
Carola Oman	*Mary of Modena*
Earl of Onslow	*Empress Maud*
E. Parry	*Queen Caroline*
K. A. Patmore	*The Seven Edwards of England*
E. Parry	*Queen Caroline*
H. Pearson	*Charles II; his Life and Times*
	Complete Peerage
Samuel Pepys	*Diary*
Sir Charles Petrie	*The Stuarts*
J. H. Plumb	*The Four Georges*
Austin Lane Poole	*Medieval England*
G. R. Potter (ed.)	*The New Cambridge Modern History*
Sir Maurice Powicke	*Life of Henry III and the Lord Edward*
Sir Maurice Powicke	*The Thirteenth Century*
H. M. F. Prescott	*Mary Tudor*
Frederick Price (ed.)	*The Textbook of the Practice of Medicine*
M. and C. H. B. Quennell	*A history of Everyday Things in England*
Peter Quennell	*Caroline of England*
G. Rattray-Taylor	*Sex in History*
Jasper Ridley	*Thomas Cranmer*
Nerca A. Robb	*William of Orange; a personal portrait*
M. V. Rosenberg	*Eleanore of Aquitaine*

R. N. Routh (ed.)	*They Saw it Happen*
A. L. Rowse	*The Later Churchills*
Victoria Sackville-West	*Knole and the Sackvilles*
M. Sanders	*Intimate letters of England's Kings*
M. Sanders	*Intimate letters of England's Queens*
Giles St. Aubyn	*The Royal George*
Romney Sedgwick (ed.)	*Lord Harvey's Memoirs*
	Social Life of Britain from the Conquest to the Reformation
Edith Sitwell	*Fanfare for Elizabeth*
Osbert Sitwell and Margaret Barton	*Brighton*
Sacheverell Sitwell and Francis Bamford	*Edinburgh*
Lacey Baldwin Smith	*A Tudor Tragedy*
Anthony Steel	*Richard II*
D. M. Stenton	*English Society in the Middle Ages*
Agnes Strickland	*Lives of the Queens of England*
D. M. Stuart	*The Daughters of George III*
D. M. Stuart	*Men and Women of Plantagenet England*
W. M. Thackeray	*The Four Georges*
C. T. S. Thompson	*Love, Marriage and Romance in old London*
G. M. Trevelyan	*History of England*
G. M. Trevelyan	*England under the Stuarts*
G. M. Trevelyan	*English Social History*
G. Treese	*Seven Queens of England*
E. S. Turner	*The Court of St. James*
	The Last Journals of Horace Walpole
W. L. Warren	*King John*
C. V. Wedgwood	*Oliver Cromwell*
C. V. Wedgwood	*The King's Peace*
C. V. Wedgwood	*The Trial of Charles II*
H. G. Wells	*History of England*
	Who's Who
C. A. Wilkinson	*Coeur de Lion*
W. H. Wilkins	*Caroline the Illustrious*
W. H. Wilkins	*Mrs. FitzHerbert and George IV*
W. H. Wilkins	*The Love of an Uncrowned Queen*
D. H. Wilson	*James VI and I*
John H. Wilson	*Nell Gwynn; Royal Mistress*